Preface

The realisation that both biology and socio-cultural attributes shape human development has an important place in the current anthropological thinking. This has on the one hand enlarged the scope of anthropological dimension and on the other has opened up new possibilities for anthropology with the induction of new persepectives and approaches of allied disciplines. North East India has always been a happy hunting ground for the natural scientists, population biologists and social scientists including anthropologists because of the rich diversity of culture and language on the one hand and a considerable degree of biogenetic variation on the other. One distinct advantage of anthropology is that it could successfully combine the cultural and biological aspects of humankind into an integrated approach. It has been said time and again, *albeit* mechanically, that anthropology aids in integrating the natural sciences, the social sciences and the humanities.

It cannot be denied that at present there has been a growing interest in human variation, stimulated by advances in genetics and evolutionary biology in the last few decades. It is common practice to explain variation or variability in terms of biogenetic differences manifested at the population level. In a situation where a number of ethnic groups share almost the same environment this is understandable. Moreover, it has been increasingly realised that genetic variability within populations is important to the variability of some special kinds of behaviour. For decades anthropology has remained confined to seeking cultural and environmental variables affecting human behavior. But biology and, more specifically, genetics will always remain a major source of variations in human beings. Adequate methods have now been developed and used to separate genetic and environmental influences on quantitative traits and behavioral differences. Since North East India manifests a considerable range of diversity in terms of human populations and social groups, it can be visualised as variation across time. In order to have a clear understanding of this variation, taking an ecological viewpoint may be necessary, where adaptive interactions among bio-cultural and environmental variables could be assessed. North East India provides ample opportunities for doing that.

Tribes with all its ramifications hold a special place in the socio-political milieu exhibited by North East India. But the social structural analysis so long pursued in case of tribal groups has now changed its methodological direction and analytical framework. Not only that, it has also extended its domain including in the process different class and caste like formations as also other minority groups. Even the formations and population compositions in the contiguous area of North Bengal including Darjeeling, Sikkim have a bearing on North East India. All in all, North East India now holds a broad canvas for those who take a keen interest in its affairs.

In a pluralistic situation as is prevalent in North East India, distribution of political power at the community level, or the access to the sources of political power involves the question of size and numerical dominance as also creating a 'political culture' of their own, emphasising their distinctiveness in the lifeways and organizational pattern. Again, within the framework of a tribe there has been a marked increase in the number of polities, which cut across the whole range of tribal system.

Real societies are the product of demographic, ecological, economic and political situations defining a specific context. But the situations do not build up into a fixed environment, but into a constantly changing environment. The changes that result from the process may usefully be brought under two heads. Firstly, there are those, which are consistent with a continuity of a formal order. Secondly, there are changes, which do reflect alterations in the formal structure. It cannot be said that all the tribal societies of North East India are of one type or another. The same society often manifests both the processes—continuity of the formal structural order and alterations in it. There is a line of thinking, which has found acceptance in some quarters, that the conflicting tendencies displayed by tribal societies are somewhat in-built in their system. As 'ideal units' too, the 'self contained' nature of tribal societies is an expression of their indigenous socio-political order, which is in a way structurally ingrained. Its representation in the present time gets distorted because of growing sectarian prejudices and factional interests, the perpetrators of which have fixed up goals going far beyond the structural limits of the traditional order. Probably internal contradictions laid down in the social structure have to work themselves out over time, particularly when different forms of external influence and different political situations are encountered. These contradictions may give rise to deceptive tendencies or bring in realignment of forces of political control at certain level. In the latter case, the tendency is to form different operational groups vying for monopoly of power. In the process some of them may even take recourse to direct violent actions in order to prove their effectiveness. This is one way of winning more followers. There is also a contradiction between the domestic units represented by villages or village-based clan groups functioning as local groups and the overall tribal system of social control. As a result of direct intervention of polities in determining the conditions of social reproduction, there have been indications that the tribal system now heads for reproduction of class relations. In the context of 'Secessionist Ethnic Conflict in South and Southeast Asia' David Carment (2003) states:

> "With respect to policy it can be said that policy options on managing secessionist ethnic conflict depend on the explanations we accept for the cause of conflict. If one emphasises root causes (for example, mass mobilisation, intra-elite competition, primordialism or relative deprivation), the list of solutions would include partition, power sharing, democratisation, constitutional entrenchment of ethnic and minority rights, proportional division of key offices, mutual vetoes and so on. On the other hand, if one emphasises dynamic interactions within a given conflict, then for finding solutions focus would have to be on first evaluating these processes (primarily the constraints and opportunities available to leaders in using force against minorities) and then taking early and preventive action."

While both the approaches have their justifications, they tend to give an impression of oversimplifying the root causes of conflicts in a manner suggestive of the stand taken by some specialists in the field that conflicts are very much amenable to management in the ordinary sense of the term. Ethnic conflicts call for deeper understanding and probe since they are inextricable part of the self-identity of the group. Suppression or containment of an ethnic conflict does not actually mean the end of it, although a nation's interest will be safeguarded as long as there is no external outburst of it.

The situation prevailing in North East India has to be linked with the dynamics of change. To understand the process of change, more emphasis is now given on formal institutions and consequently, social behaviors and cultural experience of the individual community members are rather neglected. While analysing the culture, social organisation and Asian identity in Urban East Africa, Campbell (1999) makes a valid point. He observes:

> "an emphasis on formal institutions also ignores the manner in which the various traditions and social identities have been reproduced, particularly the struggles which individuals are engaged in to ensure personal survival and cultural continuity."

Here the role of ideologies deserves mention. Though ideologies contribute to cultural constructions, these are not to be taken as 'timeless creation'. With regard to culture, there has now been a shift from 'psycho-social perspective' to 'constructionist' design. Cultural descriptions now-a-days belong mainly to the second category. The interpretative part reflects the deliberate attempt to develop a pre-conceived design on the part of cultural analyst. The larger question of group identity is involved with it. The authors of this volume have one common concern. All of them seek to describe and analyse the distinctive features or situations of some North East Indian communities as biological or socio-cultural formations representing specific entities in time and space. Of course, it has to be admitted that cultural or social estimation and bio-genetic evaluation do not always coincide. Both, however, need to be understood in a historical perspective, which may have a regional overtone.

RAJAT KANTI DAS
DEBASHIS BASU

Acknowledgements

It is difficult to ofter acknowledgements to all the contributors to this volume adequately in a brief note. However, it must be put on record that we are grateful to all of them for their active cooperation and for contributing their bit in the preparation of this volume. Their contributions are not only relevant to their respective areas of expertise, but will go a long way in enhancing our understanding of North East Indian situation. No doubt, these could successfully underline the need for looking at North East India in proper perspective. We express a sense of gratitude to the Editor, *Man in India* and Editor, Departmental *Journal of Political Science* of Vidyasagar University. Midnapur, West Bengal, who could realise the importance of the papers by Ajit K. Danda and Debnarayan Modak. Incidentally, Ajit K. Danda's paper was first published in *Man in India* and the original version of Debnarayan Modak's paper appeared in the Political Science Journal of Vidyasagar University. Special mention must be made of North East India Council for Social Science Research, Shillong for giving us permission to include R.K. Bhattacharya's Memorial Lecture in the volume. (We acknowledge our deep sense of gratitude to Prof. A.C. Bhagabati for the foreword which is of tremendous academic and personal significance to us).

We are indeed thankful to M. P. Misra of Akansha Publishing House, New Delhi for processing the production and publication of the volume. Our thanks are also due to Miss Rita Paul for doing the initial typing and composition. Lastly, we thank everyone, who is even remotely connected with the preparation of this volume.

RAJAT KANTI DAS
DEBASHIS BASU

PART THREE: TRIBE AND ETHNICITY, CULTURE AND IDENTITY, DEVELOPMENT AND PROBLEMS OF CHANGE

List of Contributors

Balgir, R.S., Deputy Director (Senior), Regional Medical Research Centre (ICMR), Chandrasekharpur, Nandankanan Road, Bhubaneswar - 751023.

Baruah, Geetanjali, Research Associate, Anthropological Survey of India, North East Regional Centre, Madanrting, Shillong - 793021

Baruah, Tiluttoma, Lecturer, Department of Anthropology, Cotton College, Guwahati, Assam.

Basu, Debashis, Research Associate (P), Anthropological Survey of India, North East Regional Centre, Madanrting, Shillong - 793021.

Bhattacharya, R.K., Director (Retd.), Anthropological Survey of India and UNESCO Professor, Indira Gandhi National Centre for Arts, 1, Janpath, New Delhi -110001.

Chakravarty, C.S., Professor, Department of Zoology, University of Burdwan, Burdwan, West Bengal.

Danda, Ajit K., Professor, "Kadam Kanan", Jhargram, West Midnapore - 721507.

Das, Rajat K., Professor, Department of Anthropology, Vidyasagar University, West Midnapore - 721102.

Das, Samir K., Reader, Department of Political Science, University of Calcutta, Kolkata - 700027.

Gassah, L.S., Professor, Department of Political Science, North Eastern Hill University, Main Campus, Mawlai, Shillong - 793008.

Gogoi, Nitul, Reader, Department of Anthropology, Dibrugarh University, Dibrugarh, Assam, - 786004.

Julius L. Marak, Museologist, State Central Museum, Government of Meghalaya, Shillong - 793001.

Kar, Sujata, Research Fellow, Biological Anthropology Unit, Indian Statistical Institute, 203, B.T. Road, Kolkata - 700108.

Kumar, Vikrant, Research fellow, Anthropology and Human Genetics Unit, Indian Statistical Institute, 203, B.T. Road, Kolkata - 700108.

Lalthantluanga, R., Professor, Department of Biochemistry, North Eastern Hill University, Main Campus, Mawlai, Shillong - 793024.

Limbu, D.K., Reader, Department of Anthropology, North-Eastern Hill University, Nongthymmy, Shillong - 793014.

Lyngdoh, C. Reuben, Lecturer, Department of Political Science, Synod College, Jaiaw, Shillong - 793002.

Modak, Debnarayan, Reader, Department of Political Science, Vidyasagar University, Midnapore, West Bengal - 721102.

Mozumdar, Arupendra, Research Fellow, Biological Anthropology Unit, Indian Statistical Institute, 203, B.T. Road, Kolkata - 700108

Mukhopadhyay, Rajat S., Professor, Department of Sociology North Bengal University, Raja Rammohanpur, Darjeeling.

Nag, Sajal, Professor, Department of History, Assam University, Silchar, Assam, - 788011.

Partha P. Majumdar, Professor, Anthropology and Human Genetics Unit, Indian Statistical Institute, 203, B.T. Road, Kolkata - 700108

Raha, M.K., Jt. Director (Retd.), Anthropological Survey of India, 10/3, Jamir Lane, Kolkata - 700019.

Reddy, B. Mohan, Professor, Anthropology and Human Genetics Unit, Indian Statistical Institute, 203, B.T. Road Kolkata - 700108.

Roy, B. Dutta, Professor, & Secretary, Northeast India Council of Social Science Research, B.T. Hostel, Laitumkhrah, Shillong -793003.

Roy, M., Anthropology and Human Genetics Unit, Indian Statistical Institute, 203, B.T. Road, Kolkata - 700108.

Roy, Subrata, Associate Professor, Biological Anthropology Unit, Indian Statistical Institute, 203, B.T. Road Kolkata - 700108.

Sengupta, N.K., Physician, Juthika Nursing Home, Chaibasa, Singbhum, Jharkhand.

PART ONE

INTRODUCING NORTH EAST INDIA

1

A Profile of North-East India and its Disadvantaged Populations

B. DUTTA ROY

For a long time North East India was tagged with the Eastern zone of India. Now it is treated as a separate zone. The bifurcation is significant. It underlies the importance of North East India as a separate entity having a viable social, political and economic representation in the country. The region is potentially rich, though economically and otherwise disadvantaged.

The resource-rich North East India is geopolitically distinguishable. It is bounded by four countries—Bhutan and China on the North, Myanmar on the East and South and Bangladesh on the West and South. The area covers 3,54,000 sq. km. and includes Assam, Arunachal Pradesh, Manipur, Meghalaya, Nagaland and Tripura with a total population of 31,547,314 (1991 Census). Sikkim is not included in the list as the main consideration is geographical contiguity. The area contains the unpredictable Brahmaputra, somewhat difficult terrain of Arunachal Pradesh, Nagaland, Manipur, Mizoram and forested hills of Meghalaya. North East India is connected with the rest of India by a strategic but vulnerable narrow corridor with North Bengal.

A feature of population of North East India is its rapid growth—both in the hills and in the valleys. Another significant feature is that more than 25 percent of its total population are scheduled tribes and about 7 percent are scheduled castes.

more than 25 percent of its total population are scheduled tribes and about 7 percent are scheduled castes.

Table 1.1 State-wise total scheduled caste and scheduled tribe populations of North-East India (1991 census)
Population

State	*Total*	*Scheduled castes*	*Scheduled tribes*
Arunachal Pradesh	864,558	4,052	550,351
		(0.47)	(63.66)
Assam	22,414, 322	1,659,412	2,874,441
		(7.40)	(12.82)
Manipur	1,837,149	37,105	632,173
		(2.02)	(34.41)
Meghalaya	1,774,778	9.872	1,517,927
		(0.51)	(85.53)
Mizoram	689,756	691	653,565
		(0.1)	(94.75)
Nagaland	1,209,546	–	1,060.82
			(87.7)
Tripura	2,757,205	451,115	853,345
		(16.48)	(30.95)
	31,574,314	2,161,448 (6.85)	8,142,624 (25.81)

The tribals constitute 87.70 percent in Nagaland, 85.53 percent in Meghalaya, 30.95 in Tripura and 34.41 percent in Manipur; only 12.82 percent of the population of Assam belong to scheduled tribes. The tribal population in Mizoram is the highest with 94.75 percent, while Arunachal Pradesh tribals constitute 63.66 percent of its population. At least every third citizen of North East India belongs either to a scheduled caste or a scheduled tribe. No other region presents such a variety of tribes and communities as North East India does. Castes and tribes from other parts of India also find a place here.

Major tribes and sub-tribes entered into North East occupying mostly hills and some fringe areas in the plains. They speak different dialects and possess their own distinctive social and cultural traditions which they jealously guard. Two major ethnic strains are found in the tribes of North East India—that of the Mongoloid and Proto-Australoid. But generally, the bulk of tribal population show strains of Mongoloid features. Linguistically, they speak a form of Tibeto-Burman and Siamese-Chinese, which have affiliation with the Thai language. The Khasis and Pnars speak dialects which belong to the Mon-Khmer linguistic group showing characteristics of Austro-Asiatic linguistic family.

The number of tribal communities, having distinctive cultures, languages, dialects including sub-tribes would be around 200 in North East India as against 460 for the whole of India. In other words, it may be inferred that about 44 percent of the Scheduled Tribes of India live in the North East region of the country, which in terms of percentage comes to 25.81 of the total population of North East India.

All the tribals are not at the same level of social and economic development. Some of them, particularly the Khasis and Mizos, have educationally and economically reached a higher level of attainment than many others. But most of them are poor as underdevelopment or lack of development is widespread and land is appropriated by a few. Industrialisation is almost unknown. Literacy rate among the Mizos is second only to the people of Kerala. Despite the progress made towards amelioration of the lot of the tribals, the impact of the successive Five Year Plans has so far been marginal.

The hill areas of North East India were uniformly administered till 1932 as a backward tract. From April 1937, there was a bifurcation of the administrative pattern. The Mizo Hills (Lushai Hills), Naga Hills, North Cachar Hills and North Eastern Frontier tracts became 'Excluded Areas', excluded from ministerial jurisdiction , and the Garo Hills, the British portion of the Khasi and Jaintia Hills and Mikir Hills (Karbi Anglong) were partially excluded areas. The excluded areas were further protected by the inner lines which prevented the entry of outsiders without permit. The last of such lines was drawn in North Cachar Hills in 1942.

The tribals of hill districts as a result developed a special kind of identity which had remained crucial for subsequent political developments. All the new political units in North East India except in Meghalaya are really old administrative tribal hill districts. Meghalaya is an amalgamation of two tribal districts—Garo Hills and Old Khasi and Jaintia Hill districts plus 25 Khasi Syiemships, which had a nominal status of princely states. Beside these Syiemships, there were two princely states of Manipur and Tripura, which had usual political connections

Tribal District Councils under state legislation are ineffective due to unequal land relations.

MEGHALAYA

Meghalaya is the amalgamation of the two old districts under British rule-that of the Garo Hills and United Khasi Hills and 25 former syiemships under the Sanad relationship during colonial rule. It is now divided into seven districts with Three Autonomous District Council, under the Sixth Schedule of the Constitution of India. The three leading tribes are Khasi, the Pnar and the Garo. A section of the Rabhas, Boro-Kacharis and Kochs are also permanently staying in Meghalaya with 5 percent government posts being reserved for them. Eighty percent of the posts, are, however, reserved for the main groups of tribals. Interests of the tribals are protected under the Meghalaya Transfer of Land (Regulation) Act, 1971, the provisions of reservation in services and provision of seat reservation in the Legislative Assembly and in Parliament. Out of a total population of 1,774,778 (1991), 9,072 (0.51 percent) are scheduled castes and scheduled tribes numbering 1,517,927 (85.52 percent). Being a tribal—dominated state, atrocities on scheduled tribes and even scheduled castes are far from a common feature. For the same reason, all the general schemes for economic, cultural and social development are earmarked, in essence, for the tribals.

The Khasi and Garo are recognised matrilineal societies. But even in a typically matrilineal society like the Khasi, the women are not allowed to participate in the traditional village *Durbar* and their representation in Autonomous District Councils is also rare. They are usually dependents on males for management of landed property. There is, however, no child and bonded labourer in Meghalaya. Agriculture is the mainstay of the economy of the people. But the total area under cultivation is only 8.75 percent of the area of the state. Only a few small scale industries exist in the state. In its present form agriculture holds little promise.

MIZORAM

Mizoram is primarily a landlocked hilly area occupying a strategic frontier. It has an area of 21,081 sq. km, about 62 percent of which is covered by forests and 10 percent of the available land is cultivable. Champhai, North Vanlaiphai and Thezawl practise rice cultivation. Though Chamdur is a plain area, it is covered by forest. The state is predominantly inhabited by scheduled tribes. Of the 13 tribes, the main tribes are Mizo, Pawi, Lakher and the Chakma. About seventy percent of the tribals depend on agriculture for their living. But it is mainly based on shifting cultivation on 189 thousand hectares accounting for 8.97 percent of the total area of the state. No major industry functions in Mizoram.

The population of Mizoram is 6,86,217 (1991) and the scheduled tribes account for 94.75 percent of the total population. The scheduled caste population is very small with 691 persons who are mostly engaged in agriculture, trade and commerce, service and construction works.

Being a tribal state, there is no special component plan or tribal sub-plan in Mizoram. There is no special scheme for the scheduled caste people also as they represent only 0.10 percent of the total population. The state government has been providing reservation in Government services for the scheduled tribes to the extent of 93.26 percent and 1.83 percent for the scheduled castes. But there is no specific legislation for it. The Government is providing reservation for scheduled tribes in proportion to their population in the state as approved by the Government of India in 1985. The interest of the tribals were protected under the Bengal Eastern Frontier Regulation of 1973 in the form of Inner Line, which used to prohibit Indian citizens from entering Mizoram without a government pass. Now the entry is not that strictly regulated. The China Hills Regulation Act of 1896, made effective from October 1951, empowers the Deputy Commissioner to expel any Indian citizen from Mizoram. The Mizo District Transfer of Land Act 1963 and Mizoram Transfer of Land Amendment Act of 1990 provide protection to the scheduled tribes of the state as regards asserting inalienable rights of the tribal people on land. The Mizoram Trading by Non-Tribal Regulation Act of 1974, 1977 protect the tribals against non-tribals in the field of trade and commerce. In Mizoram there is no municipality or Gram Panchayat. There are Village Councils numbering 671 to look after the general welfare of the people. They are important political and social bodies entrusted with village administration and development work. There are three Autonomous District Councils under the Sixth Schedule to protect tribal identity and culture. There is no special scheme as such for the development of the scheduled tribes and scheduled castes, as the state is essentially a tribal society. However, efforts are being made to protect the social and economic interest as well as the cultural identity of the people.

through the agency of Governor of Assam. There was finally an unadministered Naga tribal area beyond the boundaries of British India but within India and under the executive control of the Governor General of India exercised through the Governor of Assam. Such ethnic pockets had close affinities with neighbouring British India territories. It may be mentioned here that many tribals live along international boundaries and their ethnic and cultural affinities are with other tribes across the frontier. The tribal areas of North East India were not completely integrated with the political and economic system of the country and the Inner Line System still in vogue further reported the tribal region of North East India from the rest of the country.

Admittedly, tribes were not integrated with the political and economic system of the colonial India. After Independence also, the process of integration of the tribals with the mainstream people could never get under way, partly because of the continuation of the British legacy and partly because of the growing political consciousness of the tribal people. On the eve of Independence, the situation in the North East Hills was very fluid. The economic impact of the Second World War, the divisive policy of the colonial administration, the possibility of freedom in near future, the national movement and growing sense of ethnic identity among different ethnic groups, spread of education in the hills by Christian Missionaries and a gradual emergence of a small educated middle class among the tribals of the hills and in the plains contributed to the growth of a sense of political awareness among the different tribal groups. The political movement in these hills surfaced with the coming of Independence. With the transfer of power, the tribes became more conscious of their a political identity. The Sixth Schedule to the Constitution of India was an attempt to protect tribal interests in the hill tribes-dominated composite Assam districts in 1952. The Nagas were not impressed with the arrangement and rejected it outright. They eventually got by a hard way a territorial and political entity in 1962-63. The other tribes, the Khasis, the Pnars, the Garos, and Lushias took advantage of this new political instrument in the form of Autonomous District Council to consolidate the authority of the newly emerging liberal middle class leadership and to set about a process of political modernisation. The Lushai hills following the Naga path grew into Mizoram. By 1972, political reorganisation created Meghalaya as an amalgamation of the Garos, Khasis, Pnars, Syntengs, Jaintias among the major tribal groups. Arunachal Pradesh was formed out of the North East Frontier Tracts and Mizoram became a full state in 1986. Likewise, the two former princely states of Manipur and Tripura were accorded the status of full statehood in 1972 along with Meghalaya.

ARUNACHAL PRADESH

Arunachal Pradesh has 51 tribes and sub-tribes. Out of these, 25 tribes are identified major tribes. Deori, Kimir, Mishing, Zakhring and Lisu are not declared as scheduled tribes in this state. In Arunachal Pradesh only 0.47% of the total population belongs to schedule caste group. There is no indigenous scheduled caste in the state. However, 16 castes are recognised as scheduled castes in Arunachal Pradesh. There is no specific development scheme for them. No specific tribal sub-plan or special common plan is in operation in Arunachal Pradesh. All the developmental schemes taken up by the state government are directed towards the development of scheduled tribes. There is no separate scheme ensuring social, cultural and economic safeguards to the tribals. But the state has taken up some measures to protect the socio-cultural heritage of the scheduled tribes. Being a tribal state, there is little scope for the non-tribals to exploit the scheduled tribes. But suppression of rights and differentiating women as reflected by the presence of bonded labour and slavery in some tribal societies of Arunachal Pradesh have also to be taken note of. The original settlers of the state, however, resent the settlement of Chakma and Majong tribal refugees in Arunachal Pradesh, who took shelter in the state in the wake of disturbances in Bangladesh in sixties and seventies. If anything, the relationship between the two groups of tribals is not normal.

ASSAM

16.48 percent of the people of India belong to the scheduled castes, while in Assam it is 7.40 percent of the total population. In Assam, there are 16 scheduled castes with 9 synonyms as per Scheduled Castes and Scheduled Tribes list Modification Order, 1976. The literacy rate in Assam is 53.43 percent, while only 43.42 percent of scheduled castes and 39.12 percent of the tribals in Assam are literates. Among the scheduled castes, the Namasudras occupy the predominant position with 32.97 percent of the total scheduled caste population of Assam. They are supposed to belong to the fishing community. In fact, they are an agricultural caste in the Barak Valley. Kaibartas are equally prominent. Fishing is also an avenue for their livelihood. 53.5 percent of the scheduled caste people are agriculturists. Pottery and goldsmithy are important occupations for the Hiras and Banias respectively. Fishing is no longer an exclusive profession for the Kaibartas. They have almost lost the profession to outsiders. There is no denying the fact that in terms of economic progress the scheduled castes are much behind other people. Their children help the parents in their professional work, denying them the opportunity of schooling. They are never self-sufficient in agricultural production as cultivable land is limited and insufficient. As a result, they are in perpetual indebtedness. There is now a growing trend in them to shift to other occupations. The Assam State Development Corporation for Scheduled Castes, the Assam Plains Tribes Development Corporation and the Assam Tribal Development Authority established in 1983 are important institutions working for overall social and economic development of scheduled castes and plains tribals in Assam. A number of N.G.Os are also working in this field.

NAGALAND

Nagaland is a predominantly scheduled tribe-inhabited state with a population of 1,209,546. There are many separate tribes and sub-tribes amongst the Nagas, each with their own distinct language and culture. Of the tribes, mention may be made of the Konyak, Angami, Lotha, Chakosang, Chang, Khienungam, Phom-Sangtam, Yimchungre, Zeliang, Khezha, Chakru and Rengma. Ao, Sema, Lotha, Konyak and Angami are the leading Naga tribes. Some of the important Manipur Naga tribes like the Tangkhul, Mao, Maram have their representation in Nagaland. Besides, a small number of Kukis, Garos, Kacharis and Karbis also live here.

In Nagaland, the tribal or village councils control the social life, try minor criminal and civil cases in accordance with customary law, though a limit has been put to avoid harsh and heavy punishment.

There is no tribal sub-plan or special component plan in Nagaland as it is predominantly a tribal state. The state has, therefore, no separate or exclusive scheme for the development of scheduled tribes of the state.

The status of women in Naga society is not that low as the incidence of suppression of woman and apathy towards them are rather uncommon. Women are engaged in handloom and some cottage industries. There is no major industry in Nagaland. The paper mill is now closed. People practise *jhum*, terrace and settled cultivation. But food production is inadequate.

MANIPUR

About 10 percent of the total area of Manipur is in the valley, which comes to 223 sq. km. hills account for 90 percent of the area of the state. But about 70 percent of the people of Manipur live in the valley and the rest in the hills. Imphal, Thoubal and Bishnupur areas are mostly inhabited by the Meiteis. 68.46 percent of the population is dependent on agriculture and wet cultivation is widely practised in the valley. Shifting cultivation is still in practice in the hills. The handloom industry keeps about five lakh people engaged, who represent about 28 percent of the total population and comprise mostly women.

Out of a total population of 1,837,149, scheduled castes number 37,105, while the tribal population comes to 6,32,173 according to 1991 Census. There are 29 scheduled tribes and 7 scheduled castes.

The state government is implementing special component plans for the development of scheduled caste people. The Tribal sub-plan is directed towards the development of the tribals. Interestingly, 47.72 percent of the scheduled castes live in the villages and 52.28 percent of them live in urban areas. The literacy rate of the scheduled castes is 56.44 percent against 59.89 percent for the whole state. The population of scheduled castes in Manipur is only 2.02 percent of the total population and 2.14 percent of land belong to them. So, the share of land of the scheduled caste people is slightly more than their population. But the land holding is not equitable.

The 29 major scheduled tribes may be divided into some broad ethnic groups like Naga, Kuki-Chin, Mizo. The literacy percentage of scheduled tribes is 53.63 as against 59.89 percent for the whole state. The incidence of poverty is 56.80 percent among the tribals.

There is a regular interaction between scheduled castes, scheduled tribes with the Meiteis, which is by and large peaceful. But in recent years the relation between the Nagas and the Kuki tribes has been strained mostly because of the dispute over the exercise of control in specific areas.

The tenancy laws of Manipur exclude the hill areas where the scheduled tribes are predominant and the land traditionally belongs to the tribal chiefs. The forest policy is also directed to safeguard the customary rights and interests of the tribals. But in practice the conditions are not always maintained. Illegal felling of trees has reached an alarming proportion and in this act tribals are not always to be blamed. The five

TRIPURA

Tripura is a landlocked state, (former princely state) which had merged with India soon after India's Independence. It had, in 1951, 639000 people, a substantial portion of whom were local tribals. The Maharaja himself was a tribal. But due to unabated influx from neighbouring country (the present Bangladesh), the demographic balance was lost and in 1991 the total population rose to 2,757,205 with scheduled tribe population standing at 853,345 persons (30.95 percent). Not unexpectedly, they had lost control over a substantial portion of tribal land. Recent legislations providing for re-transfer of tribal Council under the Sixth Schedule was created to protect the identity and land of the tribals in tribal-dominated areas.

There are 19 tribes and 17 Kuki sub-tribes in Tripura. The three most important tribal communities in Tripura are Tripuri, Reang and Jamatia. The Tripuris are the most important scheduled tribe in Tripura who have been divided into two groups - The Puran Tripuris and the Deshi Tripuris. In the past, the Tripuris mostly depended on *jhum* cultivation. Now-a-days, many of them have settled down in the plains and adopted plough cultivation. In the land previously used for *jhum* cultivation, coffee and rubber cultivation have been introduced in a big way. But *jhum* cultivation still continues in many areas.

It is true that efforts are being made to protect the interests of the tribals by introducing tribal sub-plan. The scheduled castes, mostly immigrants, are also looked after by special component plan. In Tripura the scheduled caste people numbering 451,116 (1991) account for 16.48 percent of the population of the state. They are mostly migrants.

Taking North East India as a whole, one gets the impression that the tribal sub-plans and special component plans for the scheduled tribes and also for the scheduled castes have not brought about significant results. Mostly they remain non-implemented except to an extent in Tripura and Assam. The scheduled castes have almost touched the rock bottom level of existence. They lost ownership of land in many cases and became victims of exploitation as artisans, as labourers and professionals. The scheduled tribes were in a better position with command over their land and forests in their respective areas. But slowly there have been inroads of commercial ventures from outside and moneylenders and money-lending agencies have become more active. Refugees from Bangladesh had encroached upon tribal land in Tripura.

Slowly tribals began to loose command over their resources, land and forests to the emerging elites of their own communities and to the state. The emerging middle class in tribal society is indicative of the growth of an exploitative trend in their set up. The structural transformation of the tribal economy had gone in favour of a small group of tribals, who could get the benefits of political accessibility, economic and educational opportunities.

It has been estimated in 1981 that approximately 52.63 percent of the population in rural areas and 33.37 percent in urban areas in North East India live below the poverty line. The present day position has not substantially changed. In tiny Meghalaya more than 50 percent of the families live below the poverty line. The process of economic deprivation of rural people has adversely affected the scheduled castes and the scheduled tribes. Ironically, due to the policy of reservation for the scheduled tribes and scheduled castes in services, the emerging middle class in the tribal society corner most of the benefits.

Of the total population of 31,547,314 (1991) , the scheduled castes and scheduled tribes, forming 6.85 percent and 25.81 percent respectively of the total population, along with other backward communities are mostly the victims of inequality in the socio-economic field. Inequality has also emerged in the tribal society because the common villagers have lost command over land and forests. At another level, the scheduled castes have lost control over land to the advanced class. There is today a growing number of landless agricultural labourers among both scheduled castes and scheduled tribes. They are getting restive as they suffer from a sense of deprivation. The widening disparity of income within the tribal society has definitely contributed to the growing sense of frustration among the tribals. Unemployment in the sense it is understood in the complex, class-based society has gradually crept into the tribal society as well. This is probably expected. What could not be properly anticipated is the kind of reaction to such deprivations. Their biological background has not always proved to be advantageous to them, but it has at least provided them with a footing to think differently for which they alone cannot be blamed.

REFERENCES

Roy Barman, B.K. 1961. *Demographic and Socio-economic Profiles of North East India. Census of India.*

Census of India, 1991. *Special Tables for Scheduled Castes and Scheduled Tribes. Mizoram, Nagaland, Arunachal Pradesh, Manipur and Tripura.*

Singh, K.S. (ed). 1972. *Tribal Situation in India.* New Delhi: Monohar.

PART TWO

POPULATION, GENETICS, HEALTH

2

Emerging Trends in Genetic Epidemiology of Hemo-globinopathy in the Seven Sister States of North Eastern India

R. S. BALGIR

INTRODUCTION

The Indian subcontinent provides a unique opportunity to study the micro-evolutionary dynamics in human populations. The populations in India are highly inbred communities, as a result of which many distinct bio-social practices have been perpetuated creating linguistic, religious, caste and ethnic barriers.

Human heredity plays a major role in the conservation of characters. However, the genetic errors and variations do occur depending upon the geographical location, economic and familial constraints, nutrition, breeding structure and bio-social practices perpetuated in a population from time to time. An attempt has been made here to identify the emerging treads in genetic epidemiology with special reference to abnormal hemoglobins E and sickle cell (HbS) in North Eastern India.

Aims and Objectives

The study in hand has the following aims and objectives :

1. To introduce the genetic epidemiology briefly ;

2. To enlist the plausible reasons for hemoglobin beta-E mutation;
3. To highlight the factors responsible for high prevalence of hemoglobin E in North Eastern India ;
4. To review in brief the origin and spread of hemoglobin E in North Eastern India;
5. To present an update of sickle cell and E hemoglobinopathy in North Eastern India.

Genetic Epidemiology

Genetic epidemiology encompasses the study of genetic factors including the guiding principles for their ultimate control and understanding of the etiology of complex familial diseases. In other words, genetic epidemiology is a science that deals with the etiology, distribution and control of diseases in a group of relatives and for the inherited causes of a disease in a population (Morton, 1982). Genetic epidemiology is primarily concerned with the study of familial aggregation of particular phenotypes/genotypes to resolve genetic inheritance from other sources of resemblance in family. Risk factor is the most commonly used term in genetic epidemiology. It reveals the degree of susceptibility or non-susceptibility of an individual, family or, for that matter, a population towards a disease. Support for a major gene cause implies that some individuals and perhaps their relatives may be at high risk of developing a certain condition of disease. Identification of individuals at high risk may be useful for conducting further biological investigations, therapeutic tests, prevention, genetic counselling or other clinical decisions, if a plausible model of transmission is traced or made available.

Genetic epidemiology is an important tool for delineation of the genetic and non-genetic factors in the causation of a condition of disease. The resultant information is of utmost importance in planning the preventive and promotive health care strategies among the different population groups inheriting a biological trait or disease. It is, therefore, emphasized for the development of a need-based health care system in India which should include not only the curative aspects but also look into the preventive, promotive health care for the management of genetic disorders and their genetic burden in the communities (Balgir, 2000).

Genetic epidemiology is gradually advancing into the field of modern Human Genetics, where rapid scientific strides have been made in recent years. With the eradication of maladies due to infection and malnutrition, the focus has now been shifted towards diseases of genetic origin that are the sources of most of the human sufferings. It has been estimated that every individual carries 5-8 harmful genes that may be expressed in a conducive environment (Roy et al., 1986). There is a heavy risk and load of genetic diseases because of high birth rate, consanguineous marriages, caste and local endogamy and lack of rehabilitative facilities available, especially to poverty-stricken rural masses in India. Every year 80,000 infants with congenital malformation, 27,200 infants with Down's syndrome, 5,000 infants with hereditary anemia, over 9,000 thalassemia children and 4,300 babies with Duchenne muscular dystrophy are born with high morbidity and mortality in India. There are about 25 million carriers of beta-thalassemia gene in India. At least one child with this genetic disease is born every 40 seconds in India (Verma, 1991).

Now-a-days, it has become imperative for clinicians to identify and detect the human disorders due to genetic cause because upon their correct diagnosis depends the treatment, prognosis, prevention and counselling. There are several inherited abnormalities known to afflict human beings. Hemoglobinopathy is recognised as one of the most important public health problems today in Human Genetics in India. Hemoglobinopathies—a group of inherited disorders of structure and synthesis of globin part of hemoglobin molecule, are the most commonly encountered monogenic genetic disorders. There are three common hemoglobin variants, namely, sickle cell (HbS), hemoglobin E (HbE) and hemoglobin D (HbD), which are most frequently observed in the Indian patients, sometimes in association with alpha or beta-thalassemia (Balgir, 1996a).

The errors in hemoglobin synthesis do lead to considerable disease states. It becomes the cause of a disease if the abnormal hemoglobin is unstable which leads to early destruction of red cells as in sickle cell hemoglobin or hemoglobin E and also, if, it results in some way early lysis due to a structural malformation of the membrane as in thalassemia. In many cases, the abnormal hemoglobin does not produce signs and symptoms, unless the subject is under stressful condition. Even under normal conditions, sometimes the variability is recorded in the expression of a disease.

Hemoglobin Variant

Hemoglobin E is the commonest structural variant in South East Asia. It is a hemoglobin variant in which there is substitution of normal glutamine residue by lysine in the 26th amino acid position of the beta-globin polypeptide (Beta 26 Glu to Lys) and is caused by the codon 26 (GAG >AAG) mutation [OMIM NO. 141900.0071] of the beta-globin gene. Barring a few cases of sporadic appearance in India, hemoglobin E (HbE) is frequently detected in people originating from North Eastern India (Balgir, 1995a).

It is difficult to say when, where and how the hemoglobin E mutation had taken place during the course of human life. It might have either originated somewhere in the North Eastern part of India or in South East Asian countries. Some of the factors, common both to North Eastern region of India and South East Asia responsible for hemoglobin E mutation, may be elaborated here as under with special reference to North Eastern India:

Ecology

The North Eastern part of India has lush green vegetal cover throughout the year. There are thick forests, foothills, plain valleys of river Brahamputra and its tributaries, tea gardens and paddy fields. In the paddy fields, frequent waterlogging leads to mosquito breeding. Thick forests give shelter to mosquitoes. Mosquitoes are vectors of malaria, which spread the disease in the region.

Climate

For about nine months from April to September and again from December to February incessant rain keeps the weather helpful for mosquitoes to proliferate. The hot and humid climate accelerates the breeding of mosquitoes in the North Easter region of India. The high density of mosquito fauna carries the malarial parasite, which causes the disease.

Wet Cultivation

The paddy cultivation helps the growth and development of mosquito fauna which, in turn, help the migration of malarial parasite. High density of mosquito fauna and high rate of transmission of malaria cause an epidemic to spread rapidly in the region. Uncontrolled malaria takes a high toll of life in the North East region of India every year. This endemicity of lethal disease of malaria is detrimental to human population growth and its proliferation.

Human Population and Malaria

Under all conducive climatic and environmental conditions for the spread of malaria (both plain and forest malaria), which is a major cause of high human mortality, the nature provides some protective mechanism to the host against such a dreadful disease. This protection comes from a mutation in hemoglobin molecule of the red blood cell upon which the malarial parasite survives. Now, any sudden change in hemoglobin molecule is unsuitable for the survival of malarial parasite and so the host is saved and protected from the lethal malarial disease. It is presumed that the hemoglobin E gene probably developed against the malarial endemicity in North East India.

Genotoxic Effects of Environment

The globin molecule has been used as a tool in the detection of variety of mutations in human populations. It remains to be seen if the alterations seen are of any use in assessing the genotoxic potential of environmental conditions. It is equally likely that some chemicals, drugs, radioactive compounds, other ultra-violet rays, etc. may be responsible for the hemoglobin E mutation in the initial stages. It is extremely unlikely that only a malarious environment is the prime cause of such an exotic multifarious result.

The interaction pattern of an abnormal hemoglobin gene with climate, geographical condition, nutrition and other environmental factors requires thorough analysis.

Reasons for High Prevalence of Hemoglobin E Variant

There are several reasons for rapid proliferation of hemoglobin E in the North Eastern states of India.

The hemoglobin E is benign in nature and no significant adverse effects have been recorded in individuals performing their day-to-day activities with it. Moreover, it is a fact that persons possessing hemoglobin E have low level of hemoglobin than the normal cases. The low level of hemoglobin in girls adds to their beauty of the skin colour so that they have a fair complexion rather than the brown or dark brown complexion. Consequently, they develop an added physical attraction, which opens up possibilities for their marital union on a higher scale. This results in rapid proliferation of the abnormal gene. Incidentally, marriage by elopement is the most frequently practised type in North East India.

However, in some communities, the practice of local, kin group level or tribal endogamy is strictly followed with the result that the abnormal hemoglobin E gene, once entered in the population, goes on multiplying vigorously because of small population size. The genetic or marriage distance is very low in these populations. Since there is no genetic testing and counselling facilities available to the people in the rural areas where the masses exist without having a knowledge base, there is no likelihood of genetic prevention and control of the malady. Thus, the abnormal gene multiplies manifold undetected and unnoticed in the community.

The subsistence economy plays a major role in the selection of mates in North East India. On the whole, the economy of the autochthonous people of North East India is in a poor shape, partly because of work lethargy and partly because of climate sound barrier. An economic condition could sometimes break the traditional economically sound person can marry any girl belonging to any community, regardless of caste, creed, language, religion. This is further substantiated by the fact that the non-Mongoloid (Caucasoid) people in the region have assimilated the local genetic characters like hemoglobin E which was earlier prevalent only in the populations of Mongoloid origin.

The climate has also its bearing upon the nature and activities of the people. The rainy season is a prolonged one, lasting about nine months in a year in North Eastern region of India. The climate is hot and humid during these nine months. This limits the major or vital outside household activities of the people. Fertility has been observed to be high in females especially among the hemoglobin E heterozygotes (Balgir, 1992c). This contributed to a rapid population rise in the North East region of India. There is hardly any family with an average of less than 4-5 children in the region. Comparatively, higher fertility in the region is singularly important in the spread and distribution of hemoglobin E gene in the population.

The mainstay of the people is agriculture and they also depend on forest products available in the region. For cultivating paddy, they need not have to work hard as the region is well fed with rain water. They get sufficient rice and local fish to eat during the whole year. For other requirements they either procure these from locally available sources like paddy fields, forests or do not bother at all about their availability and inclusion in the dietion a regular basis. The excess of children or large family size in such a situation does not pose much of a problem. This is also a contributory factor in the spread and proliferation of abnormal hemoglobin E gene in North East India.

Regarding the prevalence and distribution of sickle cell hemoglobinopathy in the North Eastern region of India, migrations of people from the state of West Bengal, Bihar, Orissa, Andhra Pradesh, Tamil Nadu and Kerala had a definite role to play (Balgir, 1996b), Partly based on this, the origin, spread and maintenance of sickle cell gene in Indian populations have been elaborated further (Balgir, 2001, 2002).

There may be some other unnoticed and unexplored factors like founder effect, small population size, local inbreeding, illiteracy responsible for the rapid proliferation of hemoglobin E in North East India.

Origin and spread of Hemoglobin E Mutation

Although sporadic cases of hemoglobin E in Assam and West Bengal (3.9%) were mentioned by Chatterjea (1960), the first indication of a high prevalence of this abnormal in the population of North East India was the finding of 23% of Hb E carriers among in the Toto tribe the border of Assam and West Bengal by Chaudhuri et al. (1962).

In view of the observed association of high prevalence of hemoglobin E with the Austro-Asiatic speakers in South East Asia (Flatz *et al.*, 1965), the attention was directed towards the Khasi of Meghalaya, an Austroasiatic group. Initially, three populations were selected for examination: (1) Khasi of Meghalaya—an Austroasiatic group, (2) Ahom of Assam—a Tai group related to Shan of Burma (Myanmar), who had migrated from Myanmar during 13th century A.D., (3) an Assamese caste population of Lower Assam.

Till recently, the hypothesis of a single Hb -> Hb E mutation and its spread from South East Asia was generally accepted. The frequency of Hb E gene in the Caucasoid caste population is around 0.3, whereas the gene is highly prevalent in the Mongoloid populations, frequencies ranging from 0.2 to 0.6 (Table 2). The Boro (Bodo) Kachari population residing in Assam have shown 0.64 frequency of hemoglobin E allele, so far the highest in the world. The Sonowal Kachari, an allied tribal group, closely follow them (0.56). There are alternative hypotheses regarding the origin, spread and maintenance of the allele in South East Asia and in North East India.

It was believed to be maintained through an adaptive advantage in the malarious environment, but a higher incidence of the allele (0.4-0.6) among the Bodo populations than among Austroasiatic and Tai groups—the Khasi and the Ahom (0.3-0.4), who could have carried the gene from Thailand or from the Shan region Myanmar, could not be explained on the basis of the hypothesis given by Flatz et al. (1965).

The Restriction Fragment Length Polymorphism (RELF)—based four point studies bearing codon 26(G->A) showed that in spite of the expected 2^4 or 16 haplotypes, Beta-E-mutations were observed only on four haplotypes, suggesting that there exists a linkage disequilibrium between 5' and 3' haplotype cluster and also within 5' haplotype cluster. It has been hypothesized that either Beta-E originated as a single mutation in Southeast Asia or has multiple origins (Antonarakis et al., 1985; Hundrieser et al., 1988).

In fact, Beta E mutation has been observed in five different haplotypes (restriction endonucleases), three in Southeast Asia (Antonariakis et al., 1982) and two in Europeans (Kazazian et al., 1984). These haplotypes may be found in association with two different beta-globin gene framework in Europeans. On the other hand, there are reports of two different mutations of Hb E with two different DNA frameworks (Antonarakis et al., 1982; Hundrieser et al., 1988). The highest occurrence of the gene in Assam area, which is on the far end of the proposed center of distribution in Northern Laos, Northeast Thailand and Cambodia, is deviation from the expected pattern of gene distribution. Based on this observation, Deka et. al. (1988) speculated that hemoglobin E in the Tibeto-Burman populations of Assam arose by an independent mutation contributing to the high frequencies of hemoglobin E in the Northeast Indian populations.

Antonarakis et al. (1982) have demonstrated that Hb E is present in two different 'Beta-gene frameworks' in Southeast Asia, suggesting at least two mutational events. One of the mutations was found to be exclusively associated with the populations of Laos, Thailand and Cambodia. In case of multiple mutational events, a second HbE mutant may have its origin in the Tibeto-Burmans of Assam.

By analysing eight restriction sites, Hundrieser et al. (1988) studied Kachari (Bodo group) of Tibeto-Burman language group in Assam among whom the highest known prevalence of hemoglobin E has been reported.

He found a common origin of the hemoglobin beta-E gene in Southeast Asia and Assam. This is somewhat surprising since the main area of distribution of hemoglobin beta-E is Southeast Asia and some of the original populations of North East India like Ahom, of Assam, Khasis of Meghalaya and other Tibeto-Burman groups of the region have no direct link with Southeast Asians.

These findings get further support from several studies carried out among the tribals of Tripura (De et al., 1997; Das et al., 2000; Das et al., 2002). The four point haplotype (chromosome) analysis with assigned framework 2 of Beta-globin gene cluster from Hb E homozygotes in tribal population of Tripura had produced interesting results. The 5'+++B^E-3' was the most predominant haplotype in Tripura (19 Beta-E chromosomes), followed by North Bengal (4 Beta-E chromosomes), Assam (2 Beta-E chromosomes), and Bangladesh (1 Beta-E chromosome), whereas the 5'-++B^E-3' haplotype which was also found in Tripura (1 Beta-E chromosome) was observed in Northeast Thailand (Das et al., 2000) too. The 5'++-B^E-3' haplotype was detected for the first time in Tripura (7 Beta-E chromosomes) whereas the 5'---B^E3' haplotype is common in southern West Bengal (14 Beta-E chromosomes), Tripura (3 Beta-E chromosomes), Bangladesh (3 Beta-E chromosomes), but not in Assam (Das et al., 2000).

The pattern of distribution of hemoglobin beta-E and malarial infection in Southeast Asia and North East India suggest the introduction of hemoglobin beta-E from Southeast Asia and attainment of higher frequencies in certain populations probably because of continued selective pressure of malarial infection (Saha, 1990).

Cruz-Coke (1978) reported that no abnormal hemoglobin had been found among the high altitude populations. Is it due to the fact that abnormal hemoglobins carry less oxygen and so they just cannot survive or is it due to the absence of malarial parasite in high altitude areas as because the abnormal haemoglobin genes have no selective advantage are yet to be ascertained (Saha, 1990) observed a low frequency of hemoglobin Beta-E (about 0.02) among the Khasis of Cherrapunji district (Meghalaya) as compared to the Khasis of Shillong (0.22) and reported that this could be due to relaxation of selection in the absence of malaria at high altitude.

Generally speaking, endogamy, founder effect and/or local inbreeding may possibly explain the high prevalence of hemoglobin E gene in North East India.

Prevalence and geographical Distribution

The North-Eastern region of India, which comprises of seven sister states namely, Arunachal Pradesh, Assam, Manipur, Meghalaya, Mizoram, Nagaland and Tripura, is ecologically an ever-green part of the country with thick vegetal cover, having hot and humid climate, heavy rainfall, high and low hills, plateaus and plains, valleys and rivers and varied groups of people with rich traditions, songs and dances. It has attracted several researchers to undertake studies on different biological traits. On hemoglobinopathy, several studies have been carried out in the North Eastern region, except in the state of Mizoram, which have been compiled below in the form of a population synthesis.

ARUNACHAL PRADESH

Arunachal Pradesh is the easternmost part of India, surrounded on three sides by the international border with Bhutan in the West, China in the North and North-East, and Myanmar in the East, the Southern border being shared with the plains of Assam. The tribal population constitutes about 70-75% of the total population of Arunachal Pradesh. High mountains and dense forests have stood in the way of developing intercommunications between the tribes living in different river valleys. Isolation imposed by geography has also led to the formation of over 26 major tribes and a number of sub-tribes with several dialects to live and flourish with their distinct identities in dress, social life and customs (Balgir, 1995).

The prevalence of hemoglobin E gene varies between 5% to 18% in Adi, Apatani, Nishi, and other tribes in the state of Arunachal Pradesh as indicated in Table 2.1. The Arunachal tribes are Mongoloid people and belong to the Tibeto-Burman family. These populations originally were strictly endogamous, but now inter-tribal marriages are also taking place. Both fraternal polyandry and polygamy are practised by the Adi tribe, irrespective of the age of partners. The practices of bride-price in the form of mithun, a hybrid of cow and buffalo and polygamy are common with particular concern being shown to age of partners among the Nishi and Apatani tribes of Arunachal Pradesh (Balgir and Dutta, 1990).

ASSAM

In the plains of Assam, the Ahoms, belonging to the Tai-Shan group of Mongoloid racial stock, entered Assam in 1228 AD through the Patkai range. They had fierce fights with the local Bodo-Kachari population for the dominion (Balgir, 1993). They have now settled in the plains of Upper Assam. Formerly speakers of a form of Tai language, they are now culturally and linguistically assimilated to the Assamese population. They are medium in height and possess broad head with mesorrhine nose and light brown skin colour.

Table: 2.1. Prevalence of hemoglobin E hemoglobinopathy in Tribal populations of Arunachal Pradesh.

Name of Tribe	*No. Tested*	*Hb AE %*	*Hb EE %*	*Source*
Adi	35	11.4	0	Balgir & Dutta, 1990
Adi (Gallong)	113	25.7	5.3	Saha, 1990
Adi (Minyong)	42	16.7	0	-Do-
Adi (Others)	60	16.7	1.6	-Do-
Apatani	29	10.3	0	Balgir & Dutta, 1990
Apatani	79	11.4	0	Saha, 1990
Nishi	117	12	0	Balagir & Dutta, 1990
Nishi	216	13	0.9	Saha, 1990
Other mixed tribes	22	9.1	4.5	Balgir & Dutta, 1990
Other mixed tribes	58	10.3	1.7	Saha, 1990

The Kachari population belong to the Mongoloid group of Sino-Tibetan stock who have many subgroups such as Sonowal, Bodo, Mech, etc. This Bodo group of tribes belong to the Tibeto-Burman language group. They are medium statured and have yellowish-brown to dark-brown skin colour, typical flat nose and oblique eye slits. Bur considerable variation occurs among them.

The frequency of hemoglobin E gene ranges between 2% to 64% in the populations of Mongoloid origin and between 5% to 30% among the Caucasoid groups of Assam (Table 2.2). The sickle cell gene is also prevalent in Assam, but is mostly confined to the tea garden labour force (Table 2.3). However, sporadic cases of sickle cell gene are now coming up among the Muslims and Mongoloid populations of Assam (Balgir, 1993).

Table: 2.2. Prevalence of hemoglobin E hemoglobinopathy in populations of Assam

Name of Tribe	*No. Tested*	*Hb AE %*	*Hb SS %*	*Allele (E) Frequency*	*Source*
MONGOLOID GROUP :					
Ahom	129	46.5	11.6	0.349	Flatz et al., 1972
Ahom	125	41.6	10.4*	0.304	Balgir. 1991a
Ahom	399	45.4	10.0	0.327	Das et al., 1975
Ahom	119	47.1	16.8	0.403	Das et al., 1988
Karbi (Mikir)	131	27.5	6.1	0.198	Deka et al., 1980
Karbi	110	29.1	8.2	0.227	Das et al., 1988
Boro Kachari	131	47.3	31.3	0.549	Deka et al., 1980
Boro Kachari	110	38.2	45.4	0.645	Das et al., 1988
Mech- Kachari	124	44.4	31.5	0.536	Balgir, 1992a
Sonowal-Kachari	158	50.0	31.6	0.562	Balgir. 1993
Sonowal	555	49.7	26.1	0.510	Das et al., 1975
Sonowal	106	45.3	17	0.396	Deka et al., 1988
Chutiya	62	46.8	6.4	0.298	-Do-
Rajbanshi	164	39.6	15.2	0.350	Das et al., 1980
Rajbanshi	102	36.3	4.9	0.230	Deka et al., 1988
Garo	135	37.0	31.1	0.496	Das et al., 1980
Rabha	128	55.5	25.8	0.535	-Do-
Lalung (Tiwa)	114	50.9	19.3	0.447	-Do-
Tiwa	27	25.9	18.5	0.315	Balgir, 1995
Sut	22	4.6	0.0	0.023	-Do-
CAUCASOID GROUP :					
Brahmin	98	10.2	2	0.051	Deka et al., 1988
Kalita	104	19.2	1.9	0.115	-Do-
Kaibarta	101	24.8	1.0	0.134	-Do-
Daibarta	124	20.2	18.5	0.286	Balgir, 1991b
Muslim	104	19.2*	1.0	0.101	Das et al., 1980
Assamese Sikh	15	20.0	20.0	0.300	Balgir, 1995
Assamese (Lower Assam)	182	15.9	2.8	0.107	Flatz et al., 1972
Assamese (Upper Assam)	133	19.5	3.8	0.135	Das et al., 1980
Tea Garden Labourers	336	0	13.1**	0.067	Balgir, 1993

*includes one person with Hb AS.

** includes not Hb E, but only one Hb SS and 43 cases of Hb AS.

Table: 2.3. Prevalence of Sickle Cell hemoglobinopathy in Tea Garden Populations of Assam

Name of Tribe	*No. Tested*	*Hb AE %*	*Hb SS %*	*Allele (S) Frequency*	*Source*
Karmakar	31	32.3	3.2	0.193	Balgir, 1992b
Tanti	39	30.8	0.0	0.154	-Do-
Das	7	28.6	0.0	0.143	-Do-
Dusad	6	25.0	0.0	0.125	-Do-
Naik	6	25.0	0.0	0.125	-Do-
Lohar	13	23.0	0.0	0.115	-Do-
Ratia	5	20.0	0.0	0.100	-Do-
Ghatwar	6	16.7	0.0	0.083	-Do-
Kharia	6	16.7	0.0	0.083	-Do-
Mirdha	7	14.3	0.0	0.071	-Do-
Murrah	17	11.8	0.0	0.059	-Do-
Orang	26	11.5	0.0	0.057	-Do-
Gowala	11	9.1	0.0	0.045	-Do-
Bhumiz	19	0.0	0.0	0.000	-Do-
Bhuyan	12	0.0	0.0	0.000	-Do-
Rabidas	34	0.0	0.0	0.000	-Do-
Others	85	0.0	0.0	0.000	-Do-

MANIPUR

The Meiteis of Manipur valley speak a language belonging to Tibeto-Burman family. They are endogamous and claim to have Kshatriya status of the Hindu caste system. Regarding the ethnic origin of the Meiteis, may they either be tagged with Kuki-Chin immigrants from Burma (Myanmar), or they may be regarded as one of the primordial groups of the region. In any case, they certainly have Mongoloid affinities.

The Brahmins of Manipur are probably of Caucasoid origin, who had initially started settling in Manipur since the 15th century A.D. when Vaishnavism first established its roots in the state. Many of the early settlers married Meitei women and even adopted the Meitei way of life including worship of Meitei deities. It appears that initially the

Brahmins settled in Imphal and then gradually spread over to other parts of the valley.

There has been considerable admixture between Brahmins and Meiteis of Manipur, revealing both Caucasoid and Mongoloid features. The frequency of hemoglobin E gene was found to be between 2% to 10% among Meiteis and Brahmins of Manipur (Table 2.4).

Table: 2.4. Prevalence of hemoglobin E hemoglobinopathy in Populations of Manipur

Name of Tribe	*No. Tested*	*Hb AE %*	*Hb EE %*	*Allele (S) Frequency*	*Source*
Meiteis	203	11.3	1.4	0.071	Chakravartti & Roy, 1979
Meiteis	104	18.3	1.0	0.101	Singh et al.,1986
Brahmin	108	5.6	0.0	0.028	-Do-

MEGHALAYA

The state of Meghalaya is famous for the highest rainfall and the prevalence of matriarchal system among the Khasi and Garo. They are Austro-Asiatic speakers. It has been revealed that the frequency of hemoglobin E gene varies between 2% to 37% among the Khasi population of Meghalaya (Table 2.5) in the North Eastern region of India.

Table: 2.5. Prevalence of hemoglobin E hemoglobinopathy in Populations of Meghalaya

Name of Tribe	*No. Tested*	*Hb AE %*	*Hb EE %*	*Allele (S) Frequency*	*Source*
Khasi	80	38.7	2.5	0.219	Das et al., 1971
Khasi	120	36.4	4.3	0.225	Flatz et al., 1972
Khasi	157	4.5	0.0	0.022	Saha, 1990
Mixed Bodo	24	16.7	29.1	0.375	Saha, 1990

MIZORAM

So far no detailed study pertaining to hemoglobinopathy from the state of Mizoram is available.

NAGALAND

In the mountainous regions of Northeastern India, including the plains of Assam, live many Mongoloid tribes. Of these, the most numerous and prominent are the Nagas, who number about a million. Their present home is Nagaland. It is still an open question why the Nagas are called Nagas. The Sanskrit meaning of the word Naga is naked people; the other connotation is snake. How the Nagas came to their present location is not very clearly known. The traditional legend traces their migration route back to the races of the South Sea on the one hand and to China on the other hand. They have been described as related to the forest tribe of Malaya. The Nagas linguistically belong to the family of Tibeto-Chinese and the Tibeto-Burman sub-families. They speak many dialects and are divided into many clans (Saha and Tay, 1990).

The Nagas are monogamous and exogamous. The significance of head-hunting once practised by the Naga tribes rested on the belief that the head was the seat of excellence of all the life essence. The sacrifice of the head of man or animal was believed to bring prosperity to the land as well as to ward off all evil spirits, including sickness.

They practise shifting cultivation (*jhum*). Compared to some other tribal groups of the region, the social system of the Nagas is more democratic. The institution of bachelors' dormition both for the boys and girls was common among the Nagas. The religious beliefs of various tribes are not uniform. They believe in various spirits and the sky gods. The majority of Naga population have now embraced Christianity. However, the Rengma Nagas showed some inclination toward Hinduism in addition to their own traditional animistic beliefs and practices.

The Naga other than the Hmar were probably one of the minority groups of mainland China during prehistoric times. They were pushed southwards because of population pressure in the past. After a long and tortuous migration, they settled in their present locations for centuries. In spite of their sojourn, they still maintain their genetic isolation to a large extent (Saha and Tay, 1990).

The prevalence of hemoglobin E gene is 1-3.5% among the Nagas of Nagaland (Table 2.6).

Table: 2.6. Prevalence of hemoglobin E hemoglobinopathy in Populations of Nagaland

Name of Tribe	*No. Tested*	*Hb AE %*	*Hb EE %*	*Allele (S) Frequency*	*Source*
Rengma Naga	148	1.4	0.0	0.007	Saha, 1990
Urban Naga	65	3.1	0.0	0.015	Saha & Tay, 1990
Rural Naga	83	0.0	0.0	0.000	-Do-
Hmar	81	2.4	0.0	0.012	-Do-
Naga	44	6.8	0.0	0.035	Balgir, 1991a

TRIPURA

Tripura, the North Eastern state of India, has a large number of endogamous tribal populations of Tibeto-Burman stock who have a long history of political and military interaction with different parts of South East Asia. It may be useful to interpret the genetic heterogeneity among the populations of Tripura.

The tribal populations of Tripura state harbour very high frequencies of hemoglobin E gene ranging from 20% to 56% (Table 2.7). The higher frequency is very near to that of Mongoloid populations of Assam.

Recently six individuals have been reported of having other hemoglobinopathies (one beta-thalassemia trait, one sickle cell trait and four Hb SE compound heterozygotes) (Das et al., 2002).

Conclusions

The population of India is heterogeneous from the standpoint of race, ethnicity, language, religion, caste and socio-cultural practices. Genetic epidemiology is an important tool for delineation of the genetic and non-genetic factors in the causation of a condition or disease in human populations. For the development of a need-based health care system in India, which should include not only the curative aspects but must also look into the preventive, promotive health care for the management of genetic disorders and their genetic burden in the communities, the role of genetic epidemiology needs to be highly emphasized.

Table: 2.7. Prevalence of hemoglobin E hemoglobinopathy in Populations of Tripura

Name of Tribe	*No. Tested*	*Hb AE %*	*Hb EE %*	*Allele (S) Frequency*	*Source*
Chakma	162	51.8	9.9	0.358	Das et al., 2002
Darlong	57	49.1	26.3	0.509	-Do-
Debbarman	104	49.0	16.3	0.409	-Do-
Halam	60	50.0	18.3	0.433	-Do-
Jamatia	65	38.5	13.8	0.331	-Do-
Marek	64	50.0	31.2	0.562	-Do-
Mog	74	41.9	5.4	0.263	-Do-
Morasingh	20	0.0	15.0	0.15	-Do-
Noatia	27	11.1	14.8	0.204	-Do-
Riang	48	50.0	20.8	0.458	-Do-
Tripura	89	53.9	12.3	0.416	-Do-
Uchi	70	60.0	21.4	0.514	-Do-

Hemoglobinopathy is one of the inherited abnormalities of blood, which is a major public health problem today in India. There are three common hemoglobin variants, namely, sickle cell (HbS), haemoglobin E (HbE) and hemoglobin D (HbD), and beta-thalassemia commonly observed in the Indian patients. Hemoglobin E is the commonest structural variant prevalent in the populations of North Eastern region of India and in South East Asia.

There are several factors common to North East India and South East Asia which contribute to hemoglobin E mutation. These factors may be ecology, climate, wet cultivation, high endemicity of malaria and genotoxic environmental variables. For the high prevalence of hemoglobin E in North Eastern India, climate, founder effect, localism and caste endogamy, small population size, low marriage distance, high fertility, inbreeding, selective pressure, subsistence economy, bio-social practices, illiteracy, among others are responsible.

The current status indicates the origin of the hemoglobin E mutation prevalent in North Eastern region of India from South East Asia. This shows that human migrations must have taken place from South East Asia leading to genetic admixture as a result of domination of one tribe over the other in the distant past. However, RFLP sites—based molecular

(DNA) analysis has shown that some hemoglobin-beta-gene cluster haplotypes resemble with the haplotypes prevalent in South East Asia, whereas the others probably have local origin in Assam or in the entire North Eastern region of India.

The pattern of distribution of hemoglobin beta-E and malarial infection in North Eastern India suggest the introduction of hemoglobin beta-E from Southeast Asia and attainment of higher frequencies in certain populations is probably because of continued selective pressure of malarial infection. Further, a low frequency of hemoglobin Beta-E (about 0.02) among the Khasi of Cherrapunji district (Meghalaya) as compared to Khasi of Shillong (0.22) has been observed which may be due to relaxation of selection pressure in the absence of malaria at high altitude.

The frequency of Hb E gene in the Caucasoid caste populations is around 30%, whereas the gene is highly prevalent in the Mongoloid populations, frequencies ranging from 20% to 60%. The Sonowal Kachari of the Tibeto-Burman speaking Bodo ethnic group residing in Assam have recorded the frequency of hemoglobin E allele at 64%, so far the highest in the world.

ACKNOWLEDGMENTS

The author is grateful to Prof. N.K. Ganguly, Director General, ICMR, New Delhi and Dr. S.K. Kar, Director, RMRC (ICMR), Bhubaneswar for providing the necessary facilities and encouragement for this write-up. Thanks are also due to all authors whose works have been quoted here in this article.

REFERENCES

Antnarakis SE, Orkin SE, Kazazian H, Goff SC, Boehm CD, Weber PG, Sexton JP, Oster H, Fairbanks VF, Chakravarti A. 1982 *Evidence for multiple origins of the B^E-globin gene in South East Asia. Proceedings of National Academy of Science* (USA) 79: 6608-6611.

Balgir RS, 2002 *Genetic Dimension of Sickle Cell Hemoglobinopathy among Five Scheduled Caste Populations of Orissa*, India. *Indian Practr.* 55: 503-514.

Balgir RS, 2001 *Indigenous and Independent Origin of the B^S-Mutation in Ancient India: Is it a Myth or Reality? Mankind Quarterly*, 42: 99-116.

Balgir RS. 2000. *The Burden of Hemoglobinopathies in India and the Challenges Ahead. Curr. Sci.* 79: 1536-1547.

Balgir RS, 1996a. *Genetic Epidemiology of the Three Predominant Abnormal Hemoglobins in India. J. Assocn. Phys. India,* 44: 25-28.

Balgir RS, 1996b. *Biomedical Anthropological Approaches in North Eastern India : A Synthesis of the Tea Garden Population of Assam. In: Peoples of North East India : Anthropological Perspective.* Sarthak Sengupta (Ed.), Gyan Publishing House, New Delhi, pp. 91-104.

Balgir RS, 1995a. *Genetic markers in the Tribal health, development and welfare with special reference to North Eastern India. In : Anthropology, Population and Development.* Sharma JC (Ed.). Inter-India Publications, New Delhi. pp. 151-171.

Balgir RS, 1993. *Blood groups, G-6-PD enzyme and hemoglobin studies among the three endogamous populations of Assam. Indian. J. Hemat. Bld. Transf.* 11: 237-243.

Balgir RS, 1992a. *Sero-genetic variations in a Mech-Kachari Trible Population. in Man in India.* 72: 293-301.

Balgir RS, 1992b. *Distribution of serogenetic markers in the Tea Garden Tribal population of Dibrugarh district, Assam. Bull Deptt Anthrop.* Dibrugarh Univ. 18: 29-38.

Balgir RS, 1992c. *Reproductive Profile of Mothers in relation to Hemoglobin E Genotypes. Indian J Pediatr,* 59: 449-454.

Balgir RS, 1991a. *Genetic diversity among the six Mongoloid populations of North Eastern India. J. Hum. Ecol.* 2: 207-210.

Balgir RS, 1991b. *Red cell genetic polymorphism in a Non-mongoloid scheduled caste population of Dibrugarh district, Assam. Indian. J. Hemat. Blood. Transf* 9: 175-184.

Balgir RS, Dutta LP. 1990 *Distribution of genetic markers in the Mongoloid Tribal populations of Arunachal Pradesh. Indian J. Hemat* 8: 51-55.

Chakravartti MR, Roy AK, 1979. *Hb E gene in Imphal, Manipur, India. Humangenetik* 51: 209-211.

Chatterjea JB, 1960 *Hemoglobinopathy in India. J. Indian. Med. Assocn.* 34: 102-105.

Chaudhuri S, Chakravartti MR, Mukherjee B, Sen SN, Ghosh J, Maitra A. 1962 *Study of hematological factors, blood groups, anthropometric measurements and genetics of some of the tribal groups of India. Proceedings of 9th Congress of International Society of Blood Transfusion,* Mexico.

Cruz-Coke R. 1978 *A genetic description of high altitude populations. In: The Biology of High Altitude Peoples.* Baker PT (Ed.). International Biological Programme 14, Cambridge University Press, Cambridge pp. 47-63.

Das SK, De M, Sengupta B, Das N, Bhattacharya DK and Talukder G. 2002. *High incidence of hemoglobin E in Tribal populations of Tripura, North East India. Anthropologist* 4: 105-108.

Das BM, Deka R, Das R. *1980. Hemoglobin E in six populations of Assam. J Indian Anthrop, Soc.* 15: 153-156.

Das BM, Deka R, Flatz G. 1975. *Predominance of the hemoglobin E gene in a Mongoloid population in Assam (India). Humangenetik* 30: 187-191

Das BM, Chakravarti MR, Delbruck H, Flatz G. 1971 *High prevalence of hemoglobin E in two populations in Assam. Humangenetik* 12: 264.

Das SK, De M, Bhattacharya DK, Sengupta B, Das N, Talukder G. 2000. *Interaction of different hemoglobinopathies in Eastern India with a view to establish genotypephenotype correlation. Am. J. Hum. Biol.* 12: 454-459.

De M, Das SK, Bhattacharya DK, Talukder G. 1997 *The occurrence of B-thalassemia mutation and its interaction with hemoglobin E in the Eastern India. Int. J. Hemat.* 66: 31-34.

Deka R, Reddy AP, Mukherjee BN, Das BM, Banerjee S, Roy M, Dey B, Malhotra KC, Walter H. *1988 Hemoglobin E distribution in ten endogamous population groups of Assam*, India. *Hum. Hered.* 38: 261-266.

Flatz G, Chakravarti MR, Das BM, Delbruck H. 1972 *Genetic survey in the population of Assam. ABO blood groups, glucose-6-phosphate dehydrogenase and hemoglobin type. Hum. Hered.* 22: 223-330.

Flatz G, Pik C, Sringam S *1965 Hemoglobin E and Beta-thalassemia : their distribution in Thailan. Ann. Hum. Genet.* 29: 151-153.

Hundrieser J, Deka R, Gogoi BC, Papp T, Flatz G. *1988 DNA haplotypes and frameworks associated with the beta-globin gene in the Kachari population of Assam (India). Hum. Hered.* 38: 240-243.

Kazazian HH, Waber PG, Boehm CD, Lee JI, Antonarkis SE, Fairbanks VF *1984 Hemoglobin E in Europeans : Further evidence for multiorigins of Beta E globin gene. Am. J. Hum. Genet.* 36: 212-217.

Morton NE *1982 Outline of Genetic Epidemiology.* Basel Karger, New York.

Roy S, Basu S, Jindal A and Kshatriya G. *1986 Genetic epidemiological approaches to health care. Technical Report 11.* National Institute of Health and Family Welfare, New Delhi.

Saha N, *1990 Distribution of hemoglobin E in several Mongoloid populations of North East India. Hum. Biol.* 62: 535-544.

Saha N, Tay JSH. *1990 Genetic studies among the Nagas and Hmars of Eastern India Am. J. Phys. Anthrop.* 82: 101-112.

Singh KS, Mukherjee BN, Walter H, Lindenberg P, Gilbert K, Dannewitz A, Malhotra KC, Banerjee S, Roy M, Dey B. *1986 Genetic Markers among Meiteis and Brahmins of Manipur, India. Hum. Hered.* 36: 177-187.

Verma IC 1991, *Human genetics on the crest of development. Bull. Hum. Genet.* 16: 1-6.

3

Genetic Heterogeneity and Popolation Structure: A Study of North-east India with Reference to Neighbouring Populations

DEBASHIS BASU, VIKRANT KUMAR
AND B. MOHAN REDDY

INTRODUCTION

Northeastern part of India is inhabited by numerous endogamous tribes and castes of diverse ethnic and sociocultural background. These populations are affiliated to different linguistic families and have either Mongoloid or Caucasoid ethnic features. While the Mongoloids barring very few are tribal groups and, except Khasi, speak languages of Tibeto-Chinese or Tibeto-Burman family, the Caucasoids are caste groups subscribing to Indo-European languages.

All these populations have co-existed for a long period of time and therefore there is a possibility of considerable admixture between themselves as well as from outside (Das et al., 1980a, 1980b, Das, 1977, Kumar et al., 2004, Singh and Molhotra, 1970, 1971). In one of our earlier studies (Kumar et al. 2004) based on 22 populations and 11 genetic markers, we have examined the nature and extent of genetic heterogeneity in the Northeastern India and the results conform to sociological phenomenon of 'Tribe-Caste Continuum' to have reflected in their genetic structure. While on the one end of multivariate space we find the caste populations, on the other is the constellation of tribes; in between are the populations of semi-Hinduised Mongoloid caste groups, suggesting probably gene flow among these groups. We further find that Mongoloid populations come from a relatively heterogeneous background when compared to Indo-European Caucasoid populations.

In this paper we extend our earlier study on the genetic structure of the Northeastern Indian populations to include populations from the neighbouring states like Bengal, Bihar and Orissa to focus primarily on the genetic heterogeneity of the NE populations in comparison with their neighbours. Here we, however, have compromised on the number of loci to include larger number of populations. For this purpose we could get genetic data from available literature only on five traditional genetic markers (ABO, HP, AP, AK and EsD) for 39 populations.

Materials and Method

Gene frequency data for five common loci viz., ABO, HP, AP, AK and EsD commonly available in literatures for 39 populations have been taken into consideration for the present study. The genetic diversity, both intra and inter-population level, was estimated using gene diversity measures (H_S, H_T and G_{ST}) of Nei (1987). G_{ST} is a ratio of the extent of gene differentiation among the population (D_{ST}) to the extent of the total genetic variation in the entire population (H_T), while H_S is a measure of total intra-population heterozygosity.

To assess the genetic affinity among the populations of Northeastern India along with their neighbouring states Nei's D_A distances were computed and then NJ tree was drawn. Multidimensional daling (MDS) based in Nei's DA distances was also recorde to depict the genetic relationships in the multivariate space. Further, Harpending and Ward (1982) model was employed to gauge the patterns of gene flow and stochastic processes.

Population Background

The names ethnic status and linguistic affiliation are given to the studied populations in Table 3.1. Out of the 39 populations considered, 22 populations belong to Northeastern India including Sikkim.

Table 3.1. Ethnic status and the Linguistic affiliations of the thirty-nine investigated populations

Sl. No.	Name of population	Area of sampling	Ethnic status	Linguistic affiliation
1	2	3	4	5
1	Brahmin[1,2,3,4]	Assam	Caucasoid	Indo-European
2	Kaibarta[1,2,3,4]	Assam	Caucasoid	Indo-European
3	Kalita[1,2,3,4]	Assam	Caucasoid	Indo-European
4	Muslim[1,2,3,4]	Assam	Caucasoid	Indo-European
5	Rajbanshi[1,2,3,4]	Assam	Mixed	Indo-European
6	Ahom[1,2,3,4]	Assam	Mongoloid	Originally Tibeto-Chinese (Siamese-Chinese, Tai) currently Indo-European
7	Chutia[1,2,3,4]	Assam	Mongoloid	Originally Tibeto-Chinese (Tibeto-Burman, Assam-Burmese), Currently Indo-European
8	Karbi[1,2,3,4]	Assam	Mongoloid	Tibeto-Chinese (Tibeto-Burman, Assam-Burmese)
9	Sonowal[1,2,3,4]	Assam	Mongoloid	Tibeto-Burman, Assam-Burmese)
10	Kachari[1,2,3,4]	Assam	Mongoloid	Tibeto-Chinese (Tibeto-Burman, Assam-Burmese)
11	Oraon[5,6]	Bihar (Gumla & Ranchi)	Australoid	Dravidian
12	Brahmin[7]	Manipur	Caucasoid	Indo-European
13	Meitei[7]	Manipur	Mongoloid	Tibeto-Chinese (Tibeto-Burman, Assam-Burmese)
14	Lanjia Saora[8,9]	Orissa (Ganjam)	Australoid	Austro-Asiatic
15	Khord[8,9]	Orissa (Ganjam)	Australoid	Dravidian
16	Jalari[10]	Orissa (Puri)	Caucasoid	Dravidian
17	Kevto[10]	Orissa (Puri)	Caucasoid	Indo-European

1	2	3	4	5
18	Vaddabalija[10]	Orissa (Puri, Penitocotat)	Caucasoid	Dravidian
19	Vaddabalija[10]	Orissa (Puri, Vedapata)	Caucasoid	Dravidian
20	Brahmin[11]	Sikkim	Caucasoid	Indo-European
21	Chetri[11]	Sikkim	Caucasoid	Indo-European
22	Newar[11]	Sikkim	Mixed	Tibeto-Chinese (Tibto-Burman, Tibeto-Himalayan)
23	Bhutia[11]	Sikkim	Mongoloid	Tibeto-Chinese (Tibto-Burman, Tibeto-Himalayan)
24	Lepcha[11]	Sikkim	Mongoloid	Tibeto-Chinese (Tibto-Burman, Tibeto-Himalayan)
25	Gurungs[11]	Sikkim	Mongoloid	Tibeto-Chinese (Tibeto-Burman, Tibeto-Himalayan)
26	Rai[11]	Sikkim	Mongoloid	Tibeto-Chinese (Tibeto-Burman, Tibeto-Himalayan)
27	Sherpa[11]	Sikkim	Mongoloid	Tibeto-Chinese (Tibeto-Burman, Tibeto-Himalayan)
28	Subba[11]	Sikkim	Mongoloid	Tibeto-Chinese (Tibeto Burman, Tibeto-Himalayan)
29	Tamang[11]	Sikkim	Mongoloid	Tibeto-Chinese (Tibeto-Burman, Tibeto-Himalayan)
30	Vaidhya[12]	W. Bengal (24 Parganas)	Caucasoid	Indo-European
31	Rajdanshi[12]	W. Bengal (Cooch Behar)	Mixed	Indo-European
32	Garo[12]	W. Bengal (Cooch Behar)	Mongoloid	Tibeto-Chinese (Tibeto-Burman, Assam-Burmese)
33	Rabha[12]	W. Bengal (Cooch Behar)	Mongoloid	Tibeto-Chinese (Tibeto-Burman, Assam-Burmese)
34	Mech[12]	W. Bengal (Jalpaiguri)	Monogoloid	Tibeto-Chinese (Tibeto-Burman, Assam-Burmese)
35	Kaibarta[12]	W. Bengal (Kolkata)	Caucasoid	Indo-European
36	Lodha[12]	W. Bengal (Midnapore)	Austarloid	Austro-Asiatic
37	Munda[12]	W. Bengal (Maidnapore)	Australoid	Austro-Asiatic

Contd. . . .

Table 3.1 - (Concld.)

1	2	3	4	5
38	Bagdi[12]	W. Bengal (Maidnapore)	Caucasoid	Indo-European
39	Brahmin[12]	W. Bengal (N. 24 parganas)	Caucasoid	Indo-European

1. Walter et al. 1986;
2. Das et al. 1987;
3. Deka et al. 1988;
4. Mukherjee et al. 1989;
5. Kirk et al. 1962;
6. Saha et al. 1988;
7. Singh et al. 1986;
8. Chahal 1981;
9. Papiha et al. 1988;
10. Reddy et al. 1989;
11. Bhasin et al. 1986;
12. Mukherjee et al. 1987;

*The primary source of these data was Bhasin et al. 1992, although are verified from the original sources as quoted.

Figure 1 is a schematic diagram depicting the probable migratory routes of different ethnic and linguistic groups inhabiting Northeastern India. The populations of Assam are both Mongoloids speaking Tibeto-Chinese or Tibeto-Burman languages (Ahom, Chutia, Sonowal, Karbi and Kachari) and Caucasoids speaking Indo-European languages. Similarly, Chetris and Brahmins of Sikkim are be considered as Caucasoids, while the populations of Mongoloid origin are Nepalese (Subba, Rai, Tamang, Gruing), Lepcha, Bhutia and Sherpa. The Mongoloid groups of Assam and Sikkim have probably originated from two separate parental populations as suggested by the study of Kumar et al. (2004). The Meitie of Manipur, who were originally Mongoloids, had considerable admixture with the Brahmins a high caste Caucasoid population. The ethnic origin of Newar and Rajbanshi of Sikkim and West Bengal respectively are not fully established and there are a number of hypotheses focussing on this issue (Kumar et al., 2004).

Majority of the neighbouring populations considered are from West Bengal, who belong to Mongoloid (Garo, Rabha and Mech), Caucasoid (Bagdis, Brahmin Kaibarta and Vaidhya) and Proto-Australoid (Lodha and Munda) ethnic categories. The populations included from Orissa are Lanjia Saura and Khond of Proto-Australoid group, Caucasiods represented by Kevto, Jalari, Vaddabalija of Penticotta and Vaddabalija of Vadepeta. The only group included from Bihar are Oraon. These people have Proto-Australoid physical features, but speak a language which may belong to the Dravidian Linguistic family.

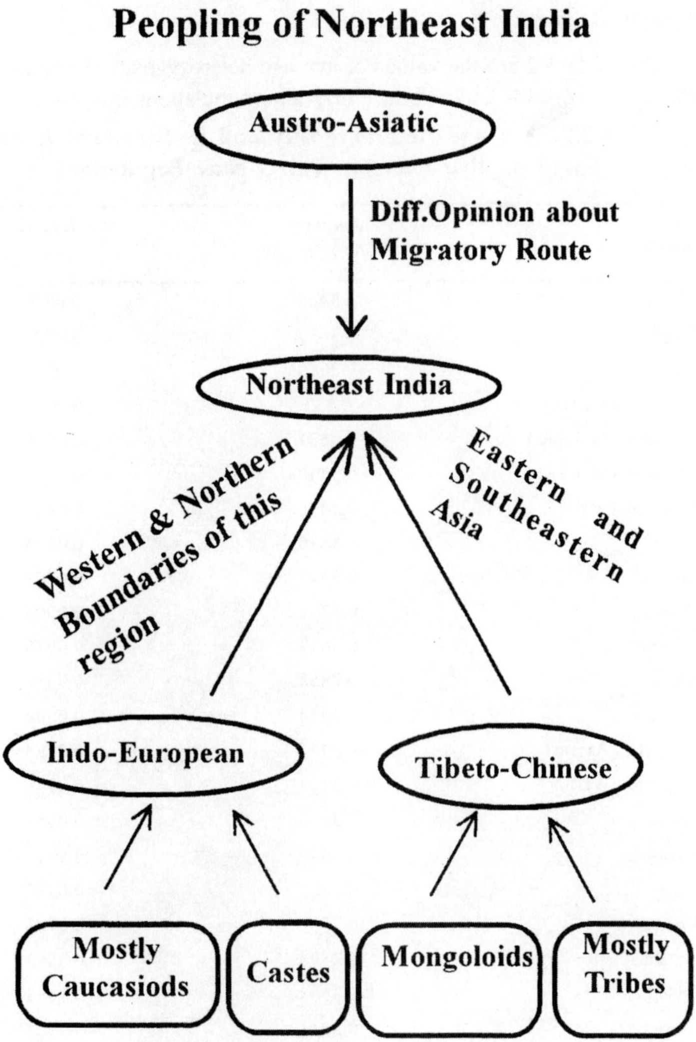

Figure 1. Schematic diagram depicting the probable migratory routes of different ethnic and linguistic groups along with their social affiliations inhabiting the Northeastern India

RESULTS

Genetic Diversity

In Table 3.2 are the values of average heterozygosity (H_s) and their standard errors for each of the thirty-nine populations based on 5 loci.

Table 3.2. Average Heterozygosity and its Standard Error based on five Loci for Thirty-Nine Populations

Name of Populations	*Average Heterozygosity*	*Standard Error*
Ahom	0.3400	0.0762
Bagdi	0.3637	0.0831
Bhutia	0.2970	0.0964
Brahmin (Assam)	0.353	0.0687
Brahmin (Manipur)	0.3871	0.0819
Brahmin (Sikkim)	0.3490	0.0534
Brahmin (WB)	0.3474	0.0925
Chetri	0.3836	0.0815
Chutia	0.3321	0.0809
Garo	0.3331	0.0909
Gurung	0.3699	0.0918
Jalari	0.2858	0.0816
Kachari	0.3474	0.0844
Kaibarta (Assam)	0.3447	0.0584
Daibarta (WB)	0.3499	0.0788
Kalita	0.3616	0.0681
Karbi	0.3630	0.0929
Kevto	0.2785	0.0785
Khond	0.3501	0.0781
Lepcha	0.2898	0.0863
Lodha	0.3568	0.1062
Mech	0.3014	0.0762
Meitie	0.3863	0.0723
Munda	0.3503	0.0879
Muslim (Assam)	0.3557	0.0581
Newar	0.3648	0.0895
Oraon	0.3711	0.0817

Name of Populations	Average Heterozygosity	Standard Error
Rabha	0.3719	0.0919
Rai	0.3494	0.0957
Rajbanshi (Assam)	0.3496	0.0751
Rajbanshi (WB)	0.3327	0.0811
Saora L	0.3547	0.0904
Sherpas	0.2988	0.0968
Sonowal	0.3795	0.0779
Subba	0.3141	0.1030
Tamang	0.3375	0.0701
Vaddabalija-P	0.3199	0.0857
Vaddabalija-V	0.2918	0.0542
Vaidhya	0.3634	0.0764

Table 3.3. The Range and the Average values of Heterozygosity for Different Groups of Populations

Groups of Populations	Range	Average Heterozygosity
All groups	0.2785-0.3871	0.3382
Austro-Asiatic	0.3503-0.3568	0.3503
Dravidian	0.2858-0.3711	0.3200
Indo-European	0.2785-0.3871	0.3470
Tibeto-Chinese	0.2898-0.3863	0.3342

The ranges and averages for different linguistic categories of populations are furnished in Table 3.3. The values of average heterozygosity, H_S are the observed to be the highest for Austro-Asiatic populations (0.3503) compared to all other linguistic categories. The range of H_S seems to be relatively wider for all the categories except for Austro-Asiatic groups where all the populations show very similar and relatively moderate value. When we categories the populations into Northeastern and non-Northeastern Indian populations we find that the value of H_S of Northeastern (0.3479) is slightly higher than the value of non-Northeastern of (0.3366) Indian populations. The G_{ST} values, locus-wise as well as averages for different categories of populations, based on 5 loci are furnished in Table 3.4. The G_{ST} value is highest for EsD locus (0.0411) and least at the AP locus (0.0141). The G_{ST} value is highest for Dravidian groups (0.0381) and least for Austro-Asiatic groups (0.0084). The G_{ST} value of Tibeto-Chinese group (0.0179) is higher than the Indo-European category, which is consistent with the hypothesis of an earlier study (Kumar et al., 2004) that these populations come from relatively heterogeneous backgrounds than the Indo-Europeans.

Table 3.4. Locus-wise and Average Gene Diversity (G_{ST}) Values among Different Categories

Locus	*All Groups*	*Austro-Asiatic*	*Dravidian*	*Indo-European*	*Tibeto-Chinese*
ABO	0.0209	0.0052	0.0187	0.0207	0.0157
Hp	0.0205	0.0051	0.0461	0.0102	0.0164
AP	0.0141	0.0036	0.0092	0.0065	0.0171
AK	0.0227	0.009	0.0108	0.0106	0.0282
EsD	0.0411	0.0175	0.0974	0.0231	0.0214
Average	0.0241	0.0084	0.0381	0.0155	0.0179

Genetic Affinities

To visualize the nature of population relationships Nei's D_A distances based on the allele frequency data were computed for different pairs of populations. Although we have computed both the NJ and the UPGMA trees based on Nei's D_A distance matrix (Table 3.5) were computed. We present here only the NJ dendrogram (Figure 2) as both of them reflect the similar pattern of interrelationships. In the genetic distance matrix the maximum distance (0.047) is observed between the Rai of Sikkim and the Kevto of Orissa, while there is no distance observed between the Ahom and Khond. In the NJ tree, broadly speaking, two clusters can be discerned: one formed mostly by the Tibeto-Chinese Northeastern Mongoloids *i.e.* the upper half of the tree (from Rai to Mech) and the rest of the populations forming another cluster. Within the 1st cluster three sub-clusters can be discerned. The first formed by the Mongoloids of Nepal (Rai, Subba, Bhutia, Lepcha, Sherpa) and the second by Mongoloids of Assam (Kachari, Gurung, Sonowal, Rabha and Karbi). The Rajbanshi of Assam and West Bengal form a third sub-

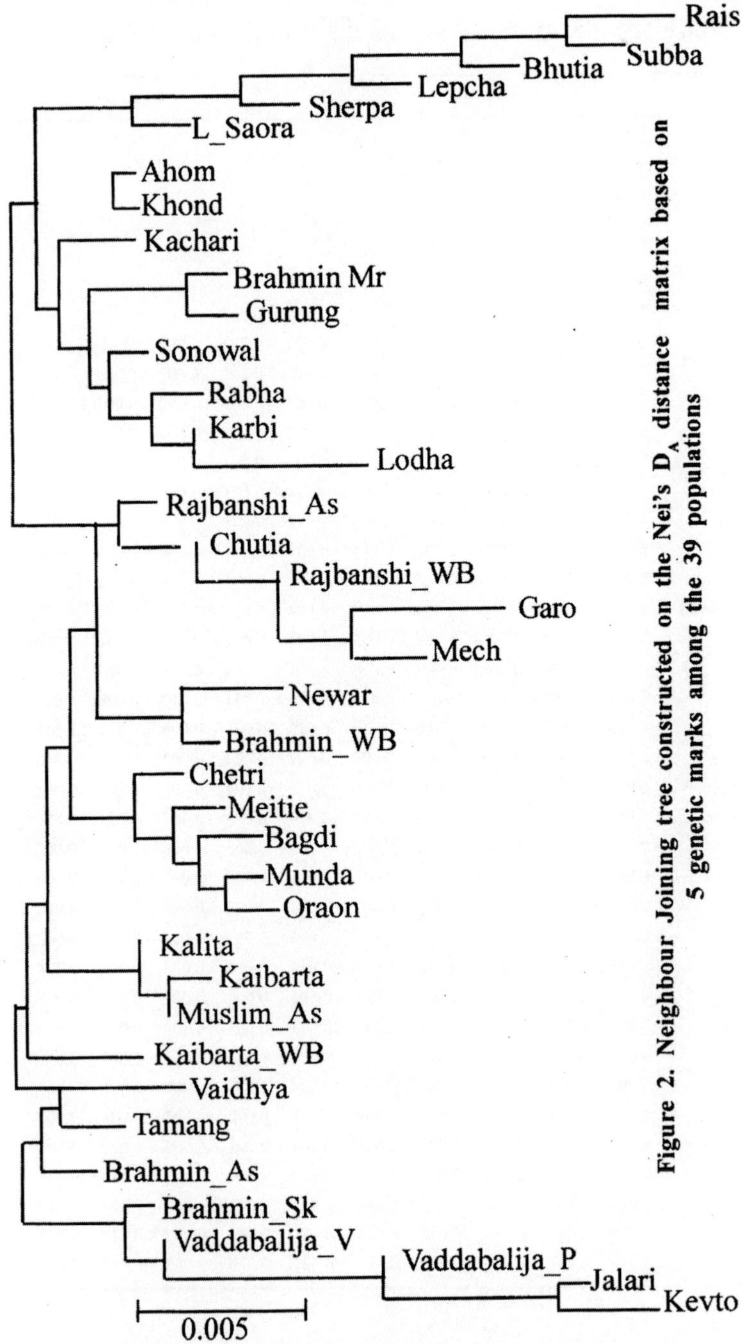

Figure 2. Neighbour Joining tree constructed on the Nei's D_A distance matrix based on 5 genetic marks among the 39 populations

Table: 3.5. DA Distance for all the Thirty-Nine Populations

	1	2	3	4	5	6	7	8	9	10
Brahmin-Mr	0.000									
Meitei	0.002	0.000								
Brahmin-As	0.005	0.004	0.000							
Kalita	0.006	0.005	0.004	0.000						
Kaibarta	0.009	0.006	0.004	0.001	0.000					
Muslim-As	0.006	0.004	0.004	0.001	0.001	0.000				
Khom	0.003	0.003	0.004	0.003	0.004	0.002	0.000			
Karbi	0.005	0.005	0.009	0.005	0.007	0.005	0.003	0.000		
Kachari	0.003	0.004	0.005	0.004	0.005	0.003	0.001	0.002	0.000	
Sonowal	0.002	0.002	0.006	0.003	0.005	0.003	0.001	0.002	0.002	0.000
Chutia	0.007	0.008	0.005	0.002	0.003	0.003	0.002	0.004	0.002	0.005
Rajbanshi-As	0.005	0.004	0.004	0.001	0.002	0.001	0.001	0.002	0.001	0.002
Lepcha	0.012	0.013	0.013	0.010	0.011	0.010	0.005	0.008	0.006	0.010
Bhutia	0.012	0.015	0.011	0.014	0.015	0.015	0.008	0.010	0.006	0.013
Sherpa	0.009	0.008	0.007	0.008	0.008	0.008	0.005	0.008	0.005	0.009
Tamang	0.008	0.007	0.002	0.001	0.001	0.002	0.004	0.008	0.005	0.007
Brahmin-Sk	0.012	0.010	0.006	0.005	0.004	0.004	0.007	0.013	0.009	0.009
Chetri	0.003	0.003	0.004	0.002	0.005	0.004	0.004	0.006	0.004	0.004
Newar	0.005	0.006	0.006	0.003	0.006	0.005	0.004	0.006	0.004	0.005
Rais	0.008	0.014	0.017	0.021	0.025	0.020	0.011	0.012	0.008	0.012
Subba	0.010	0.012	0.015	0.018	0.020	0.017	0.008	0.008	0.007	0.011
Gurung	0.002	0.006	0.006	0.007	0.009	0.007	0.003	0.004	0.001	0.003
Brahmin-WB	0.005	0.007	0.004	0.004	0.006	0.005	0.004	0.005	0.002	0.005
Vaidhya	0.005	0.004	0.001	0.003	0.004	0.004	0.005	0.007	0.004	0.005
Bagdis	0.006	0.003	0.004	0.004	0.005	0.005	0.005	0.006	0.006	0.005
Kaibarta-WB	0.006	0.005	0.002	0.002	0.003	0.003	0.004	0.007	0.004	0.006
Rajbanshi-WB	0.005	0.008	0.006	0.006	0.007	0.005	0.002	0.004	0.001	0.004
Rabha	0.003	0.005	0.011	0.006	0.009	0.006	0.003	0.002	0.002	0.002
Garo	0.015	0.016	0.016	0.011	0.011	0.011	0.008	0.004	0.006	0.009
Mech	0.011	0.013	0.009	0.006	0.005	0.005	0.004	0.006	0.003	0.007
Munda	0.005	0.002	0.007	0.004	0.006	0.004	0.003	0.004	0.005	0.003
Lodha	0.008	0.007	0.016	0.014	0.017	0.014	0.008	0.004	0.009	0.007
Oraon	0.006	0.002	0.008	0.003	0.005	0.004	0.003	0.003	0.005	0.003
Khond	0.003	0.002	0.004	0.002	0.004	0.002	0.000	0.003	0.001	0.001
Lanjia Saora	0.003	0.002	0.005	0.004	0.006	0.004	0.001	0.002	0.002	0.002
Vaddabalija-P	0.022	0.024	0.014	0.021	0.019	0.020	0.019	0.020	0.016	0.021
Vaddabalija-V	0.017	0.017	0.008	0.013	0.010	0.011	0.012	0.020	0.013	0.017
Jālari	0.026	0.028	0.014	0.025	0.022	0.023	0.023	0.032	0.022	0.029
Kevto	0.033	0.031	0.015	0.020	0.016	0.021	0.025	0.030	0.025	0.031

Table 3.5 - (Contd.)

11	12	13	14	15	16	17	18	19	20
0.000									
0.001	0.000								
0.007	0.007	0.000							
0.007	0.010	0.005	0.000						
0.006	0.006	0.005	0.004	0.000					
0.002	0.002	0.009	0.011	0.005	0.000				
0.007	0.006	0.009	0.016	0.012	0.004	0.000			
0.005	0.003	0.012	0.012	0.007	0.003	0.008	0.000		
0.004	0.003	0.006	0.008	0.006	0.004	0.005	0.003	0.000	
0.016	0.016	0.012	0.009	0.014	0.021	0.025	0.016	0.015	0.000
0.013	0.012	0.007	0.005	0.007	0.018	0.023	0.016	0.014	0.005
0.005	0.004	0.009	0.007	0.008	0.008	0.012	0.005	0.005	0.005
0.002	0.003	0.008	0.005	0.005	0.003	0.010	0.003	0.003	0.013
0.004	0.004	0.013	0.010	0.006	0.003	0.008	0.002	0.005	0.018
0.006	0.004	0.012	0.012	0.004	0.004	0.010	0.002	0.004	0.020
0.003	0.003	0.011	0.010	0.004	0.001	0.006	0.001	0.003	0.020
0.003	0.003	0.006	0.007	0.008	0.007	0.010	0.008	0.007	0.008
0.006	0.004	0.009	0.012	0.010	0.009	0.013	0.005	0.005	0.010
0.006	0.007	0.009	0.010	0.012	0.014	0.018	0.015	0.012	0.018
0.001	0.003	0.005	0.007	0.008	0.005	0.009	0.010	0.007	0.015
0.006	0.003	0.008	0.011	0.004	0.005	0.010	0.003	0.005	0.017
0.014	0.010	0.014	0.014	0.009	0.017	0.023	0.010	0.012	0.015
0.006	0.003	0.012	0.015	0.007	0.006	0.010	0.004	0.006	0.021
0.003	0.001	0.006	0.009	0.004	0.003	0.007	0.002	0.003	0.012
0.004	0.002	0.007	0.007	0.003	0.005	0.010	0.002	0.003	0.011
0.016	0.018	0.019	0.016	0.022	0.019	0.015	0.024	0.019	0.026
0.011	0.012	0.010	0.014	0.013	0.009	0.004	0.016	0.011	0.025
0.021	0.024	0.021	0.019	0.023	0.019	0.014	0.027	0.022	0.031
0.017	0.021	0.024	0.022	0.021	0.015	0.013	0.025	0.021	0.047

Contd. . . .

Table 3.5 - (Contd.)

	21	22	23	24	25	26	27	28	29
Brahmin-Mr									
Meitei									
Brahmin-As									
Kalita									
Kaibarta									
Muslim-As									
Khom									
Karbi									
Kachari									
Sonowal									
Chutia									
Rajbanshi-As									
Lepcha									
Bhutia									
Sherpa									
Tamang									
Brahmin-Sk									
Chetri									
Newar									
Rais									
Subba	0.000								
Gurung	0.007	0.000							
Brahmin-WB	0.012	0.003	0.000						
Vaidhya	0.015	0.006	0.003	0.000					
Bagdis	0.015	0.009	0.005	0.003	0.000				
Kaibarta-WB	0.017	0.007	0.002	0.001	0.002	0.000			
Rajbanshi-WB	0.007	0.002	0.004	0.007	0.0011	0.008	0.000		
Rabha	0.011	0.003	0.006	0.009	0.007	0.008	0.005	0.000	
Garo	0.011	0.009	0.009	0.014	0.016	0.014	0.005	0.009	0.000
Mech	0.012	0.006	0.005	0.009	0.012	0.007	0.002	0.008	0.005
Munda	0.011	0.008	0.006	0.006	0.002	0.004	0.009	0.004	0.012
Lodha	0.008	0.010	0.012	0.012	0.008	0.014	0.013	0.007	0.013
Oraon	0.015	0.009	0.007	0.006	0.002	0.005	0.010	0.005	0.012
Khond	0.009	0.003	0.003	0.004	0.003	0.003	0.004	0.003	0.010
Lanjia Saora	0.007	0.003	0.003	0.004	0.002	0.004	0.005	0.003	0.009
Vaddabalija-P	0.023	0.016	0.017	0.015	0.026	0.020	0.013	0.028	0.019
Vaddabalija-V	0 022	0.016	0.014	0.011	0.017	0.012	0.012	0.022	0.023
Jalari	0.029	0.023	0.022	0.018	0.029	0.021	0.020	0.036	0.034
Kevto	0.038	0.029	0.019	0.016	0.024	0.017	0.024	0.038	0.029

Table 3.5 - (Concld.)

30	31	32	33	34	35	36	37	38	39
0.000									
0.010	0.000								
0.019	0.005	0.000							
0.011	0.001	0.005	0.000						
0.005	0.002	0.008	0.002	0.000					
0.007	0.001	0.004	0.002	0.001	0.000				
0.016	0.028	0.033	0.028	0.021	0.022	0.000			
0.011	0.018	0.031	0.020	0.013	0.016	0.009	0.000		
0.021	0.032	0.044	0.035	0.025	0.028	0.006	0.004	0.000	
0.019	0.030	0.044	0.030	0.025	0.028	0.011	0.008	0.009	0.000

cluster with Chutia Garo and Mech. which is expected as Rajbanshis are considered to be originally Mongoloids.

The second broad cluster also consists of three sub-clusters, the first one comprising of Dravidian Caucasoid populations of Orissa (Vaddabalija V. Vaddabalija P. Jalari and Kevto), and the second constituted by Indo-European Caucasiods of Assam and West Bengal (Kalita. Kaibarta of Assam and West Bengal. Muslim of Assam, Vaidhya and Brahmin of Assam). Rest of the populations in this cluster form a loose conglomeration (Newar and Brahmin of West Bengal, Chetri, Meitei, Bagdi, Munda and Oraon). Overall, it seems that the pattern of population relationship is, by and large, consistent with their ethnic affiliations and within this they seem to cluster based on geographic affiliations.

Multidimensional Scaling

The limitations inherent in the dendogram resulting from the imposition of bifurcation topology can be partially overcome by using multidimensional scaling (MDS) for depicting relationships among populations based on frequency or distance. Although MDS tends to generate conclusions similar to those obtained by the tree, they are likely to be more faithful describer of the data than trees when there is considerable genetic exchange between close geographic neighbours (Cavalli-Sforza et al., 1994). In Fig. 3 we present two-dimensional plot of populations based on multidimensional scaling of Nei's D_A distance matrix. The two dimensions of the MDS plot accounts for 93% of the total variation with the stress value of 14% suggesting a reasonable fitness. In the plot the Kevto, Vaddabalija (V), Vaddabalija (P) and Jalari, who are Dravidian Caucasoid groups, are outliers and all are differentiated from the rest of the populations on 1st dimension but are relatively closer to Indo-European Caucasiods when compared to other Mongoloids or Austroloids. Broadly speaking, most of the Indo-European speaking Caucasoid groups, irrespective of their geographic affiliation, form a loose constellation and are differentiated from rest of the populations on both the dimensions. The non-clustering of the populations such as Brahmins of Manipur with the Caucasoid cluster strongly suggest their admixture with the Meitei of Manipur. As far as the Mongoloids are concerned, it is apparent that the Mongoloids of Sikkim are differentiated from the Mongoloids of Assam, Manipur and West Bengal on the 2nd dimension both forming a loose conglomeration. The Austro-Asiatic speaking groups. (Lodha. Munda and Lanjia Saura), though are

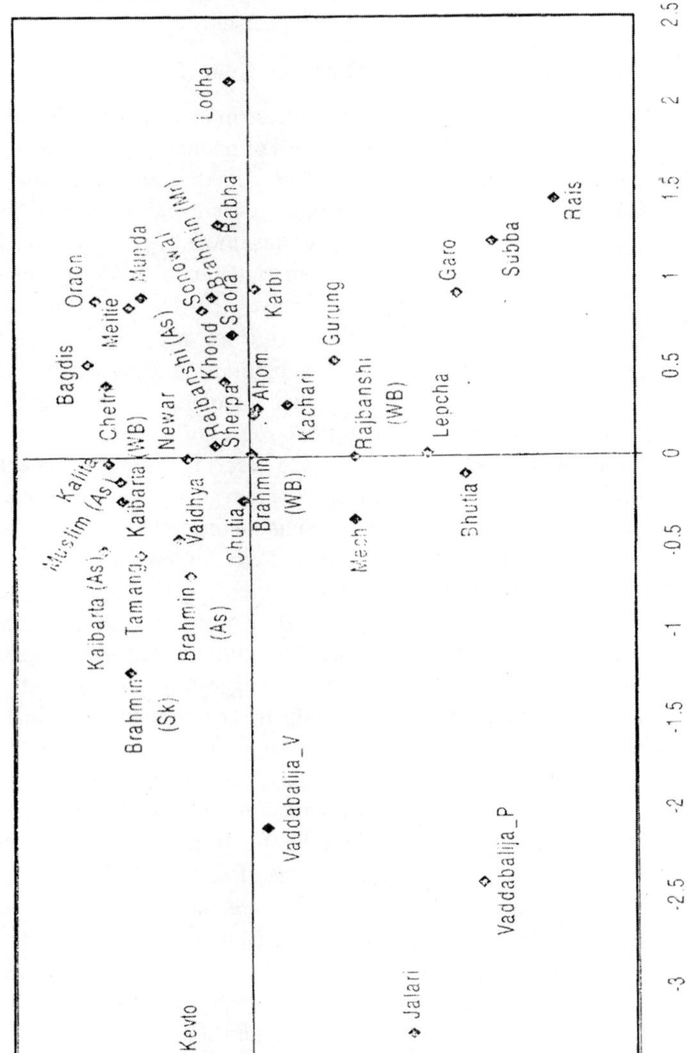

Figure 3. Plot of 39 populations on the first two dimensions derived from the multidimensional scaling of the Nei's D_A distance matrix.

in the 2nd quadrant with most of the Mongoloids of Assam, Manipur and West Bengal, do not form a compact cluster.

Population Structure and Patterns of Gene Flow

To understand the local genetic differentiation and the underlying process responsible for the present pattern of population structure among the groups of Northeastern India and its neighbouring states we have used Harpending and Ward (1982) model, somewhat analogous to the Wright's island model. According to this model, given the uniform systematic pressure (gene flow) from outside, the average genetic heterogeneity within a population is negatively correlated with its genetic distance from the centroid of the gene frequency array (R_{ii}). Higher than average gene flow into any of the subgroups is expected to reflect higher than average heterozygosity than predicted by the regression model and lie above the theoretical regression line. Conversely, populations experiencing isolation and less than average gene flow from outside show lower values of heterozygosity and lie below the regression line. The values of observed and expected heterozygosity for all the 39 populations and their distances from the centroid are furnished in Table 6. Regression plot of average heterozygosity versus distance from the centroid for all the groups is shown in Fig. 4, along with the theoretical regression line. In the regression plot most of the populations are lying on or near the regression line suggesting no effect of gene flow and stochastic process of genetic drift. The populations, which are moderate outliers above the regression line, are Brahmin and Meitei of Manipur, suggesting relatively higher than average external gene flow into them compared to other populations. The populations that are outliers below the regression line are Kevto, Jalari, Vaddabalija-P from Orissa and Lepcha, Sherpa, Subba, Bhutia of Sikkim and Mech of West Bengal. While Kevto and Vaddabalija-P are the migrant populations from Andhra Pradesh, Sherpa, Subba and Bhutia are the migrants from Nepal and therefore their position below the regression line may reflect a bottleneck effect of certain degree. The Lepcha remain still isolated and are probably affected by genetic drift, hence its position is outlined as below the regression line.

DISCUSSION

From the NJ tree and MDS plot it is clear that the pattern of clustering of populations are consistent with their ethnic denominations and within the clusters they are grouped on the basis of their geographic

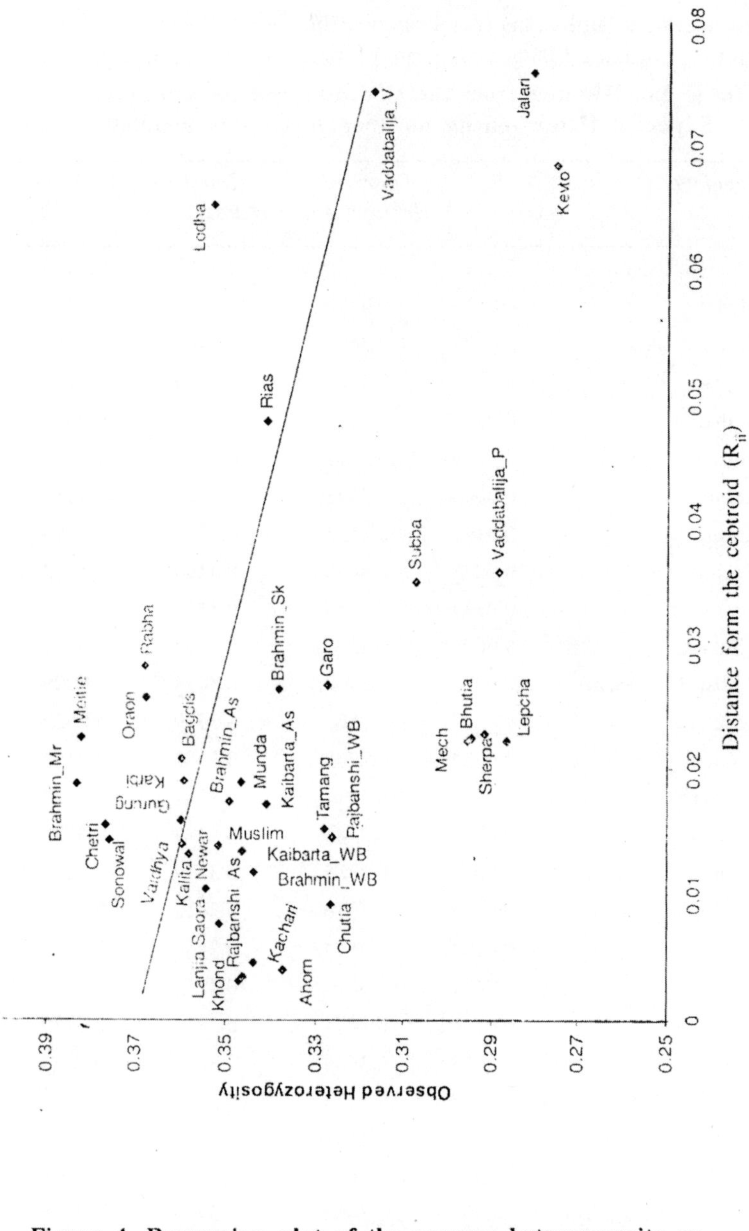

Figure 4. Regression plot of the average heterozygosity vs. distance from the Centroid of the 39 populations

and linguistic affiliations. For example, the Tibeto-Chinese or Tibeto-Burman speaking Mongoloids form a separate broad cluster and within

Table 3.6. Distance from the Centroid and the Observed and Expected Heterogeneity for the Thirty-Nine Populations

Populations	R_{ii}	*Observed Hetrozygosity*	*Expected Hetrozygosity*	*Difference*
Brahmin (Manipur)	0.0189	0.3835	0.3400	0.0435
Meitie	0.0225	0.3824	0.3388	0.0437
Brahmin (Assam)	0.0175	0.3494	0.3405	0.0089
Kalita	0.0133	0.3582	0.3420	0.0162
Kaibarta	0.0172	0.3412	0.3406	0.0006
Muslim (Assam)	0.0139	0.3517	0.3418	0.0099
Ahom	0.0040	0.3371	0.3452	-0.0081
Karbi	0.0191	0.3595	0.3399	0.0196
Kachari	0.0045	0.3437	0.3450	-0.0013
Sonowal	0.0143	0.3759	0.3416	0.0343
Chutia	0.0092	0.3267	0.3434	-0.0166
Rajbanshi (Assam)	0.0035	0.3462	0.3454	0.0009
Lepcha	0.0222	0.2866	0.3389	-0.0522
Bhutia	0.0224	0.2948	0.3388	-0.0441
Sherpa	0.0227	0.2971	0.3387	-0.0470
Tamang	0.0152	0.3281	0.3413	-0.0132
Brahmin (Sikkim)	0.0264	0.3385	0.3374	0.0010
Chetri	0.0155	0.3770	0.3412	0.0359
Newar	0.0104	0.3543	0.3430	0.0113
Rais	0.0481	0.3412	0.3299	0.0113
Subba	0.0350	0.3074	0.3344	-0.0270
Gurung	0.0158	0.3600	0.3600	0.0189
Brahmin (West Bengal)	0.0118	0.3438	0.3438	0.0013
Vaidhya	0.0140	0.3598	0.3598	0.0181
Bagdis	0.0208	0.3601	0.3601	0.0208
Kaibarta (West Bengal)	0.0134	0.3464	0.3464	0.0045
Rajbanshi (West Bengal)	0.0145	0.3264	0.3264	0.0151

Populations	R_{ii}	*Observed Hetrozygosity*	*Expected Hetrozygosity*	*Difference*
Rabha	0.0283	0.3683	0.3683	0.0316
Garo	0.0267	0.3276	0.3276	-0.0097
Mech	0.0222	0.2956	0.2956	-0.0433
Munda	0.0189	0.3467	0.3467	0.0067
Loaha	0.0654	0.3528	0.3528	0.0289
Oraon	0.0257	0.3681	0.3681	0.0304
Khond	0.0031	0.3470	0.3470	0.0015
Lanjia Saora	0.0076	0.3515	0.3515	0.0076
Vaddabalija (Penticotta)	0.0745	0.3172	0.3172	-0.0035
Vaddabalija (Vadapeta)	0.0358	0.2885	0.2885	-0.0456
Jalari	0.0762	0.2809	0.2809	-0.0393
Kevto	0.0686	0.2756	0.2756	-0.0472

this, Mongoloids of Assam and Sikkim form two separate and distinct sub-clusters (Figs. 2 and 3). One important point that emerges out of the foregoing analysis is that probably the genetic structure of the populations primarily reflects ethnic affiliations of the constituent groups within which geographic and linguistic affiliations are only subtly implied. This scenario is well reflected in our analysis with formation of two broad clusters of population *i.e.*, Mongoloids and Caucasoids and within them we have two sub clusters, one formed by Assamese and Burmese groups of Assam and the other by Tibeto-Himalayan groups of Sikkim. The former represent a Mongoloid cluster and the latter the Caucasoid cluster with sub-clusters of Dravidian Caucasoids and Indo-European Cuacasiods. In the MDS plot and NJ tree, there is a distinct disjointed distribution of the populations of Orissa, which have migrated from Andhra Pradesh, and the rest of the populations of Eastern and Northeastern India. At the same time, the genetic continuity among the populations of the Northeast with the geographically contiguous populations from the Eastern India as a whole is also subtly reflected. At a lower level of geographic hierarchy within the Eastern India, the Mongoloids of Assam are genetically closer to the Mongoloids of West Bengal, when compared to the Mongoloids of Sikkim. Similarly, the

Caucasoids of Assam are closer to the Caucasoids of West Bengal as compared to the Caucasoids of Orissa. This kind of pattern has emerged probably because of the migration of Mongoloids of Assam into West Bengal and that of Caucasoids from West Bengal to Assam as has been hypothesised in the schematic diagram (Fig. 1). It is also apparent that neither the Caucasoids nor the Mongoloids of Sikkim are genetically closer to other Northeastern or Eastern Indian populations, suggesting probably their distinct origin and/or their long history of separation from the rest of the Northeastern or Eastern Indian populations.

REFERENCES

Bhasin, M.K., Walter, H., Chahal, M.S., Bharadwaj, V., Sudhakar, K., Danker-Hopfe, H., Dannewitz, A., Singh, I.P., Shil, A.P., Sharma, M.B. and Wadhavan, D. 1986 *Biology of the People of Sikkim, Inia,* 1. Studies on the variability of genetic markers. *Z. Morph. Anthrop.* 77:49-86.

Bhasin, M.K., Walter, H. and Danker-Hopfe, H. 1992 *The Distribution of genetical, morphological and behavioural traits among the peoples Indian origin.* Delhi, India: Kamla-Faj Enterprises.

Cavalli-Sforza. L.L., Menozzi, P. and Piazza, A. 1994 *The History and Geography of Human Genes.* Princeton N.J.University Press. New Jersey.

Chahal, S.M.S. 1981. *Genetic Variation and Sturcture in Selected Populations of India.* Ph.D.Thesis. University of Newcastleupon Tyne, England.

Das BM. 1977. *Inheritance of Cerumen Type and its Importance in Population Study. Man in India.* 57:305-312.

Das, B.M., Walter, H., Gilvert, K., Lindenbrg,P., Malhotra, K.C., Mukherjee, B.N., Deka, R., and Chakraborty, R. 1987 *Genetic Variation of Five Bloed Group Polymorphisms in ten populations of Assam, India. Inter. J. Anthrop.,* 2: 325-340.

Das, B.M., Deka , R., and Das, R. 1980a, *Haemoglobin E in Six Populations of Assam. J. Indian Anthrop. Soc. 15*: 153-156.

Das, B.M., Deka, R., and Das, R. 1980b. *Haemoglobin E in North-East India.* A review. *Indian J. Phys. Anthrop. Hum. Genet. 6:* 55-82.

Deka, R., Reddy, A.P., Mukhrjee, B.N., Das, B.M., Banerjee, S., Roy. M., Dey. B., Malhotra, K.C. and Walter, H. 1988 *Hemoglobin E Distribution in Ten Endogamous Population Groups of Assam,* India. *Hum. Hered. 38:* 261-266.

Harpending, H.C., and Ward. R. 1982 *Chemical Systematics and Human Evolution. In M. Nitecki (ed.): Biochemical Aspects of Evolutionary Biology,* Chicago, IL: University of Chicago Press, PP. 213-256.

Kirk, R.L., L.Y.C., Vos, G.H. And Vidyarthi, L.P. 1962. *A Genetical Study of the Oraons of the Chotanagpur Plateau (Bihar, India). Am. J. Phys.* Anthrop., 20: 375-386.

Kumar, V., Basu, D. and Reddy, B.M. 2004 *Genetic Heterogeneity in the North-Eastern India:* Reflection of tribe-caste continuum in the genetic structure. *Biol. Am. J. Hum. Biol. 16:334-345.*

Mukherjee. B.N., Malhotra, K.C., Roy, M. Banerjee, S., Walter, H. and Chakraborty, R. 1989 *Genetic Heterogeneity and Population Structure in Eastern India:* Red cell enzyme variability in ten Assamese populations. *Z. Morph. Anthrop. 77: 287-296.*

Mukherjee, B.N., Wa lter, H., Malhotra, K.C., Chakraborty, R., Sauber, P., Banerjee, S. and Roy, M. 1987 Population Genetic Study on Ten Endogamous groups of West Bengal, India. *Anthrop. Anz., 45: 239-254.*

Nei M. 1987. *Molecular Evolutionary Genetics.* New York:Columbia Univ. Press.

Papiha, S.S., Roberts, D.F., and Mishra, S.C. 1988. Serogenetic Studies Among an Urban and two Tribal Populations of Orissa. India. *Ann. Hum. Biol., 15:* 143-152.

Reddy, B.M., Chopra, V.P., Rodewaldt, A et al. 1989. Genetic Differentiation among Four Groups of Fishermen of the Eastern Coast, India. *Ann. Hum. Biol. 16:* 321-333.

Saha. N., Tay, J.S.H., Das, M.K., Piplai. C., Gupta, R. and Roy, S.K., 1988. Genetic Studies among the Sedants and Migrant Oraons of Eastern India. *Am. J. Phys. Anthrop., 76: 321-330.*

Sharma, S. K, Gogoi, S., Dutta, R. And Mahanta, I. 2003. Humoglobin D in Mongoloid Non-tribal family : A report from North East India. *Current Science. 84.* (6). 752-753.

Singh, K.S., Mukherjee, B.N., Waletr, H., Lindenberg, P., Gilbert, K., Dannewitz, A., Malhotra, K.C., Banrjee. S., Rou, M., and Dey, B. 1986 Genetic Markers among Meitei and Brahmins of Manipur, India. *Hum. Hered., 36:*177-187.

Walter, H.. Mukherjee, B.N., Gilbert, K., Lindenberg, P., Dannewitz, A., Malhotra, K.C., Das, B.M., and Deka, R. 1986. Investigations on the Variability of Haptoglobin, trensferrin anf Gc Polymorphisms in Assam, India. *Hum. Hered., 36:* 388-396.

4

Genetic Relationships of Two Tibeto-Burman Speaking Tribal Groups of North East India with Two Other Indian Tribal Groups Speaking Different Languages

C.S. CHAKRABARTI, M. ROY, N.K. SENGUPTA,
R. LALTHANTLUANGA, P.P. MAJUMDER

INTRODUCTION

People of Indian subcontinent represent a great diversity of morphological, genetic, cultural and linguistic features (Majumder, 1998). To the characteristics of the indigenous populations of India, many exogenous features have been added due to immigrations that have taken place in historical times. As a result, the present Indian population comprises indigenous tribes with traditional life styles, along with many non-tribal groups. The number of tribal groups have been estimated to be about 450 (Singh, 1992). Some of the tribal groups are numerically large and found in various parts of India, while some groups are very small who inhabit restricted geographical territories. The tribal groups of India speak dialects that belong primarily to three major language families—Austro-Asiatic (a branch of Austric), Dravidian and Tibeto-

Burman (a branch of Sino-Tibetan). There are, however, a few tribal groups who speak dialects that belong to the Indo-European linguistic family. The Dravidian-speaking groups are primarily confined to the southern region of India, while the Tibeto-Burman speaking tribals are restricted to the northwestern region of India. In this study, we have attempted to estimate genomic diversities and relationships between two morphologically Mongoloid, Sino-Indian speaking tribal groups (Toto, Mizo) and have compared these with those of an Indo-European speaking tribal group (Tharu) inhabiting the sub-Himalayan region and a morphologically Proto-Australoid, Austro-Asiatic speaking tribal group (Ho).

The Tharu are a numerically large (about 30,000 individuals) tribe of Uttar Pradesh. Their origin is largely unknown. Their name may have been derived from 'Terai', a region in western Himalayan foothills, or from 'Thar" meaning 'forestation', or from 'Thar', a desert in western India. The Tharus claim to be descendants of the Rajputs, a dominant caste population of northern India, who are supposedly ancestors of many of the present-day Hinduised sections of the northern Indian ethnic groups. Some anthropologists (Majumdar, 1944) have claimed that they have a mixed ancestry. Because they have Mongoloid morphological features, it has been suggested that they may have been derived from admixture between the Proto-Australoid Indian tribals and some Mongoloid tribal group of Nepal. They are primarily agriculturists, although some are fishermen and some continue to be hunter-gatherers. They are divided into 5 main largely exogamous, subgroups. We have sampled individuals from two of these subgroups—Rana and Katharia.

The Totos are a very small, secluded primitive tribe comprising less than 1000 individuals confined to a particular village called Totopara (Sanyal, 1973). Totopara is situated 228—282 m. above sea level. in the district of Jalpaiguri in West Bengal, India, covering an area of approximately 2000 acres (Sanyal, 1973; Sarkar, 1993; Sinha and Pal, 1984). The Totos are morphologically, linguistically and culturally very different from the tribes and communities living around them, which include Koch, Rajbanshi, Mech, Garo, Tephy, Panikoch, Bhutia (Sanyal, 1973). Gates (1963) considered them as a distinct isolated tribe having Mongoloid features. The Toto society is male dominated, though women prefer husbands younger to them (Sinha, 1988). The Totos are an endogamous group having 13 exogamous clans (Sarkar, 1993). Inter-clan marriage is prohibited. Monogamy is the normally practiced (Sinha,

1988). Cross-cousin marriages, both maternal and paternal, are common (Debnath, 1982). Although there are many views regarding the origin of the Toto, the dominant view is that the Totos are a faction of the Bhutia community, having Tibetan ancestry.

The people who live in the north-eastern Indian State of Mizoram designate themselves as the Mizo ("the highlanders"). The State of Mizoram shares borders with Bangladesh and Myanmar. The origin of the Mizo tribals remains uncertain. But it is a fact that they entered from the direction of Myanmar in large numbers. The word 'Mizo' appears to be a blanket term and probably comprised many tribes, *e.g.*, Lushai, Punte, Poi, Roite, Darlong, Thado, Hmar, etc. Some of these tribes are no longer separately identifiable (*e.g.*, Darlong and Roite). However, the languages spoken by these groups, which belong to the Kuki-Chin sub-family, are dialectically and structurally so similar that it points to their belonging to a common ancestral stock (Goswami, 1979). They possess Mongoloid morphological features. Agriculture is the principal occupation of the Mizos. Most Mizos are followers of Christianity; a significant fraction also follow Buddhism. The total population size is about 450,000.

The Hos are an Austro-Asiatic speaking tribal group, predominantly inhabiting the eastern Indian region. Many anthropologists believe that the numerically large Austro-Asiatic tribals of this region were once a single tribe. Subsequently, in the course of migration to different areas, they assumed different names. The Austro-Asiatic speaking tribals are supposedly the most ancient inhabitants of India. The Hos have been living in isolation for a long time (Roy Chaudhury, 1958), in spite of the fact that they number over 400,000 individuals. Most are ancestor worshippers, although some have adopted Hinduism or Christianity. Their society comprises a number of exogamous clans. Cross-cousin marriages are not a taboo, if not one of the most preferred unions.

MATERIALS AND METHODS

Blood samples (5-10 ml in EDTA) were collected from individuals with prior their consent. All sampled individuals were unrelated at least to the first cousin level. The locations of sampling are indicated in Fig. 1. Blood samples were transported in ice to the laboratory of the Anthropology and Human Genetics Unit, Indian Statistical Institute. High molecular weight DNA was isolated from the blood samples by salting out procedure (Miller et al. 1988). Each DNA sample was

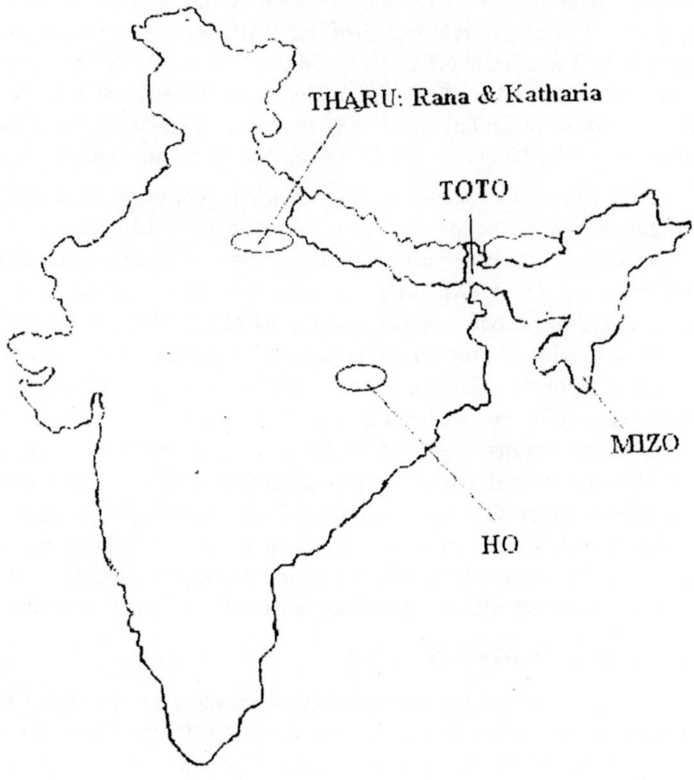

Figure 1. Map of India showing the locations of sampling of populations under study

analysed for polymorphisms at 25 loci, of which 8 were insertion/deletion polymorphisms (IDPs) and remaining 17 were RELPs. The names and GDB accession numbers or ALFRED (http://alfred.med.yale.edu) UID of the RSP loci are: ESRI (GDB:185229); NAT (GDB:187676); CYPIA (GDB: 9956062)-Mspl; PSCR (GDB:182305); T2 (GDB: 196856); LPL (GDB: 285016); ALB(GDB: 178648); ALAD-Mspl (GDB: 155925); ALAD-Rsal (GDB:155924); HBYB-Hinc *II* (GDB: 56084); HB 3ΨB-HincII; HB 5B—Hinfl; Hox B4-Mspl (UID; SI0001670); DRD2 (UID: SI000191L)- TaqIB, TaqID, Taq1A; ADH2-RsaI (UID: SI000002C). The names of the IDPs are given in Table 1. Primers and protocols used for screening of the IDPs were as given in Majumder et al. (1999a) and Tishkoff et al. (1996), and those for RSPs were as given in Jorde et al. (1999a) and Tishkoff et al. (1996), and those for RSPs were as given in Jorde et al. (1995), Majumder et al. (1996b) and K. Kidd (personal communication). All DNA isolations and analyses have been performed in the laboratory of the Indian Statistical Institute, Kolkata.

Allele frequencies at each of these *biallelic loci* were estimated for each population by the maximum likelihood method. Chi-squared tests of significance between the observed genotype frequencies and those expected under Hardy-Weinberg equilibrium were performed. For the three sets of linked loci in and around the ALAD, DRD2 and Hb genes, maximum likelihood estimates of haplotype frequencies were estimated by the EM algorithm, using the HAPLOFREQ package (Majumder and Majumder, 2000). For analyses of genomic diversities, differentiation and distances, estimated haplotype frequencies at these three sets of linked loci were used. Observed gene diversities and the coefficient of gene differentiation G_{ST}, were estimated (Nei, 1973). Genetic distances between populations were estimated using the D_A, distance measure (Nei, 1983), An unrooted neighbour-joining tree (Saitou and Nei, 1987) was constructed to identify affinities among the tribal populations.

RESULTS AND DISCUSSION

Sample sizes and the + allele (Insertion allele for the Indel loci and presence of the restriction site for the RFLP loci) frequencies are given in Table 1. All the loci except *Alu* CD4 show high degrees of polymorphism across most populations. All populations at most loci show statistically non-significant differences of observed genotype frequencies and those expected under Hardy-Weinberg equilibrium Table 4.1.

However, all populations are significantly deviated from the Hardy-Weinberg equilibrium at the Alu D1 locus. At this locus, there is a significant excess of homozygotes over the expected. There are striking differences in allele frequencies at the PSCR locus; the Mizos are monomorphic at the locus. Among the 25 loci, there are three sets of linked loci in and around the ALAD, DRD2 and HB genes (gene clusters). Extimated haplotype frequencies for these sets of linked loci are given in Table 4.2.

Table: 4.1. Sample sizes, genotype and allele frequencies at 25 loci among tribal populations of India.

Locus		*Katharia Tharu*	*Rana Tharu*	*Toto*	*Mizo*	*Ho*
Alu MtNuc	n	36	53	30	27	53
	+/+	9	20	15	5	10
	+/-	11	13	11	13	28
	-/-	16	20	4	9	15
	p ± s.e.	0.403 ± .058	0.500 ± .043	0.683 ± 0.060	0.426 ± 0.067	0.453 ± 0.048
	X^2	4.793*	13.755*	0.700	0.006	0.232
Alu PV92	n	36	53	30	29	54
	+/+	19	36	26	21	17
	+/-	12	15	4	8	27
	-/-	5	2	0	0	10
	p ± s.e.	0.694 ± .548	0.821 ± .037	0.933 ± 0.032	0.862 ± 0.045	0.565 ± 0.048
	X^2	1.657*	.077	0.153	0.742	0.0016
Alu FX3B	n	36	53	29	27	53
	+/+	22	35	24	10	53
	+/-	13	17	5	15	15
	-/-	1	1	0	2	3
	p ± s.e.	0.729 ± 0.478	0.821 ± .037	0.914 ± 0.037	0.648 ± 0.065	0.802 ± 0.039
	X^2	.323	.431	0.258	1.284	0.633

Contd. . . .

Table 4.1 - (Cond . . .)

Locus		*Katharia Tharu*	*Rana Tharu*	*Toto*	*Mizo*	*Ho*
Alu DI	n	36	53	30	28	52
	+/+	12	19	8	7	18
	+/-	6	9	4	2	11
	-/-	18	25	18	19	23
	p ± s.e.	0.417 ± .058	0.443 .048	0.333 ± 0.060	0.452 ± 0.049	
	X^2	15.546*	22.806*	14.700*	19.058*	17.072*
Alu APO	n	36	53	30	29	53
	+/+	25	26	23	29	53
	+/-	11	25	5	5	16
	-/-	0	2	2	2	0
	p ± s.e.	0.847 ± 0.42	0.726 ± .043	0.850 ± 0.046	0.845 ± 0.048	0.849 ± 0.035
	X^2	1.171	1.848	3.600	3.400	1.675
Alu ACE	n	36	53	30	29	54
	+/+	12	21	9	10	30
	+/-	17	24	16	15	19
	-/-	7	8	5	4	5
	p ± s.e.	0.569 ± .058	0.629 ± .047	0.567 ± 0.064	0.603 ± 0.064	0.731 ± 0.043
	X^2	.049	.070	0.222	0.189	0.588

Locus		Katharia Tharu	Rana Tharu	Toto	Mizo	Ho
Alu CD4	n	36	54	30	26	54
	+/+	35	52	30	26	54
	+/-	1	2	0	0	0
	-/-	0	0	0	0	0
	p ± s.e.	0.986 ± 0.14	0.981 ± .013	1.000	1.000	1.000
	X^2	.007	.019	-	-	-
Alu PLAT	n	36	53	30	29	54
	+/+	24	32	0	10	26
	+/-	11	20	2	14	25
	-/-	1	1	28	5	3
	p ± s.e.	0.819 ± .045	0.792 ± .039	0.033 ± 0.023	0.586 ± 0.065	0.713 ± 0.04
	X^2	.038	1.148	0.036	0.001	0.928
ESR	n	37	54	30	29	54
	+/+	15	17	4	13	26
	+/-	16	30	15	16	22
	-/-	6	7	11	0	6
	p ± s.e.	0.622 ± .056	0.593 .047	0.383 ± 0.063	0.724 ± 0.059	0.685 ± 0.04
	X^2	.241	1.224	0.099	4.209*	0.167

Contd. . . .

Table 4.1 (Concld.)

Locus		*Katharia Tharu*	*Rana Tharu*	*Toto*	*Mizo*	*Ho*
NAT	n	37	54	30	26	54
	+/+	17	27	28	26	30
	+/-	20	24	2	0	20
	-/-	0	3	0	0	4
	p ± s.e.	0.730 ± 0.52	0.722 ± .043	0.967 ± 0.023	1.000	0.741 ± 0.004
	X^2	5.075*	.626	0.036	-	0.069
CYPIA	n	37	52	30	26	54
	+/+	5	10	7	3	13
	+/-	15	28	12	10	25
	-/-	17	14	11	13	16
	p ± s.e.	0.338 .055	0.462 ± .049	0.433 ± 0.064	0.308 ± 0.064	0.472 ± 0.048
	X^2	.326	.361	1.033	0.246	0.274
PSCR	n	37	54	30	26	53
	+/+	3	1	0	0	4
	+/-	9	17	3	0	20
	-/-	25	36	27	26	29
	p ± s.e.	0.203 ± .047	0.176 ± .037	0.050 ± 0.028	1.000	0.264 ± 0.043
	X^2	2.266	.397	0.083	-	0.046

Table 4.2. Haplotype frequencies at linked sets of loci in and around genes in tribal populations of India

Locus	*Haplo-type*	*Katharia Tharu*	*Rana Tharu*	*Toto Ho*	*Mizo*	*Ho*
ALAD	+/+	0.145	0.010	0.000	0.000	0.000
	+/-	0.313	0.188	0.033	0.111	0.071
	-/+	0.147	0.235	0.633	0.315	0.214
	-/-	0.395	0.567	0.333	0.574	0.714
DRD2	+/+/+	0.351	0.293	0.201	0.211	0.731
	+/+/-	0.079	0.204	0.164	0.163	0.000
	+/-/+	0.160	0.021	0.000	0.039	0.000
	+/-/-	0.035	0.011	0.000	0.000	0.000
	-/+/+	0.143	0.102	0.017	0.126	0.019
	-/+/-	0.052	0.014	0.000	0.000	0.000
	-/-/+	0.180	0.273	0..432	0.461	0.231
	-/-/-	0.000	0.082	0.185	0.000	0.019
Hb	+/+/+	0.216	0.084	0.300	0.130	0.040
	+/+/-	0.131	0.045	0.000	0.105	0.000
	+/-/+	0.041	0.152	0.000	0.026	0.000
	+/-/-	0.071	0.068	0.000	0.025	0.000
	-/+/+	0.115	0.220	0.050	0.132	0.180
	-/+/-	0.024	0.000	0.000	0.000	0.000
	-/-/+	0.239	0.346	0.650	0.569	0.760
	-/-/-	0.163	0.085	0.000	0.013	0.020

It is seen from the table that there is a large variation in estimated frequencies of haplotypes across populations. The differences in haplotype frequencies are not only significantly different at the 5% level among the 5 groups, but are also significantly different between the two Tharu subgroups. However, the two Tharu subgroups show similarities between themselves which is distinctive from the remaining three groups. The ALAD +/+ haplotype is only present among the two Tharu subgroups, but not in the other populations. Similarly, the DRD2 +/+/- and the -/+/- haplotypes are not present among Totos, Mizos and

Hos, but are present among Rana and Katharia Tharus. The gene diversity for each of the study populations is given in Table 4.3. Gene diversity values range from 0.368 (Toto) to 0.467 (Katharia Tharu). It is not surprising that the Toto should have the lowest gene diversity, in view of its smallest population size among the study populations. It is also not surprising that the two subgroups of the Tharu have remarkably similar values of gene diversity.

Table 4.3. Gene diversities (on diagonal) and genetic distances between tribal populations of India

	Katharia Tharu	*Rana Tharu*	*Toto*	*Mizo*	*Ho*
Katharia Tharu	0.467 ± 0.041				
Rana Tharu	0.0164	0.462 ± 0.038			
Toto	0.0773	0.0517	0.368 ± 0.046		
Mizo	0.0213	0.0172	0.0536	0.448 ± 0.032	
Ho	0.0736	0.0634	0.0820	0.0576	0.376 ± 0.040

Genetic distances calculated on the basis of allele and haplotype frequencies at the 20 loci are provided in Table 3. A neighbour-joining tree (Fig. 2) was constructed. Bootstrapping was done using 1000 replications. It is seen from the reconstructed genomic affinities that the two subgroups of the Tharu are closer to each other. Even though most Tibeto-Burman speakers of northeast India are said to have originated from closely-related ancestral groups of southern China or southeast Asia, the Totos and the Mizos do not seem to be genetically close. The Tharu subgroups are closer to the Ho. The bootstrapped estimates of the confidence associated with these branches are quite high (Fig. 2). This confirms the earlier observations of anthropologists (Majumder, 1944) that the Tharu may be a mixed population. As a matter of fact, the speculation that the Tharu may have been derived from admixture between a Proto-Australoid tribal population of India and a Mongoloid tribal population of Nepal seems to be consistent with the findings of the present study. We have been unable to test this hypothesis of admixture formally and to obtain statistical estimates of admixture proportions because comparable genotype data from Mongoloid tribal populations of Nepal are not currently available. It would be worth attempting in future.

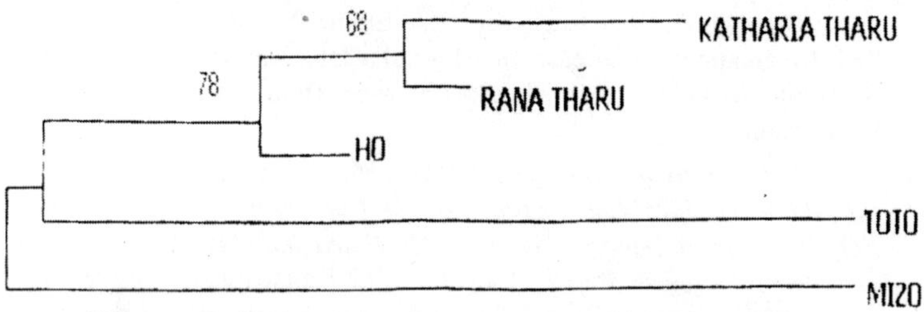

Figure: 2. Neighbour-joining tree depicting genomic relationships among tribal populations of India

ACKNOWLEDGMENTS

This study was supported by grants from the Department of Biotechnology, Government of India, and the Indian Statistical Institute. We are grateful to Dr. Ken Kidd and Dr. Lynn Jorde for sharing some laboratory protocols with us and to all members of the laboratory of the Anthropology & Human Genetics. Unit, Indian Statistical Institute, for help and co-operation throughout the course of this study.

REFERENCES

Debnath, S.K. (1982). *Courtship and Ceremonial Aspect of marriage among Totos : a tribal isolated of Indo-Bhutan Border. Vanyajati*, XXX : 49.

Gates, R.R. (1963). The Totos (Cited by Sanyal, C.C.1973. In: *Meches and the Totos : two sub-Himalayan tribes of the North Bengal*. Darjeeling: North Bengal University Press.

Goswami, B.B. (1979). *Mizo Unrest: A Study of Politicization of Culture*. Jaipur: Aalekh Publishers.

Jorde, L.B., Bamshad, M.J., Watkins, W.S., Zenger, R., Fraley, A.E., Krakowiak, P.A., Carpenter, K.D., Soodyall, H., Jenkins, T. & Rogers, A.R. (1995) Origins and Affinities of Modern Humans: a Comparison of Mitochondrial and Nuchlear Genetic Data. *Am. J. Hum. Genet.*, 57,523-538.

Majumdar, D.N. (1944). *The Fortunes of Primitive Tribes*, Lucknow: Universal Publishers.

Majumder, P.P. (1998). People of India : Biological Diversity and Affinities. *Evol. Anthropol.*, 6, 100-110.

Majumder, P.P., Roy, B., Banerjee, S., Chakraborty, M., Dey, B., Mukherjee, N., Roy, M., Guha Thakurta, P. & Sil, S.K. (1999a) Human-specific insertion/deletion Polymorphisms in Indian Populations and their possible Evolutionary implications. *Eur. J. Hum. Genet.* 7,435-446.

Majumder, P.P., Roy, B., Balgir, R.S. & Dash, B.P. (1999b) Polymorphisms in the Beta-globin Gene Cluster in some Ethnic Populations of India and their Implications on Disease. In: Molecular Intervention in Disease (eds. S. Gupta & O.P. Sood), pp. 75-83. New Delhi: Ranbaxy Science Foundation.

Majumder, P.P. & Majumder, P. (2000) *HAPLOFREQ: A Computer Program for Maximum Likelihood Estimation of Haplotype Frequencies in a Population from Genotype data on Unrelated individuals via the EM* algorithm. Technical Report, Calcutta: Indian Statistical Institute.

Miller, S.A., Dykes, D.D. & Polsky, H.F. (1998) A Simple Salting out Procedure for extracting DNA form human nucleated cells. *Nucl. Acids Res. 16*, 1215.

Nei, M. (1973) Analysis of Gene Diversity in Subdivided Populations. *Proc. Natl. Acad. Sci.* USA 70,3321-3323.

Roy Chaudhury, P.C. (1958) *Bihar District Gazetteers* : Singhbhum. Patna: Secretariat Press.

Saitou, N. & Nei, M. (1987) The Neighhbour-Joining Method: A new method for reconstructing phylogenetic trees. *Mol. Biol. Evol. 4*, 406-425.

Sanyal, C.C. (1973). *The Meches and the Totos : Two sub-Himalayan Tribes of North Bengal.* Darjeeling : North Bengal University Press.

Sarkar, A. (1993). *Toto : Society and change* (A sub-Himalayan Tribe of West Bengal). Calcutta: Firma KLM Private Ltd.

Singh, K.S. (1992). *People of India.* Delhi: Oxford India Press.

Sinha, D. (1988). Ethno-Zoological Studies of the Sub-Himalayan Tribal area of North Bengal with emphasis on Ecological and Bio-energetics of the Totos. Ph.D.Thesis. Siliguri: North Bengal University.

Sinha, D. & Pal, B.C. (1984). A study of Eco-sociological Change among and Underdeveloped Tribes : the Totos of North Bengal. *Bulletin of Cultural Research Institute,* Vol. XVI, No. 1-4.

Tishkoff, S.A., Ruano, g., Kidd, J.R. & Kidd, K.K. (1996) Distribution and Frequency of a Polymorphic Alu insertion at the Plasminogen Activator Locus in Humans. *Hum. Genet. 97*, 759-764.

5

Distance Between the Semsa and other Mongoloid Populations of Assam and Meghalaya in Respect of Certain Genetic Traits

D. K. LIMBU

The Semsa are an offshoot of the Dimasa tribe of North Cachar hills. Semkhor village is their only sylvan settlement. They have been maintaining their cultural isolation for more than two hundred years (Danda and Ghatak, 1985). The Semsa still maintain their traditional cultural traits, including the language of the Dimasa tribe. Marriage rule among the Semsa is strictly guided by the principle of double descent system. They also strictly follow village endogamy. The Semsa of Semkhor village are having five patri-clans and sixteen matri-clans. At the time of marriage a man is not allowed to take a bride from his own patri-clan and it is also the rule that a man should not marry a girl who belongs to the same matri-clan (Danda and Ghatak, 1985). However, cross cousin marriage, though not practiced, is not prohibited among the Semsa. Their primary concern is to maintain village endogamy at any cost.

The Semkhor village is situated in the hills of Barail range of Assam (Fig. 1.) It covers an area of 406 hectares and lies between 93°15'E and 93°22'6"E latitude and 25°20'N and 25°15'27"N longitude.

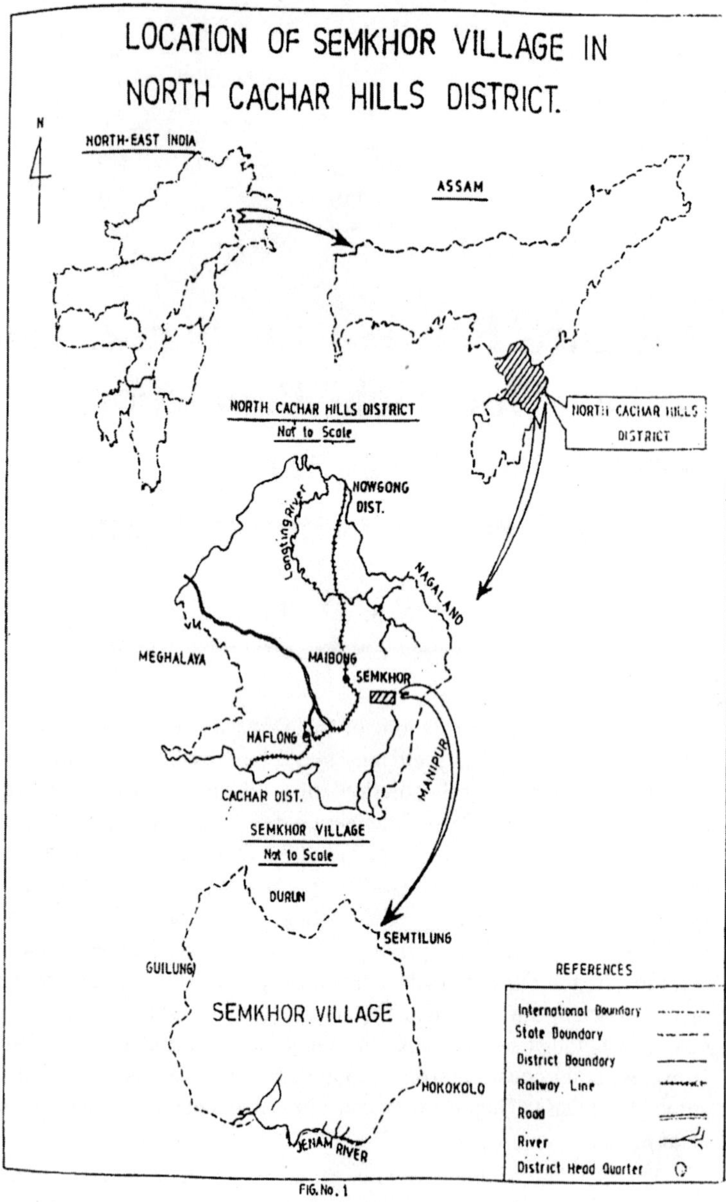

FIG. No. 1

Figure: 1

The village is bounded by hills and rivers from all sides (*District Handbook of United Mikir and North Cachar Hills, 1972*). In this village there were five saline pits (*semdikhor*), but at present only three are in usable condition. The name of the village has been derived from these natural saline pits. It happens to be one of the oldest villages in the district (Danda and Ghatak, 1985).

It is said that the people from nearer villages came to Semkhor and settled here. There is another view that a section of the Dimasa people took shelter in this village during the Kachari King's encounter with the Ahom (Danda and Ghatak, 1985). As the village is bounded by hills on all sides, the inhabitants of the village still maintain a relative cultural isolation. The Semsa population of this village is said to have been derived from the name of the village Semkhor.

There are two purposes of this study, which are:

(a) to describe the genetic characteristics of the Semsa population, and,

(b) to find out biological variations between the Semsa and the other Mongoloid populations of Assam and Meghalaya in respect of some genetic characters.

MATERIALS AND METHODS

Data for the present study were collected between January and September, 1992. The present sample on ABO and Rh blood groups consisted of 106 individuals, of whom 65 were males and 41 females; on taste sensitivity to phenylthiocarbamide, 156 individuals were tested, of whom 97 were males and 59 females; and on colour-blindness 119 males were examined.

(i) ABO and Rh (D) blood groups: Blood grouping was done following the standard techniques suggested by Lawler and Lawler (1951) and Mourant (1954).

(ii) Taste sensitivity to phenylthiocarbamide: A serial dilution technique, prescribed by Harris and Kalmus (1949), was followed.

(iii) Colourblindness: The Ishihara colour plates were employed in adequate daylight.

RESULTS

In Table 1, the results of four genetic markers, *viz*, ABO and Rh blood groups, PTC-taste blindness and colour blindness among the Semsa

Table 5.1. Genetic markers among the Semsa.

Genetic markers	*No. tested*	*Phenotype frequencies*	*%*	*Gene frequencies*	*Inferences*
ABO blood groups	106	A = 23	21.70	p = 0.1424	D/ δ = ± 0.0078 Insignificant
		B = 29	27.36	q = 0.1760	X^2 = 2.8441, df = 1, P > 0.05 Insignificant
		AB = 5	4.72	r = 0.6816	
		O = 49	46.23		
Rh blood groups	106	Rh (+) = 105	99.06	D = 0.9030	X^2 0.00001, df = 1, P > 0,05 Insignificant
		Rh (-) = 1	0.94	d = 0.0970	
PTC taste blindness	156	Tasters = 102	65.38	T = 0.5884	X^2 = 0.00012, df = 1, P > 0.05 Insignificant
		Non-tasters = 54	34.62	t = 0.4116	
Colour blindness	119	Normal = 110	92.44		
	(male)	Colour blind = 9	7.56		
		Protan = 5	55.56		
		Deutan = 3	33.33	$\bar{C}$ = 0.0756	
		Total Colour blind = 1	11.11	(male)	

have been set out. It is found that the phenotypic frequencies of A. B, AB and O blood groups are 21.70%, 27.36%, 4.72% and 46.23%, respectively. The gene frequencies p, q, r have been worked out and found to be 0.1424, 0.1760 and 0.6816, respectively. The D/δ value is 0.0078 and the X^2 value is 2.8442 (d.f. = 1 and $p>0.05$). So both the D/δ and X^2 values indicate that the population is in genetic equilibrium in respect of ABO blood groups.

Table 5.1 also shows the results of Rh blood groups carried out among the Semsa. Out of 106 individuals tested with anti-D antisera, only one individual is found to be of Rh type. So, the frequencies of Rh^+ and Rh^- individuals are 99.06% and 0.94%, respectively. The frequencies of D and d genes are 0.9030 and 0.0970, respectively. The X^2 value (X^2 = 0.00001, d.f.=1, $p>0.05$) shows that so far as the Rh blood group system is concerned, this population is in genetic equilibrium. It may be mentioned that generally the frequency of Rh gene, *i.e.* d is generally absent or if present, of occurs in a very low dose among the Indian Mongoloid populations (Bhattacharjee, 1968).

Altogether 156 individuals have been tested for PTC taste-blindness, following the method suggested by Harris and Kalmus (1949). The antimode falls on No. 6. So all the individuals, having threshold value between 0 and 6, have been taken as non-tasters and the rest of individuals are taken as tasters (Fig. 2). It is found that out of 156 Semsa individuals, 65.38% are tasters and 34.62% are non-tasters. The frequencies of T and t genes are 0.588 and 0.412 respectively. The X^2 value (0.00012, d.f.=1, $p>0.05$) indicates that the population in respect of this trait is in equilibrium.

Table 5.1 further shows the result of colourblindness among the Semsa. Altogether 119 males have been examined with the Ishihara chart. It is found that 110 (92,44%) are normal and 9 (7.56%) are colourblind. It is also found that out of 9 colourblind individuals among the Semsa, 5 (55.56%) are protan and 3 (33.33%) are deutan and I (11.11%) is complete or total colourblind. However, the frequency of colourblind gene (c) among the Semsa males is found to be 0.0756. Since, in the present study, no effort has been made to detect colourblind females among the Semsa, it is difficult to calculate the equilibrium of gene frequency for colourblindness (Cavalli-Sforza and Bodmer, 1971) among the Semsa.

Table 5.2 shows the pattern of incompatible matings among the Semsa. It has been observed on the basis of the ABO blood groups that nearly 42.47% of all matings are incompatible. Since the frequency of Rh blood groups is less than 1%, incompatible matings in respect of Rh system cannot be significant among the Semsa. However, it may be postulated that through ABO-incompatible matings, selection still finds ample opportunity to play its role in this population.

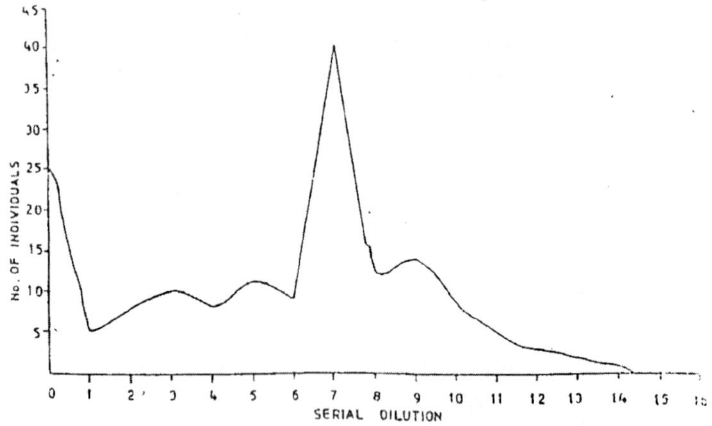

Figure: 2. Distribution of PTC Taste blindness among the Semsa

Table 5.2. Incompatible matings among the Semsa

Male x Female	*Frequency*
A x O	0.1238
B x O	0.1816
AB x O	0.0083
A x B	0.0394
B x A	0.0660
AB x A	0.0030
AB x B	0.0026
Total	0.4247 OR 42.47%

For the Dimasa, data on ABO blood groups are available. So in Table 3 a comparison has been made between the Dimasa with the Semsa. It is found that in respect of ABO blood groups, there is a significant difference between the Dimasa and Semsa (X^2=8.7672, d.f.=3, p>0.05).

Table 5.4 presents the data on colourblindness among the Semsa, Garo, Khasi, Ahom, Mikir, Boro-Kachari, Miri and Hajong. It is seen that among the Mikir and Miri no colourblind individual has been reported. Excluding the Mikir and the Miri, the Garo, Khasi, Ahom, Boro-Kachari and Hajong have been taken for comparison with the Semsa. The X^2 values indicate that in respect of this trait, no difference is observed among these populations (X^2=6.4820, d.f.=5, p>0.05). It is also observed that the Semsa do not differ from the Garo, Khasi, Ahom, Boro-Kachari or from the Hajong in respect of colourblindness (X^2 values have been given at the bottom of the Table 4).

Table 5.5 shows the gene frequencies of ABO, Rh and PTC tasteblindness among the Semsa, Koch, Rabha, Garo, Chutia, Lalung, Khasi, Ahom, Mikir and Khamyang. It may be noted that data on PTC tasteblindness among the Khamyang are not available. However, this table is self explanatory. On the basis of these data, along with those of Semsa, distance matrix has been calculated and the results are given in Tables 5.6 and 5.7.

Table 5.6 shows the distance matrix, calculated on the basis of ABO and Rh blood groups and PTC tasteblindness for the populations, *viz.*, the Koch, Rabha, Garo, Chutia, Lalung, Khasi, Ahom, Mikir and Semsa. The Khasi sample has been taken as given by Das in 1968. However, Das (1978) has also published data on ABO blood groups separately for each of the Khasi sub-groups, but he has not given data on Rh blood groups and PTC tasteblindness. So, it has not been able to consider each of the Khasi sub-groups separately. From Table 6, it is seen that the minimum distance takes place between the Semsa and Lalung (0.002). It is then followed by a distance between the Chutia and Semsa (0.003), between the Ahom and Semsa (0.004) and between the Koch and Semsa (0.005). But the Semsa stand apart from the Khasi (0.027) as well as from the Garo (0.024). On the basis of this distance matrix, calculated by the method of Sokal and Sneath (1963), the dendrogram, showing the relationships among these populations, has been drawn and reproduced in Fig. 3. The dendrogram shows that the Semsa are nearer to the Lalung and Koch but stand apart from the Khasi, Garo, Ahom and others.

Table 5.3. ABO blood groups in Dimasa and Semsa

Populations	*No.*	*ABO blood groups*							*Reference*
		Phenotypic frequency				*Gene Frequency*			
		0	*A*	*B*	*AB*	*p*	*q*	*r*	
Dimasa	100	32	16	41	11	0.1446	0.3.50	0.5508	Phukan, 1975
Semsa	106	49	23	29	5	0.1424	0.1760	0.6816	Present study

$X^2 = 8.7672$, df = 3, $P < 0.05$. Significant.

Table 5.4. Comparison of frequencies of X-linked colour-blindness between the Semsa and other populations of Assam and Meghalaya

Populations	*No. Tested*	*Normal*		*Colour-Blind*		*Authors*
		No.	*%*	*No.*	*%*	
Semsa	119	110	92.44	9	7.56	Present study.
Garo	102	97	95.10	5	4.90	Rizvi, 1974.
Khasi	495	476	96.16	19	3.84	Mukherjee, 1963.
Ahom	167	160	95. 81	7	4.19	Das et al., 1986
Mikir	125	125	100.00	0	0.00	Mukherjee, 1963.
Boro-Cachari	201	186	92.54	15	7.46	Mukherjee and Guha, 1990.
Miri	37	37	100.00	0	0.00	Srivastava, 1969.
Hajong	183	176	96.18	7	3.82	Barua, 1985.

X^2 (between all populations) = 6.4820, df = 5, $P > 0.05$, Insignificant.

X^2 (between Semsa and Garo) = 0.6541, df = 1, $P > 0.05$, Insignificant.

X^2 (between Semsa and Khasi) = 3.0510, df = 1, $P > 0.05$, Insignificant.

X^2 (between Semsa and Ahom) = 1.4919, df = 1, $P > 0.05$, Insignificant.

X^2 (between Semsa and Boro-Cachari) = 0.0114, df =1, $P > 0.05$, Insignificant.

X^2 (between Semsa and Hajong) = 2.0154, df = 1, $P > 0.05$, Insignificant.

Table 5.5. Gene frequencies of ABO, Rh and PTC by populations

	ABO				*RH*			*PTC*			
Population	*No.*	*p(A)*	*q(B)*	*r(O)*	*No.*	*D(+)*	*d(-)*	*No.*	*T*	*t*	*Reference*
Semsa	106	0.1424	0.1760	0.6816	106	0.9030	0.0970	156	0.4120	0.5880	Present study
Koch	104	0.2294	0.2420	0.5286	104	0.9020	0.0980	121	0.4546	0.5454	Sengupta, 1991
Rabha	600	0.2570	0.238	0.505	126*	0.9111	0.0889	108	0.5920	0.4080	Das, 1970; Das et al. 1980a
Garo	143	0.1780	0.2990	10.5230	144	1.000	0.0000	125	0.5350	0.4650	Das et al., 1980.
Chutia	184	0.2000	0.1120	0.6880	64	0.8751	0.1249	190	0.4520	0.5480	Das et al., 1985
Lalung	114	0.1940	0.2280	0.5780	114	0.9062	0.0938	94	0.4640	0.5360	Das et al., 1980
Khasi	821	0.1930	0.1110	0.6860	315	1.0000	0.0000	838	0.6080	0.3920	Das, 1968
Ahom	348	0.1640	0.1390	0.6790	123	0.8720	0.1276	204*	0.4620	0.538	Das et al. 1980; Das et al. 1985
Mikir	245	0.2460	0.2030	0.5510	106	0.8779	0.1221	209	0.5960	0.4040	Das and Deka, 1985
Khamyang	248	0.1060	0.2260	0.6740	248	0.9368	0.0632	-	-	-	Singh and Phukan, 1990

Table 5.6. Genetic distances* for nine populations of Assam and Meghayaya

	Semsa	*Koch*	*Rabha*	*Garo*	*Chutia*	*Lalung*	*Khasi*	*Ahom*	*Mikir*
Semsa	0.000								
Koch	0.005	0.000							
Rabha	0.011	0.003	0.000						
Garo	0.024	0.019	0.018	0.000					
Chutia	0.003	0.006	0.011	0.032	0.000				
Lalung	0.002	0.000	0.004	0.018	0.005	0.000			
Khasi	0.027	0.029	0.024	0.012	0.027	0.025	0.000		
Ahom	0.004	0.008	0.013	0.033	0.004	0.006	0.031	0.000	
Mikir	0.010	0.004	0.001	0.024	0.007	0.004	0.0027	0.010	0.000

*Based on ABO, Rh and P.T.C.— taste blindness.

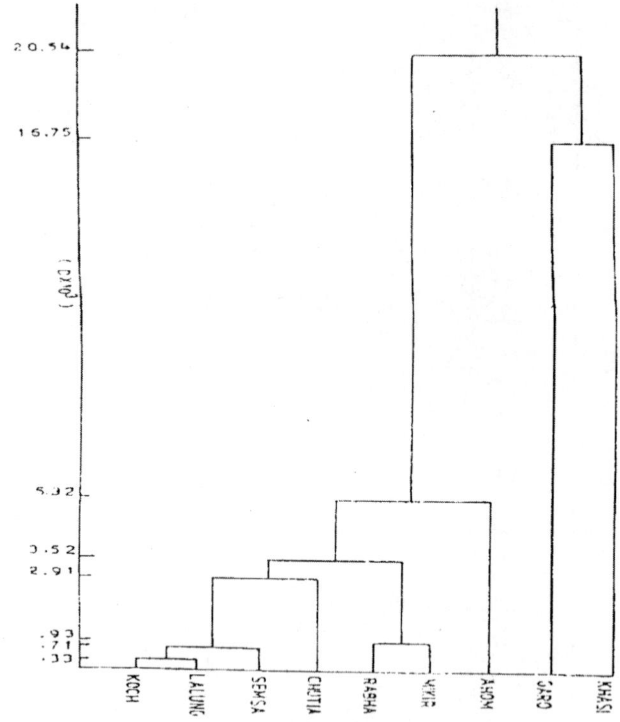

Figure: 3. Dendrogram for the populations of Assam and Meghalaya based on ABO and RH blood groups and P.T.C. taste sensitivity

Table 5.7 shows the distance matrix, based on ABO and Rh blood groups systems, among the Semsa, Koch, Rabha, Garo, Chutia, Lalung, Khasi, Ahom, Mikir and Khamyang. This distance matrix has been calculated following the method of Sokal and Sneath (1963). It shows that the Semsa stand very close to the Khamyang (0.001), followed by the Lalung (0.003), Chutia (0.004), Koch, Ahom and Mikir (0.006). They, however, remain distant from the Garo (0.032) and Khasi (0.030). The dendrogram, drawn on the basis of this genetic distance matrix, has been given in Fig. 3, which shows that the Semsa and Khamyang came very close to each other.

Table 5.7. Genetic distances* for ten populations of Assam and Meghalaya

	Semsa	*Koch*	*Rabha*	*Garo*	*Chutia*	*Lalung*	*Khasi*	*Ahom*	*Mikir*	*Khamyang*
Semsa	0.000									
Koch	0.006	0.000								
Rabha	0.009	0.000	0.000							
Garo	0.032	0.027	0.025	0.000						
Chutia	0.004	0.010	0.011	0.047	0.000					
Lalung	0.003	0.001	0.002	0.026	0.007	0.000				
Khasi	0.030	0.037	0.036	0.017	0.035	0.033	0.000			
Ahom	0.006	0.012	0.015	0.048	0.005	0.009	0.041	0.000		
Mikir	0.006	0.001	0.001	0.035	0.006	0.002	0.0040	0.010	0.000	
Khamyang	0.001	0.008	0.010	0.021	0.010	0.004	0.025	0.010	0.010	0.000

*Based on ABO and Rh blood groups.

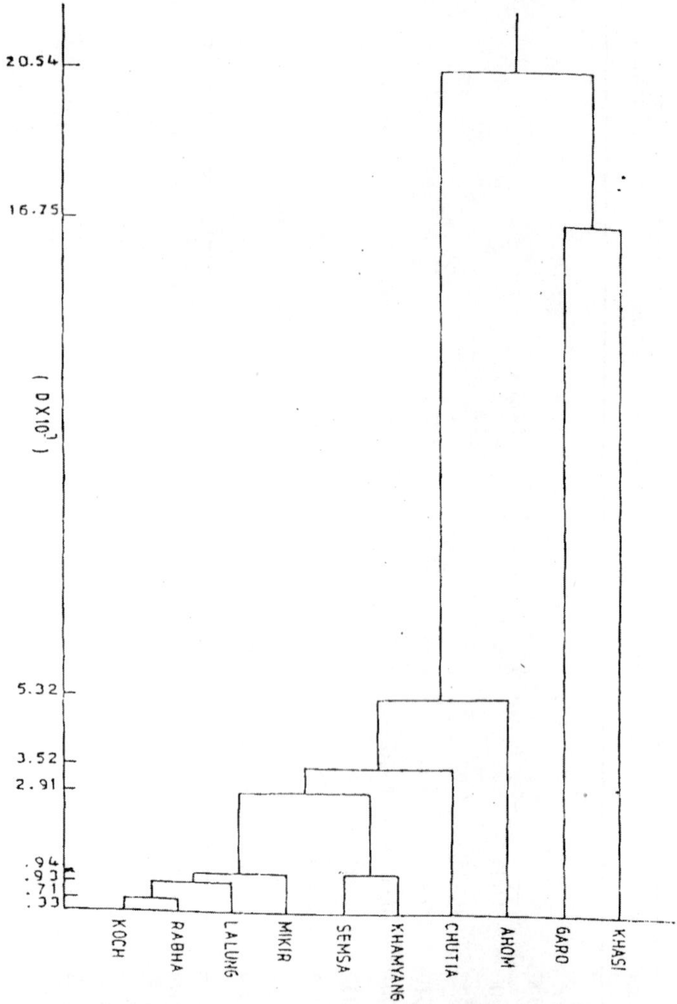

Figure: 4. Dendrogram for ten populations of Assam and Maghalaya (based on ABO and RH blood groups)

CONCLUSION

As mentioned earlier, Danda and Ghatak (1985) have suggested Semsa to be an offshoot of the Dimasa. So it is expected that in genetic traits also they would resemble the Dimasa. When a comparison has been made between the Semsa and Dimasa in respect of ABO blood groups, it is found that there is significant difference between them. Unfortunately, data on other genetic markers from the Dimasa are not available for further comparison.

The three genetic markers (ABO, Rh and PTC) have been taken into consideration to find out the genetic relationship between the Semsa and other Mongoloid populations. The dendrogram shows that the Semsa are much closer to the Lalung and Koch than to other populations (Fig. 3). When only two blood groups, *i.e.* ABO and Rh are taken into consideration, the dendrogram (Fig. 4) shows that the Khamyang and Semsa are closer to each other, but the Semsa stand somewhat separate from the other populations. It is true that on the basis of two or three genetic markers the exact phylogenetic relationship among the populations is difficult to assess. However, on the basis of whatever data on genetic markers are available, one may infer that the Semsa do not resemble the Dimasa, in spite of the fact that according to various suggestions, based on some cultural traits, the Semsa appear to be an offshoot of the Dimasa.

In the present study a very limited number of traits have been used through which it is really difficult to assess the phylogenetic relationship of the Semsa with the Dimasa in particular and with the other Mongoloid populations of Assam and Meghalaya in general. At present, with our limited data we may say that the Semsa are a separate endogamous group, taking the form of a genetic isolate, which has no direct relationship with the Dimasa or any other population. The present genetic structure of the Semsa could have been shaped due to the effect of Founder Principle (Mayr, 1963). Indeed, at the genetic level relationships between specific groups or communities tend to follow a direction, which may not always follow a cultural line of seeing things from a broader perspective.

REFERENCES

Barua, S. 1985. Red-green Colour-blindness and Earlobe attachment among the Hajongs of Meghalaya (India). *Indian Jr. phys. Anthrop. and Hum. Genet.* 11:151-154.

Bhattacharjee, P.N. 1968. Sero-genetical Variations in the Lepcha of Darjeeling District with Special reference to the Indian Mongoloid. *Bull. Anthropological Survey of India.* 17: 382-392.

Cavalli-Sforza, L.L. and W.F. Bodmer. 1971. *The Genetics of Human Populations.* W.H. Freeman and Company, San Francisco.

Danda, D.G. and S. Ghatak. 1985. *The Semsa and their Habitat.* Anthropological Survey of India, Calcutta.

Das, B.M. 1960. *Ethnic Affinities of the Rabha.* Department of Publication, Guwahati University, Guwahati.

Das, B.M. 1968. ABO Blood Groups in the Tribal Populations of North-East India with special reference to the Khasi. *Anthropologist,* Special Volume: 85-92.

Das, B.M. 1978. *Variation in Physical Characteristics in the Khasi Population of North East India.* Dutta Barua and Co., Guwahati.

Das, B.M., P.B. Das and R. Das. 1980a. *The Lalungs: Their Physical Features and Biosocial Profile.* (Mimeographed). Anthropology Department, Gauhati University, Guwahati.

Das, B.M., P.B. Das, R. Das. 1980b. *A Comparative Study of Physical Anthropology of Five Mongoloid Populations of Assam.* (Mimeographed). Anthropology Department, Gauhati University, Guwahati.

Das, B.M., P.B. Das, R. Das, H. Walter and H. Danker-Hopfe. 1985. Anthropological studies in Assam, India. Observations on Five Mongoloid Populations. *Anthrop. Anz.* 43: 193-204.

Das, B.M., R. Deka and R. Das. 1980. ABO Blood Groups and Rh Factor in six Populations of Assam. *Bull. Anth. Surv. India.* 29: 1-3.

District Handbook of United Mikir and North Cachar Hills District, 1972.

Harris, and K. Kalmus. 1949. The Measurement of Taste Sensitivity to PTC. *Ann. Eugen.* (Lond.) 15: 24-31.

Ishihara, S. 1962. *Tests for Colour-blindness.* Kannehara Shuppan Co. Ltd., Tokyo.

Lawler, S.D. and L.I. Lawler. 1951. *Human Blood Groups and Inheritance.* William Heinemann, London.

Mayr, B. 1963. *Animal Species and Evolution.* The Belknup Press of Harvard University Press, Cambridge.

Mukerjee, D.P. 1963. Variation in defective colour vision among some tribes of Assam. *Bull. Anth. Surv. India.* 12: 39-42.

Mukherjee. D.P. and A. Guha. 1990. Colour-blindness, Manual mid-phalangeal hair and Attached Earlobe among Boro-Cacharis. *J. Indian Anthrop.* Soc. 25: 153-163.

Phukan, M.N. 1975. Biological Distances among some Sub-divisions of the Kachari of Assam in respect of ABO Blood Groups and their Position among other Tribes of North Eastern India. *Bull. Deptt. Anthrop. Dibrugarh Univ.* 4: 28-34.

Rizvi, S.H.M. 1974. Unpublished Report Submitted to Anthropological Survey of India, North-Eastern Regional Station, Shillong.

Sengupta, S. 1991. A Physical Anthropological Profile of the Koch of Darrang District, Assam, *Indian J. Phys. Anthrop and Hum. Genet.* 17: 65-72.

Singh, T.S. and M.N. Phookan. 1990. A Note on the Frequency Distribution of ABO and Rhesus Blood Group in four Thai Populations of Assam (India) and their Position among the Mongoloids of this region, *Anthrop. Anz.* 48: 29-35.

Sokal, R.R. and P.H.A. Sneath. 1963. *Principles of Numerical Taxonomy.* W.H. Freeman, London.

Srivastava, R.P. 1969. Finger Prints, Colour-blindness and other Features of the Miris of Assam. *Man in India,* 49: 398.

6

Dermatoglyphics of the Tai-Phakes of Assam

TILUTTOMA BARUAH

INTRODUCTION

The Tai-Phakes, also known as Phakils, are a small group of people of Tai-origin. They entered Assam in the later part of the 18th century through a common route of Patkai range of hills. During the British rule, the phakes were divided into two broad groups of 'Borphakial' and 'Namphakial' who had settled along the Buridihing river. At present, near Joypur Tipamphakae, close to Naharkatia Namphakae and at a short distance from Margherita, there are Borphakial and Manmowmukh villages. Beside, near Ledo there are Tai-Phake villages like Nonglai, Long and Mounglang whereas Phaneng and Ngingam villages are located near Tirap.

DERMATOGLYPHIC TRAITS

Finger and palm prints of 150 individuals (75 males and 75 females) belonging to Tai-Phakae population were collected. However, a few palm prints had not been included in the analysis as these were indistinct. The age of the subject varied between 12 and 50 years. The prints were obtained by using printer's blank ink. The ridge counts were scored from the prints and pattern types were classified by standard methods as designed by Cummins and Midlo (1961). Statistical significance of the differences between samples in the present study was calculated with respect to traits considered here by the Chi-square test and by the test for quantitative variables.

FINGER

The finger patterns are classified according to Galton's threefold classification *i.e.* whorl, loop and arch. In the present study, the lateral pocket loops, twin loops, central packet loops and accidentals are all recorded as *whores*. Plain and tented arches are also recorded as arch.

The rules formulated by Cummins and Mlido (43) and followed here for ridge counting are as follows:

The number of ridges that cross a straight line connecting the tri-radius to the core of a pattern is termed the ridge-count of the pattem. Arches do not have any ridge count, loops have one and whorls and composites have two. If a pattem has two ridge counts, the larger at the two is used. The point of the triradius and the core is not counted in determining the ridge count. All ridges actually crossed by an imaginary line joining the tri-radius and the core are counted.

The values of pattem type have been found out by Furuhata's index, Dankmeijer's index and the index of pattern intensity. These are,

1. Furuhata's index = (Whorls : Loops) X 100
2. Dankmeijer's index = (Archs ÷ Whorls) X 100
3. Pattern Intensity index = {(Whorls X 2) ÷ Loops} ÷ n

PALM

The palm is studied to find out the following :

1. Termination of mainlines
2. Position of the proximal medial tri-radius
3. Configuration of hypothenar and thenar areas
4. Configuration of thenar interdigital areas
5. Atd. Angle.

Another tri-radius is usually found at the base of the palm which is known as axial tri-radius. To determine the position of axial tri-radius, a line is drawn from the proximal radiant of the mainline C towards the proximal and then it is further extended up to the bracelet crease. It may have three positions. The distal most part is t", the proximal is t and the intermediate is t'.

The main line index for each palm is the sum of the values of the endings of mainline A & D.

The angle 'atd' has been extensively used by Penrose (1954) in his study of the correlation of the incidence of an axial tri-radius which occurs near the center of the palm and Mongolism. Roughly, an 'ant' angle of over 50° is of equivalent quality in scoring the tri-radius at t'', while an angle less that 45° is equivalent to t and an intermediate angle is ranked as t'.

RESULTS

The data collected from the Tai-Phake population have been analysed and the following results are obtained.

Table 6.1. Finger Patterns of Tai-Phakes (Males & Females): all fingers combined

Sex	Table number (N)	Percent-age	Total No. of whorls	Percent-age	Total No. of ulnas loops	Percent-age
Male	*75*	*75.00*	*264*	*35.20*	*434*	*57.86*
Female	*75*	*75.00*	*274*	*36.53*	*423*	*56.40*

Sex	*Table radial*	*Percent-age*	*Total loops*	*Percent-age*	*Total arches*	*Percent-age*
Male	14	1.86	448	59.53	38	5.06
Female	18	2.40	441	58.80	35	4.66

Table 6.1 shows that the presence of loop is higher than the whorl and arch in both males and females. The percentages of whorls present are 35.20 and 36.53 in males and females respectively. Whorls are less in males than in females. The presence of loop and arch is again less in females than males. Among the males the percentages of loops and arches are 59.73 and 5.06 respectively, while the percentages of loops and arches in females are 58.80 and 4.66 respectively.

Table 6.2(a) shows that digit I of the right hand, I has more number of whorls than the digit I of the left hand. The percentage of whorls in the digit I of the right hand is 4.40 and it is 4.00 in the left hand. In digit I of the left hand ulnar loop is more than the digit I of the right hand. Their percentages are found to be 5.33 and 5.20 respectively.

Table 6.2. (a) Percentile frequencies of finger print pattern of maleTtai-Phakes (N=75)

Finger Pattern	*Right*						*Left*				*Total*		
	I	*II*	*III*	*IV*	*V*	*Total*	*I*	*II*	*III*	*IV*	*V*	*Total*	*Rt + Lt*
Whorl No.	33	26	16	42	17	134	30	26	20	38	16	130	264
Percentage	4.40	3.46	2.13	5.60	2.26	17.86	4.00	3.46	2.66	5.06	2.13	17.33	25.2
Ulnar Loop No.	39	39	57	31	55	221	40	34	47	37	55	213	434
Percentage	5.20	5.20	7.60	4.13	7.33	29.46	5.33	4.53	6.26	4.93	7.33	28.4	57.86
Radial Loop No.	-	4	1	-	-	5	-	6	21	-	1	9	14
Percentage	-	0.53	0.13	-	-	0.66	-	0.80	0.26	-	0.13	1.20	1.86
Total Loop No.	39	43	58	31	55	226	40	40	49	37	56	222	448
Percentage	5.20	5.73	7.73	4.13	7.33	30.13	5.33	5.33	6.33	4.93	7.46	29.6	59.73
Arch No.	3	6	1	2	3	15	5	10	5	-	3	23	38
Percentage	0.40	0.80	0.13	0.26	0.40	2.00	0.66	1.33	0.66	-	0.40	3.06	5.06

There is no radial loop in digit I of both right and left hands. The digit I of the left hand shows more arch than the right. Its percentage is 0.66 in the left hand and 0.4 in the right hand.

In the digit II number of finger having whorl is the same in both right and left hands, its percentage being 3.46. The percentage of ulnar loop in the digital II of the right hand is 5.20 which is more than the percentage of ulnar loops in left hand which is 4.53. The digit II of the left hand shows more radial loops than the right. Its percentage is 0.80 in the left hand and 0.53 in the right hand. The digit II of the left hand shows more arches than the right, its percentage being 1.33 in the left hand and 0.30 in the right hand.

The digit III of the left hand whorl are more than the digit II of the right hand. Their percentages are 2.66 and 2.13 respectively. The digit III of the right hand shows more ulnar loops than the left, their percentages being 7.60 and 6.26 respectively. Also, digit III of the left hand shows more redial loops and arches than the right. Their percentages are 0.26 and 0.66 in the left hand and 0.13 for both radial loops and arches in the right hand.

In the digit IV of the right hand more number of fingers have whorls than in the left hand. The percentage of fingers having whorls in the digit IV is 5.60 in the right hand and it is 5.06 in the left hand. The digit IV of the left hand has more number of fingers having ulnar loops than of the right hand. The percentage of fingers having ulnar loop in the digit IV is 4.93 in the left hand and it is 4.13 in the right hand. There is no any radial loop in digit IV of both right and left hands. Also there is no arch in the digit IV of the left hand.

Table 6.2(b) shows that the digit I of the right hand (6.40%) of females has more number of ulnar loops than the digit I of the left hand (5.46%), but digit I of the left hand has more number of whorls than the right hand. Their percentages are 3.60 and 3.20 in left and right hand digits respectively. There is no radial loop in the digit I and both right and left hands have 0.13% redial loops. The percentage of arch in the digit I of the left hand is 0.80, while it is 0.40 in the right hand.

The digit II of the left hand has more number of whorls than the digit II of the right hand. Their percentages are 4.00 and 3.60 in the left and right hand digits respectively. The digit II of the right hand has more number of ulnar loops than the digit II of the left hand and

Table 6.2(b). Percentile frequencies of finger print pattern of female Tai-Phakes (N=75)

Finger Pattern	*Right*						*Left*					*Total*	
	I	*II*	*III*	*IV*	*V*	*Total*	*I*	*II*	*III*	*IV*	*V*	*Total*	*Rt + Lt*
Whorl No.	24	27	18	45	22	136	27	30	20	4	17	138	274
Percentage	3.20	3.60	2.40	6.00	2.93	18.13	3.60	4.00	2.66	5.86	2.26	18.4	36.53
Ulnar Loop No.	43	41	55	29	49	222	41	26	50	29	55	201	423
Percentage	6.40	5.46	7.33	3.86	6.53	29.6	5.46	3.46	6.66	3.86	7.33	26.8	56.40
Radial Loop No.	-	3	-	-	1	4	1	10	-	2	1	14	18
Percentage	-	0.40	-	-	0.13	0.53	0.13	1.33	-	0.26	0.13	1.86	2.40
Total Loop No.	48	44	55	29	50	226	42	36	50	31	56	215	441
Percentage	6.40	5.86	7.33	3.86	6.66	30.13	5.60	4.80	6.66	4.13	7.46	28.66	58.80
Arch No.	3	4	2	1	3	13	6	9	5	-	2	22	35
Percentage	0.40	0.53	0.26	0.13	0.40	1.73	0.80	1.20	0.66	-	0.26	2.93	4.66

their percentages are 5.46 and 3.46 in the right and left hand digits respectively. The radial loops and arches are more in the left hand than the right hand in digit II with percentages of 1.33 and 1.20 in the left hand and 0.40 in the left and right hands respectively. The percentage of ulnar loops in digit III of the right hand is higher than the left hand. Their percentages are 7.33 and 6.66 in the right and left hands respectively. There is no radial loop in the digit III of both right and left hands. In the digit III of the left hand there is more number of arches than could be finale in the right hand. Their percentages are 0.66 and 0.26 in the left and right hands respectively. In the digit IV of the right hand there is more number of whorls than the left hand as confirmed by the percentages are 6.00 and 5.86 in the right and left hands respectively. In the digit IV of both left and right hands there is equal number of fingers having ulnar loops (3.86%). In the digit IV of the right hand radial loop is absent. But radial loop in the left hand occurs (0.26%).

In the digit V of the right hand there is more number of whorls than could be found in the left hand. There percentages in the right and left hands are 2.93 and 2.26 respectively. The percentage of ulnar loop in digit V is more in the left hand than in the right. Their percentages are 7.33 in the left and 6.53 in the right hand. In the digit V of both right and left hands there are equal number of fingers having radial loops. But is more in the right hand than the left hand. Their percentages are 0.40 and 0.26 in the right and left hands respectively.

Table 6.2 (b) shows that the highest concentration of whorl is found only in digit IV of both left and right hands. The percentages in the right and left hands are 6.00 and 5.86 respectively. The highest concentration of whorl is found only in digit IV of both left and right hand. The percentages in the right and left hands are 6.00 and 5.86 respectively. The highest concentration of ulnar loop is found in digit III and V of right and left hands, their percentage being the same (7.33%) in both cases.

The highest concentration of arch is found only in digit II of both right and left hands. Their percentages in the right and left hands are 0.33 and 1.2 respectively. The radial loop is concentrated more in digit II of both right and left hands.

From Table 6.3 it is revealed that the highest percentage of whorls occurs in males and females in digit IV of both right and left hands. In both the sexes right hand whorl occurs in the highest percentage.

Table 6.3(a) Distribution of Main Line Formulae of Tai-Phakes Male

	Right		*Left*		*Combined*	
Formulae	*No.*	*%*	*No.*	*%*	*No.*	*%*
11 7 7 5'	3	4.00	1	1.33	4	2.66
11 7 7 4	1	1.33	3	4.00	4	2.66
11 7 7 3	1	1.33	2	2.66	3	2.00
11 7 9 5'	1	1.33	-	-	1	0.66
11 9 7 5'	7	9.33	2	2.66	9	6.00
11 9 7 5"	2	2.66	-	-	2	1.33
11 9 7 4	1	1.33	3	4.00	4	2.66
11 9 5" 5'	1	1.33	-	-	1	0.66
11 9 8 4	1	1.33	-	-	1	0.66
11 11 9 4	1	1.33	-	-	1	0.66
9 9 5" 5'	1	1.33	1	1.33	2	1.33
9 9 5" 4	1	1.33	-	-	1	0.66
9 9 5" 3	1	1.33	1	1.33	2	1.33
9 7 5" 5'	8	10.66	1	1.33	9	6.00
9 7 5" 4	14	18.66	11	14.66	23	16.66
9 7 5' 4	6	8.00	2	2.66	8	5.33
9 7 5" 3	4	5.33	10	13.33	14	9.33
9 7 5' 3	2	2.66	2	2.66	4	2.66
9 7 5" 2	-	-	1	1.33	1	0.66
9 7 5" 1	-	-	1	1.33	1	0.66
9 7 5' 1	-	-	1	1.33	1	0.66
9 7 4 3	-	-	1	1.33	1	0.66
7 9 5" 5'	1	1.33	-	-	1	0.66
7 9 5" 4	1	1.33	-	-	1	0.66
7 9 5" 3	-	-	1	1.33	1	0.66
7 7 5" 4	1	1.33	-	-	1	0.66
7 7 5" 3	1	1.33	1	1.33	2	1.33
7 5" 5" 5'	1	1.33	1	1.33	2	1.33
7 5" 5" 4	3	4.00	8	10.66	11	7.33
7 5" 5" 3	2	2.66	3	4.00	5	3.33
7 5" 5' 4	4	5.33	1	1.33	5	3.33

Contd. . . .

Table 6.3(a) - (Concld.)

Formulae	Right		Left		Combined	
	No.	%	No.	%	No.	%
7 5" 5' 3	4	5.33	7	9.33	11	7.33
7 5" 5' 2	-	-	1	1.33	1	0.66
7 5" 5' 1	-	-	2	2.66	2	1.33
7 5" 5' 11	1	1.33	-	-	1	0.66
7 5" 4 4	-	-	1	1.33	1	0.66
7 5" 4 3	1	1.33	-	-	1	0.66
7 5" 4 2	-	-	2	2.66	2	1.33
7 5" 4 1	-	-	1	1.33	1	0.66
7 5' 5' 3	-	-	2	2.66	2	1.33
7 5' 4 3	-	-	1	1.33	1	0.66
7 5' 4 1	-	-	2	2.66	2	1.33
7 5' 11 1	-	-	1	1.33	1	0.66

The lowest percentage of whorls occurs in both males and females in digit III and IV (2.13 in the male left hand). In females the lowest percentage occurs in the right and left hands in the digit III (2.40 and 2.66); and in the digit V (2.93 and 2.26 in the right and left hand respectively).

The highest concentrations of loop occurs in male right hand in digit III with the percentage of 7.73 and in the left hand in digit V with the percentage of 7.46. The lowest percentage occurs in digit IV of both hands (4.13 and 4.93 for the right and left hands respectively).

Loops occur more in female right hand in the digit III and in the left hand digit V, the percentages being 7.33 and 7.46 in the right and left hands respectively.

The highest percentage of arch occurs in males and females in the digit II of both right and left hands showing a percentage of 0.80 and 1.33 in male right and left hands and 0.53 and 1.20 in female right and left hands respectively.

The palm print of the Tai-Phakes (male) have been analysed in order to find out the frequencies of the various main line formulae as seen in Table 6.3(a).

Altogether 38 combinations are observed among the males. In the male right hand 29 combinations are observed as against 27 combinations in the left hand.

The table shows that when similar main line formulae of both left and right palms of male individuals are combined it figured more in number among all other formulae found in Tai-Phakes male individuals. Its occurrence in terms of percentage is 16.66. Next to the above main line formula, the formula 9 7 5" 3 is found to be more in number than the other formulae. Its occurrence in palms of Tai-Phake male people is 9.22 percent.

The palm prints of the Tai-Phakes (female) have been analysed in order to find out the frequencies of the various main line formulae as seen in Table 6.3(b).

Among the females, altogether 44 combinations are observed. The right hands of the females show 23 combinations as against 33 combinations in the left hand.

Table 6.3(b) Distribution of Main Line Formulae of Tai-Phakes Female

	Right		*Left*		*Combined*	
Formulae	*No.*	*%*	*No.*	*%*	*No.*	*%*
11 9 8 4	2	2.66	-	-	2	1.33
11 9 7 5"	2	2.66	-	-	2	1.33
11 9 7 5'	8	10.66	6	8.00	14	9.33
11 9 7 4	4	5.33	2	2.66	6	4.00
11 9 7 2	1	1.33	-	-	1	0.66
11 9 5" 5'	1	1.33	-	-	1	0.66
11 9 5" 4	1	1.33	-	-	1	0.66
11 7 7 5'	-	-	1	1.33	1	0.66
11 × 7 4	-	-	1	1.33	1	0.66
11 7 7 3	1	1.33	1	1.33	2	1.33
9 9 5" 4	-	-	1	1.33	1	0.66
9 9 5" 3	1	1.33	-	-	1	0.66
9 7 5" 5'	5	6.66	1	1.33	6	4.00
9 7 5" 4	16	21.33	2	2.66	18	12.00
9 7 5' 4	4	5.33	3	4.00	7	4.66

Contd. . . .

Table 6.3(b) - (Concld.)

Formulae	Right No.	Right %	Left No.	Left %	Combined No.	Combined %
9 7 5" 3	9	12.00	8	10.66	17	11.33
9 7 5' 3	1	1.33	-	-	1	0.66
9 7 5" 1	-	-	4	5.33	4	2.66
9 7 4 1	-	-	1	1.33	1	0.66
9 · 5" 4	-	-	1	1.33	1	0.66
7 9 7 4	-	-	2	2.66	2	1.33
7 9 5" 5'	-	-	1	1.33	1	0.66
7 9 5" 4	-	-	1	1.33	1	0.66
7 9 5' 4	1	1.33	-	-	1	0.66
7 9 4 3	-	-	1	1.33	1	0.66
7 7 5" 3	-	-	2	2.66	2	1.33
7 7 5' 1	-	-	1	1.33	1	0.66
7 5" 5" 5'	2	2.66	3	4.00	5	-
7 5" 5" 4	3	4.00	3	4.00	6	4.00
7 5" 5' 4	1	1.33	3	4.00	4	2.66
7 5" 5" 3	4	5.33	9	12.00	13	8.66
7 5" 5' 3	1	1.33	10	13.33	11	7.33
7 5" 5' 1	-	-	1	1.33	1	0.66
7 5' 4 3	-	-	1	1.33	1	0.66
7 5" 4 1	-	-	1	1.33	1	0.66
5" 9 5' 11	-	-	1	1.33	1	0.66

The above Table 6.3(b) shows that when similar main line formulae of both left and right palms of female individuals are combined together the formulae 9 7 5" 4 figures more in number than any other formulae found in Tai-Phake female individuals. Its occurrence in terms of percentage is 12.00. Next to the above main line formulae, the formulae 975"3 is found in greater number than other formulae. Its occurrence in the palms of Tai-Phake females is 11.33%.

Table 6.4. Wilder's Three Principal Main Line Formulae

Sex	*Symbol*	*3 PMLF*	*Right*		*Left*		*Combined*	
			No.	*P.C.*	*No.*	*P.C.*	*No.*	*P.C.*
Male	a	11.9.7	14	18.66	5	6.66	19	12.66
		11×7	-	-	-	-	-	-
		11.0.7	-	-	-	-	-	-
	b	9.7.5	34	45.33	29	38.66	63	42.00
		9×.5	-	-	-	-	-	-
		9.0.5	-	-	-	-	-	-
	c	7.5.5	10	13.33	29	38.66	39	26.00
Female	a	11.9.7	15	20.00	8	10.66	23	15.33
		11.×7	-	-	-	-	-	-
		10.0.7	-	-	-	-	-	-
	b	9.7.5	35	46.66	18	24.00	53	35.33
		9.×.5	-	-	-	-	-	-
		9.0.5	-	-	-	-	-	-
	c	7.5.5	16	21.33	27	36.00	43	28.66

Table 6.4 shows the percentile frequency of Wilder's three main line formulae of 75 males and 75 females. The highest percentage in the males has been noticed in 'b' (42.00%) followed by 'c' (26.00%) and 'a' (12.66%). Hence, the order of preponderance is b>c>a. Among the formulae also, 'b' occurs (35.33%) in the highest frequency which is followed by 'c' (28.66%) and 'a' (15.33%). The order of preponderance is b>c>a. The lowest percentage in the females has been noticed in 'a' (0.66%) and 'b' (0.66%). Anomg the males, the highest number of ending occurs in position 9 (46.00%), followed by position 7 (30.00%) and position 11 (23.33%). Among the females also, the ending occurs in position 7 in the highest number (40.66%) and it is followed by 9 (38.66%) and 11 (20.55%).

LINE - C

Among the males, line C terminates in positions 7.5" and 9 in 52.66%, 25.33% and 20.66% of the cases; the ending occurs in positions 5' and 11 in same number (0.66%). In females 7.5" 9 and 5' appears in 40.00%, 30.66% 24.00% and 4.00% of the cases. There is no ending occurring in position 11.

Table 6.5. Termination of Palmar Mainlines D, C, B and a in Percentage Line=D

	Male (N = 75)			*Female (N = 75)*		
Position	*Left*	*Right*	*L + R*	*Left*	*Right*	*L + R*
7	41.33	18.66	30.00	57.33	24.00	40.66
9	42.66	49.33	46.00	28.00	49.53	38.66
11	14.66	32.00	23.33	14.66	26.66	20.66
			LINE = C			
5'	1.33	-	0.66	8.00	-	4.00
5"	37.33	13.33	25.33	38.66	22.66	30.66
7	49.33	56.00	52.68	32.00	48.00	40.00
9	12.00	29.00	20.66	18.66	29.33	24.00
11	-	1.33	0.66	-	-	-

LINE - B

The line B ends most frequently in position 5" (56.00%). Equal number of endings occur in positions 5' and 7". The percentage is 20.00%. It is followed by 4 and 9 in 2.00% and 1.33% of the cases. But in females it ends in positions 5", 5", > and 4 at 50.00% 23.33%, 19.33% and 6.66% respectively. In females no ending occurs in position 9.

LINE = A

In males, line A ends most frequently in position 4 (38.00%) and it is followed by 3 (37.33%). 5" (19.33%) 1 (2.66%) and 5" (1.33%). In females the highest position is seen in 4 (39.33%), which is followed by 3 (29.33%), 5" (10.66%), 1 (6.00%) and 5" (1.33%).

In Table 6.6(a) t (68.66%) shows the highest percentage among the males. The next highest percentage is shown by tt" (16.66%) and it is followed by t' (11.33%) and t" (3.33%) respectively.

LINE = B

	Male (N = 75)			*Female (N = 75)*		
Position	*Left*	*Right*	*L + R*	*Left*	*Right*	*L + R*
4	4.00	-	2.00	12.00	1.33	6.66
5'	26.66	13.33	20.00	25.33	21.33	23.33
5"	54.66	57.33	56.00	46.66	53.33	50.00
7	14.66	25.33	20.00	17.33	21.33	19.33
9	-	2.66	1.33	-	-	-

LINE = A

	Male (N = 75)			*Female (N = 75)*		
Position	*Left*	*Right*	*L + R*	*Left*	*Right*	*L + R*
1	5.33	-	2.66	16.00	-	8.00
3	50.66	24.00	27.33	33.33	25.33	29.33
4	33.33	42.66	38.00	30.66	48.00	39.63
5'	8.00	30.66	19.33	16.00	21.33	18.66
5"	-	2.66	1.33	-	2.66	1.33

Table 6.5 shows that the mean value of mainline index is higher in males (6.95 ± 0.92) than in females (4.05 ± 0.22).

Table 6.5. Main Line Index

	Male Main Line Index		*Female Main Line Index*	
Hands	*Mean ± S.E.*	*S.D. ± S.E.*	*Main ± S.E.*	*S.D. ± S.E.*
Right	5.39 ± 0.30	3.50 ± 0.21	4.31 ± 0.24	2.04 ± 0.08
Left	5.11 ± 0.20	2.31 ± 0.14	3.94 ± 0.20	1.15 ± 0.14
Rt + Lt	6.95 ± 0.92	14.98 ± 0.68	4.05 ± 0.22	1.91 ± 0.16

Table 6.6(a): Frequencies of Types Combination of Axial Triradius in males (N=75)

	Right		*Left*		*Right + Left*	
Types	*No.*	*P.C.*	*No.*	*P.C.*	*No.*	*P.C.*
t	51	68.00	52	69.33	103	68.66
t'	8	10.66	9	12.00	17	11.33
t	3	4.00	2	2.66	5	3.33
tt''	13	17.33	12	16.00	25	16.66

Table 6.6(b) reveals that among the females the highest percentage is recorded by t (70.66%). The next highest percentage is shown by t' (19.33%) followed by tt'', (9.33%) and t (0.66%) respectively.

Table 6.6(b): Frequencies of Types Combination of Axial Triradius in Females (N=75)

	Right		*Left*		*Right + Left*	
Types	*No.*	*P.C.*	*No.*	*P.C.*	*No.*	*P.C.*
t	52	69.33	54	72.00	106	70.66
t'	17	22.66	12	16.00	29	19.33
t''	-	-	1	1.33	1	0.66
tt''	6	8.00	8	10.66	14	9.33

From Table 6.7(a) it is revealed that occurrence of pattern A^U in the hypothenar area of both left and right palms of male individuals is more than any other pattern that occurs in male Tai-Phake people. The total percentage of A^U is (45.33%). The next highest percentage is shown by L^U (24.66%) and it is followed by V (14,66%) W^u, (7.33%) (4.66%) and A^U/L^U (3.33%) respectively.

The predominant pattern in the hypothenar area in males is arch. However, loops are quite common in this area.

Table 6.7(a): Pattern Frequency in the Hypothenar area: Males (N=75)

Pattern	Right		Left		Combined (Right + Left)	
	No.	P.C.	No.	P.C.	No.	P.C.
A^U	32	42.66	36	48.00	68	45.33
V	7	9.33	4	5.33	11	7.33
L^U	16	21.33	21	28.00	37	24.66
L^R	13	17.33	9	12.00	22	14.66
W^U	4	5.33	3	4.00	2	4.66
A^U/L^U	5	1.00	2	2.66	5	3.33

Table 6.7(b) reveals that occurrence of pattern A^U in the hypothenar area of both right and left palms of female Phake people is more than any other pattern that occurs in female Tai-Phake people. The total percentage of A^U is 45.33. The next highest percentage is shown by L^U in females (22.00) and it is followed L^R, W^U, V and A^U/L^U, the percentages being 20/00, 6.66, 4.66 and 3.33 respectively.

Table 6.7(b): Pattern Frequency in the Hypothenar area: Females (N=75)

Pattern	Right		Left		Combined (Right + Left)	
	No.	P.C.	No.	P.C.	No.	P.C.
A^U	34	45.33	31	41.33	65	43.33
V	4	5.33	3	4.00	7	4.66
L^U	15	20.00	15	24.00	33	22.00
L^R	14	18.66	16	21.33	30	20.00
W^U	6	8.00	4	5.33	10	6.66
A^U/L^U	2	2.66	3	4.00	5	3.33

From the above Table 6.8 it is evident that in the thenar/1st interdigital area open field is predominant in both the sexes (male 63.66%, female 74.00%). In males it is followed by vestiges (11.33%) and whorls (0.66%).

Except open fields, a negligible frequency of pattern has been observed in both the sexes.

TABLE 6.8: Pattern Frequency in thenar/IST Interdigital area in Males and Females

Pattern	Male (N = 75)						Female (N = 75)					
	Right		Left		Combined (Rt + Lt)		Right		Left		Combined (Rt + Lt)	
	No.	P.C.	No.	P.C.	No.	P.C.	No.	P.C.	No.	P.C.	No.	P.C.
O	51	68.00	52	69.33	103	68.66	58	77.33	53	70.66	111	74.00
V	14	18.66	10	13.33	24	16.00	10	13.33	7	9.33	17	11.33
L^R	9	12.00	12	16.00	21	14.00	7	9.33	14	18.66	21	14.00
W	1	1.33	1	1.33	2	1.33	-	-	1	1.33	1	0.66

TABLE 6.9: Pattern Frequency in II, III and Interdigital area in Males and Females

Pattern	Male (N = 75)						Female (N = 75)					
	Right		Left		Combined (Rt + Lt)		Right		Left		Combined (Rt + Lt)	
	No.	P.C.	No.	P.C.	No.	P.C.	No.	P.C.	No.	P.C.	No.	P.C.
OOO	-	-	1	1.33	1	0.66	-	-	1	1.33	1	0.66
OOL	11	54.66	49	65.33	90	60.00	44	58.66	46	61.33	90	60.00
OLL	6	8.00	7	9.33	13	8.66	9	12.90	13	17.33	22	14.66
LLO	1	1.33	-	-	1	0.66	4	5.33	1	1.33	5	3.33
OLO	26	34.66	18	24.00	44	29.33	18	24.00	14	18.66	32	21.33
LOL	1	1.33	-	-	1	0.66	-	-	-	-	-	-

As regards the pattern frequency in II, III and IV inter-digital area as revealed in Table 6.9, the combination OOL is observed to be the most frequent in both the sexes (male 60.00% and female 60.00%). In the males, this is followed by OLO (29.33%), OLL (8.66%). In the females the next highest pattern combinations are found to be OLO (21.33%), OLL (14.66%), LLO (3.33%) and OOO (0.66%). OOO, LLO and LOL have the same pattern frequencies (0.66%) among the males.

Inter-digital II

Open fields are the most dominant pattern type in II inter-digital area. Other patterns are rarely found in this area.

Inter-digital III

The other patterns are found in higher number than the open field in right hand of both the sexes.

Inter-digitate IV

In this area other patterns occur more frequently than open field in both hands of the two sexes.

It is seen from Table 6.10 that the range of 'atd' angle varies from 30°-56° in both the sexes. The females show a higher mean value 42.14 ± 81 than the males (40.10±75).

TABLE 6.10: New values of 'atd' angle in Males and Females

	Male (N = 75)			*Female (N = 75)*		
Hands	*Range*	*Mean ± S.E.*	*S.D.*	*Range*	*Mean ± S.E.*	*S.D.*
Right	30-56	39.96 ± 0.54	4.67	30-56	42.94 ± 0.58	4.99
Left	30-56	40.18 ± 0.52	4.49	30-56	42.24 ± 0.57	4.88
Combined (Rt + Lt)	30-56	40.10 ± 0.75	6.48	30-56	42.14 ± 0.81	6.99

In both right and left hands, the digit V has equal number of ulnar loops and arches, while whorl is more in the right hand than in the left hand. Their percentages are 2.26 and 2.13 in the right and left hands respectively. There is no radial loop in digit V of the right hand.

In the Table it is seen that the highest concentration of whorl is in digit IV of both right and left hands (5.60% and 3.06%). Similarly, the highest concentration of ulnar loop is in digit III (7.60%) of right hand and it is higher in digit V (7.33%) of the left hand, There is no radial loop in digit I, IV and V of the right hand and digit IV of the left hand. Concentration of radial loop is higher in digit II of both right and left hands (0.53% and 0.80%). Concentration of arch is the highest in the digit II of both left and right hands and their percentages are 0.80 and 1.33 respectively.

REFERENCES

Bhattacharya, P.N. 1955. *(Dermatoglyphics of the Abor people of Assam) The Anthropologist*, Vol. II, No., 2

Cummins, H. and Midlo, C. 1961. *Finger Prints, Palms & sales, An Introduction of Dermatoglyphics.* Dover Publications, New York.

Dankmijer, J. 1938. Some anthropological data on finger prints. *Am. J. Phy. Anthro* p. 23; pp. 377-388

Hold, S. B. 1955. *Genetics of dermal ridges, frequency distribution of total finger ridge count. Ann. Hum. Genet.* London 20, 323-339.

Sharma Thakur , G. C. 1982 *The Tai-Phakes of Assam.* B.R. Publishing Corporation; New Delhi.

7

A Framework for Studying Health Maintenance Behaviours among the Meiteis of Cachar District of Assam

ARUPENDRA MOZUMDAR, SUJATA KAR
AND SUBRATA K. ROY

All communities practise a set of health maintenance behaviours to keep themselves healthy and adopt with the changing environment. The beliefs, traditions and customs handed down through many generations usually play a major role in determining individual and community health care in most of the Indian societies. People strive for close integration within the family, clan, and/or community and live in harmony with their environment and develop their own culture as a reflection of their adaptive capacity to cope with situation. Health could be considered simultaneously at physical, mental and spiritual levels. Therefore, individual well-being is considered as a state symbolising harmony and perfect balance between mind, body, spirit and environment. However, from the standpoint of medical history, illness and health are viewed as "physical" issues, where little distinction is made between illness and disease. Consequently disease is attributed to malfunctioning atoms, molecules, cells and tissues; health is conceived as the outcome of their proper functioning. But it has now been realised that people experience illness more as a function of subjective perceptions, symobolic meanings, supernatural intervention, or value judgements that arise from one's cultural traditions (Aichtar and Izhar, 1986).Therefore, the maintenance of health and treatment of illness could be better controlled and managed by cultural tools and the inherent beliefs of the people or the community (Bloom, 1990).

There is a wider recognition in many quarters that health is a dynamic state, which includes both well-being as well as absence of illness. Accordingly, health may be defined as "a state of well-being and the capability to function in the face of changing circumstances". Health is, therefore, is a positive concept emphasising social and personal resources as well as physical capabilities. The diminution of health underscores the important contributions to health that have been made outside the formal medical care and public health systems. For both individuals and populations, health depends not only on medical care but also on other factors including individual behaviors and genetic make up as well as social and economic conditions of individuals and communities. In many communities, health may be conceived as a product of many factors, as many segments of the community contribute to and share the responsibility for its maintenance and improvement.

In the study of health and disease, the role of health maintenance is generally ignored or neglected. Illness, however, is the marked subject for concern today, particularly the way it could be related with health. Knowledge relating to health may be subject to stronger corrective and selective pressures than those which act on a people's knowledge of illness and its treatment. Knowledge to guide normal health practice must work upon its survival that can serve to maintain a reasonable health. Rules harmful for the healthy (say, food and drink) would be disastrous for a population in ways similar rules applied only to the ill might not be. Only a relatively small part of people's lives forms the illness component. Illness is an occasional event. The rules, which concern normal life and most people most of the time, must be successfully adapted to their needs. This is why, corrective and selective pressures may act on the knowledge for health more stridently than on that for illness (Lewis, 1979).

Health maintenance is defined in terms of social/cultural practice and behaviours of a particular social group in the sphere of basic health care. It includes several basic health services like food habit, hygienic practices, perception to disease and illness and supplemental health services consisting of medical man, quack doctor, homeopathic doctor, allopathic doctor and primary health centers attached the system of health care to a population in a geographic area (Banerjee, 1981). A wide range of factors beyond basic health care has significant impact on health. During the process of growing up, individuals learn the concepts of sickness and health along with religious faith from their families. Beside these, individuals also learn about the basic health care practices at the time of any crises. Some of the general health services have been implemented by the government in different pockets of the country and some services are also available from local medical practitioners. Calnan (1987) on the basis of his study suggested that government, general practitioners and individuals—all have a role to play in the maintenance of health.

India is a nation of vast contrasts-socially, geographically and culturally. It is home to many religions, Hinduism being the most common form of religion. There are a multitude of ethnic groups and social classes. It has over a dozen recognized languages and hundreds of local dialects. In spite of the progress made by India in the field of science and technology, around half of its population live without access to clean drinking water, adequate food, sanitation, employment or education. It has an extraordinarily complex political and social structure, in which the traditional caste hierarchy competes with egalitarian democratic traditions. But these differences are hardly reflected in the field of health. There is, however, lack of systematic information about the concept of health and manifestation of disease. Side by side, it is also necessary to know about the perception of one's own health status and the felt need for achieving ideal health status in the community.

All communities have a system of health care of its own, which must be judged as adequate at least for the survival of the community in that specific socio-economic and ecological setting. Such a system may be difficult to comprehend by others. But it is necessary to assess the existing knowledge about what makes people healthy and what practical approaches have proven successful in different areas and among different communities in India.

In view of the above realisation, the objectives of the present article are set with a view to look into the health maintenance behaviours among the Meiteis of Cachar district, Assam. More specifically, it focuses on the following:

1. To study health behaviours (including maintenance and

treatment of illness) of the Meities;

2. To note it there is any difference between urban Meities and their rural counterpart in this regard;
3. To develop a suitable framework for studying health maintenance behaviours.

POPULATION AND AREA

The present data have been collected as a part of a larger bio-medical program in the North-Eastern region. The data have been collected from the migrant Meiteis of Cachar district Assam. Generally the term 'Meitei' is used for the Manipuris, the original inhabitants of Manipur. From that point of view, Meiteis are synonymous with the Manipuris. They are recognized as non-tribal inhabitants, Though their major concentration is in Manipur, they are now distributed in different parts of Assam and Tripura. It is believed that they have an Indo-Chinese origin with an admixture with the Aryan invaders (Johnstone, 1971). Some of the linguists mentioned them as an offshoot of Tibeto Burman family (Grierson, 1967). There are two groups of Manipuris, *viz.* Meitei and Vishnupriya. Both the groups consider themselves as Hindu and Krishna is a popular form of god among them. They are Vaishnavites and followers of Sri Chaitanyadev, who was a of a religious movement in Bengal to uplift the low caste Hindus and bring them within the fold of Hinduism during the 15th century. Their religious performances and ways of life bear testimony to that.

Prior rapport was established with the Meiteis inhabiting the two settlements, *viz.* Boaljor and Nowaraj. These two settlements are situated approximately two kilometers away from Silchar town, the capital of Cachar district, Assam and referred here as urban group, while the rural Meiteis have been selected from Bontarapur area of Kuchudorong police station, about 40 kilometers away from Silchar town. The present Meitei groups (both urban and rural) are supposed to have been migrated from Manipur to their present habitat some 100 years back.

METHODS OF STUDY AND THE TYPE OF DATA COLLECTED

There is no standard objective measure as to know individual behaviors in the maintenance of health, although it is true that the physical functioning of health, pain or discomfort or even perception of health can be measured objectively to some extent, but emotional well-being cannot be measured objectively. No standard measure has been developed so far to objectively treat the health maintenance behaviours as behaviours are completely subjective impressions and/or perfections. Therefore, a pre-tested questionnaire focussing on different aspects of health maintenance behaviors has been utilized for the present data collection. The questionnaires have been prepared in two sections—a greater part containing common questions applicable to either sex and others for females only. In the present article, data on common health problems have been utilized. Data on morbidity were also collected through a pre-tested questionnaire and the subjects were asked to recall his/her own health problems (ailment/symptoms) during previous 3-month. Therefore, the morbidity data may have some unavoidable limitations due to recall lapse. All the data have been collected from only adult individuals of both sexes. The analysis has been done on a total number of 260 individuals (147 from urban and 113 from rural)) of both sexes. However, the chances of reporting, under-reporting or over-reporting in the present data can not be ruled out. The endeavour was to cover all the households of the respective settlement, and for the present data, individuals who could be persuaded to participate in the present study and who were present in their respective houses at the time of survey were included in the sample without any bias. There is probably little justification to present data separately for each of the sexes because neither of the traits used in the analysis seems to have sex effects.

Results

Perception of the present health status by the adult Meiteis have been presented in Table 7.1. When questioned about their health status, most of the urban individuals answered either 'Fair' (44.9%) or 'Good' (31.29%). Only, a small number of individuals perceived their health as 'Bad'. The picture is not very different in case of rural Meities, who also perceived it as 'Fair' (38.05%) or 'Good' (34.51%) like their urban counterparts. There is very little or no difference at all between urban and rural Meiteis in this respect. Out of many hygienic practices, only two types of data have been presented in conforming with the overall theme of the article. Source of drinking water and the type of toilet used by the Meiteis have been presented in Table 7.2.

A large number of urban Meiteis use pond water (63%) for drinking. Although urban groups enjoy the facilities of tap water and tube well, the users are relatively poor in number, Tap water users account for 26.53% of the total and tube well water users number still less (10.20%). In the rural area, people mostly use river water (46.9), pond water

(24.78%), and water from well (28.32%) for drinking. In the rural areas, people do not have a tube well in and around the village and tap water is completely absent. However, the use of pond water in both urban and rural areas shows a similar trend, which brings home the point that even in an urban situation people's habits have not changed much.

Table: 7.1. Perceived health status

	Urban		*Rural*	
	N	*%*	*N*	*%*
Very good	3	2.04	1	0.88
Good	46	31.29	39	34.51
Fair	66	44.90	43	38.05
Bad	28	19.05	28	24.78
Very bad	4	2.72	2	1.77

Table: 7.2. Hygienic practices

Sources of *drinking water*	*Urban*		*Rural*	
	N	*%*	*N*	*%*
Tap water	39	26.53	0	0.00
Tube well	15	10.20	0	0.00
Pond	93	63.27	28	24.78
River	0	0.00	53	46.90
Well	0	0.00	32	28.32
Types of toilet				
No. Bathroom	1	0.68	12	10.62
Katcha toilet (including use of open space)	140	95.24	101	89.38
Sanitary latrine	6	4.08	0	0.00

Most of the urban individuals use 'katcha' toilet (95.24), which does not have any treatment facility (enclosed open space). Only small number of individuals use 'sanitary' type toilet (4.08%). On the other hand, more than 10% rural people do not have the existence of any separate space for toilet and 89.38% of the rural Meiteis use 'katcha' toilet. None of the households was found to have a 'sanitary' toilet in the rural area. There is no difference in the toilet of both urban and rural Meiteis.

Table: 7.3. Occurrence of different ailments/symptoms

	Urban (N=147)		*Rural (N=113)*	
	Frequency	*%*	*Frequency*	*%*
	39	38.78	30	26.55
Abdominal pain	15	10.20	8	7.08
Headache	6	4.08	10	8.85
Caugh	24	16.33	21	18.58
Fevwe	19	12.93	22	19.47
Lack of appetite	7	4.76	5	4.42
Vomitting	3	2.04	3	2.65
Body pain	1	0.68	5	4.42
Fainting	0	0.00	1	0.88
Weakness of the body	4	2.72	12	10.62
Diarrhoca	1	0.68	1	0.88
Shivering	1	0.68	1	0.88
Constipation	6	4.08	2	1.77
Head reeling	8	5.44	11	9.73
Eye problem	13	8.84	22	19.47
Throat problem	0	0.00	1	0.88
Others	6	4.08	14	12.39

Table 7.3 shows the frequency of ailment/symptoms suffered by the Meiteis during previous three months prior to the survey. A good number of urban Meiteis (38.8%) reported absence of any ailment during the period, while some of them had suffered from one or more than one ailment. It should be made clear that the frequency of ailments/symptoms as calculated in the Table are important indications than the percentages as the percentage has been calculated on the basis of total

number of individuals interviewed. However, a few of them had experienced some ailments or developed some symptoms, which were less frequent. These include common 'cough and cold' (16.33%), fever (12.93%) and abdominal pain (10.20%). Other ailments/symptoms reported to be rare include headache (4.08%), lack of appetite (4.76%), vomiting (2.04%), weakness (2.72%), constipation (4.08%), and head reeling (5.44%). However, these were very few diagnosed cases of disease. In the rural area also, more people reported absence of ailments (26.55%) during the period. However, a few of them did experience some ailments or develop symptoms, which fall in the less frequent category. Fever (19.47%), eye problems (19.47%) and common cough and cold (18.58%) belong to this category. Other ailments/symptoms reprted to be rare include headache (8.85%), lack of appetite (4.42%), vomiting (2.65%), body pain (4.42%) and head reeling (9.73%). Apparently, in this respect there is not much difference between urban Meiteis and their rural counterpart, except for the fact that more number of rural people have problems relating to their eyes and such debilitating or deficiency symptoms as bodily weakness occur in a greater frequency among them. One gathers the impression that the general health of the rural Meiteis is relatively poor when compared to the urban section of the population.

Table 7.4 shows the choice of treatment of the Meiteis and possible reasons for such a choice. The analysis has been done on those individuals who had experienced illness and had undergone treatment during three months prior to the survey. Beside these, some of the individuals had undergone treatment from one or more than one medical personnel and those individuals have been included more than once in the Table. Generally, a good number of urban Meiteis opted for allopathic (47.78%) treatment, followed by pharmacist's suggestions (22.22%) and treatment of local medication (13.33%) including home remedies. On the other hand, a large segment of the Meiteis of the rural area opted for allopathic (57.83%) treatment, followed by pharmacist's suggestions (19.28%) and self-medication including home remedies (21.69%). Few people also followed the treatment of local traditional healers (13.25%). There are, however, some differences between urban and rural Meiteis, which are as follows: (1) a number of urban Meiteis have opted for homeopathic medicine but rural group have very little concern for that; (2) more urban people have visited local traditional healers than the rural people.

Table: 7.4. Choice of treatment and the reasons for the choice

Choice of treatment	*Urban (N=90)*		*Rural (N=83)*	
	Frequency	*%*	*Frequency*	*%*
Self-medication	12	13.33	13	21.69
Local traditional healers	18	20.00	11	13.25
Pharmacist	20	22.22	16	19.28
Quack	1	1.11	0	0.00
Allopath	43	47.48	48	57.83
Homeopath	14	15.56	1	1.20

Choice of Medical practitioner	*Urban*		*Rural*	
	N=78	*%*	*N=65*	*%*
Personal relation	33	42.31	27	41.54
Referred by relatives	9	11.54	3	4.62
On duty doctor	3	3.85	3	4.62
Only available doctor	1	1.28	5	7.69
Nearest	13	16.67	12	18.46
Faith upon the doctor	16	20.51	14	21.54
Less expensive	1	1.28	0	0.00
Specialist	2	2.56	1	1.54

Regarding the choice of medical practitioner (Table 7.4), both urban and rural Meiteis gave almost similar reasons. Choice of medical practitioners was primarily guided by personal relationship of the patient's family with the medical practitioner and secondarily, by the reputation of the medical practitioner in treating patients, and physical distance between the patient and the medical practitioner. Known medical practitioners, with good reputation and living nearby, seem to be the ideal criteria for choice.

Table: 7.5. Level of satisfaction and the reasons for dissatisfaction with treatment

Choice of treatment	*Urban*		*Rural*	
	N=78	*%*	*N=65*	*%*
Satisfied	63	80.77	49	75.38
No relief	11	14.10	10	15.38
Expensive medicine	0	0.00	1	1.54
Time consuming	4	5.13	3	4.62
Temporary relief	0	0.00	1	1.54
Others	0	0.00	1	1.54

The level of satisfaction of treatment has been presented in Table 7.5. Individuals, who had undergone treatment during three months prior to the survey, have been included in the analyses. A good number of individuals were fully satisfied (80.77% in urban area and 75.38% in rural area) with the treatment followed by the medical practitioner they had chosen during their illness. The reason for dissatisfaction with the treatment was mainly because of lack of relief in spite of the continued treatment, both in urban (14.1%) and in rural (15.38%) areas.

DISCUSSION

The present article aims at looking into the health maintenance behaviours of the Meitei community of Cachar district, Assam. Two groups (urban and rural) have been studied and the findings have been compared between urban and rural groups in order to pinpoint the differences in health maintenance.

The Meiteis usually prefer to answer as 'fair' or 'good' health, when asked about the current health condition and this is true irrespective of urban or rural living. It has also been observed that in many instances when the people were suffering from high blood pressure, skin diseases, deformities, long standing gastro-intestinal disorder, they still answered in terms of good or fair health. This may be due to their mode of talking with other persons outside the close circle. It may also be possible that this was a ploy employed by them. If their answer was 'bad', they would have faced with some follow-up questions, which could easily be avoided by expressing 'good' or 'fair' health. However, the Meiteis by and large ignore small ailments and long standing chronic diseases, which has been reflected in their overall health perception as indicated from their replies. This result corroborates the study of Roy (1991).

Hygienic practice is considered as one of the health maintenance behaviours of the community, which develops through traditions and sometimes as a mark of adaptation. There are many hygienic behaviours, but here two important behaviours sources of drinking water and types of toilet have been presented as these seem to play the major role in causing most of the illness. Pond water is the principal source of drinking water in both urban and rural areas; this seems to be the traditional system of the Meiteis. Although the urban Meiteis could avail tap water supplied by the local town administration and also tube well facilities, they are still reluctant to use such sources for drinking purpose and they have many excuses to offer as to why they are not using water from those sources. In recent times only a fraction of urban Meiteis have started using tap water and tube well as a result of the growing awareness among them. In the rural areas, people use two other sources of drinking water—river and wells in place of water taps and tube wells. It has been observed that tap water and tube wells are absent in rural areas. Rural Meitei settlements are concentrated along the river banks and ponds are not so uncommon. People prefer to use river water, which they consider to be safe. They do not take the trouble of boiling the river water before drinking. Even with increasing resources, the age-old habit of the community with regard to drinking water has remained almost unchaged. Better awareness has led to change in the outlook in some quarters, but its overall effects are rather nominal. Regarding toilets in use, it has been observed that only a small number of urban households have sanitory toilets; they normally use an enclosed space for covering, denoted here as 'katcha' toilet (without sanitation and treatment system). Rural Meiteis do not have sanitory toilets, some of the households have katcha toilets and most of the households do not have any specified area demarcated for toilet purpose. They generally use open and free spaces, which again are not earmarked for day-to-day use. Most of the Meitei households in both urban and rural areas have brick built houses and the households have the financial capacity to make sanitary toilets, but people are reluctant to spend on this, to which they attach very little importance. This may be due to lack of awareness of the people and their traditional habit of using free and open space for toilet purpose. In the urban area, due to lack of free and open space, households have been forced to prepare a specified area for toilet purpose and this seems to be an adaptive strategy developed to cope with the urban situation.

The Meiteis of both urban and rural areas show similar ailments/ symptoms, although it was expected that there would be a greater frequency of ailments/symptoms among the rural group. However, a large majority of urban individuals reported absence of ailments/ symptoms during the period of survey. Generally speaking, ailments/ symptoms do not show any significant difference between the urban and rural Meiteis. It appears that certain health problems are very common in nature and are prevelent in most of the communities but are not always reported. Rural Meiteis reported the problems of the eyes, which were comon among the females. The problems might have causal relation with the use of firewood in cooking, which is generally done by the females. The kitchen of the Meiteis is almost a closed room and it lacks proper ventilation, with the firewood generating a lot of smoke. This creates problems to the eyes. But urban Meiteis are now using cooking gas instead of firewood and as a result, problems related to eyes are relatively less among them.

A number of Meitei individuals suffered from different ailments symptoms during months prior to the survey, for the treatment of which some of them had visited medical persons. Generally, the choice of medical personnel depends on many factors, financial capacity being one of the major determinants (Frans et al, 1981). Apart from financial capacity, there are some other important social determinants like personal relation with the medical personnel, reputation of the medical practitioners in treating diseases or ailments their availability, which would contribute to the popularity of modern medical system. Much depends on the distance to be covered to call a doctor. However, both urban and rural Meiteis rely more on the allopathic treatment than traditional mode of treatment. Rural Meiteis have developed the habit of self-medication prompted more by the absence of suiatable medical personnel in the near vicinity or which may be the result of the spiralling cost of treatment including doctor's fees and transport. It is worth while to note that though the rural Meiteis have the facility for treatment in a Public Health Centre (PHC) located nearby, still the people are rather reluctant to go there as the doctors are not generally available because, most of the time they remain busy with private practice. Faith in local traditional healers seems to be more among urban Meiteis than those living in rural areas, which is rather intriguing. This may be due to the uncertainity and tensions of urban life. Although local traditional healers are not always helpful in curing illness, they prove to be helpful in releasing tensions as they show greater concern with the problems (physical, social or mental) faced by the individuals rather than the symptoms of the specific ailment.

Individual satisfaction with the treatment by medical personnel depends on many factor like the nature of disease, cost of medicine, frequency of visit to medical practioners, their behavior, time taken for recovery and so on. However, a large segment of the population, both urban and rural, who had consulted medical personnel for their illness, expressed their satisfaction in the treatment irrespective of the reputaion of the concerned doctors. A small segment of rural Meiteis, however, expressed their dissatisfaction over the treatment they had received. This may be because of their habit of self-medication including easy home-made remedies for any ailment, which sometimes complicate the illness or disease. Moreover, there is dearth of qualified physicians in the rural area.

Most of the Meiteis believe in their own indigeneous medical systems developed and followed by the community. Use of common medicinal plants or consultation with traditional healers and knowledgeable individuals within the community are the usual practice. The solutions suggested are affordable and their social cost is also not high. Common medicinal plants are readily available in the region. Of these, mention may be made of *Aloe vena, Asparagus,* plants of *Solanaceae, Libiaceae, Oxalidaceae, Apocynaceae families, Terminalia arjuna, Phyllanthus emblica (amloki), Adhatoda vesica (Vasak), Rawalfia serpentina (sanpagandha), Azadirachta indica (neem), Centella asiatica (thankuni), Ananos cosmosus* (pine apple). Some common herbs and creepers may also be included in the list. But knowledge of indigenious medical system has lost its value and usefulness within the community because of various reasons. The main reasons are: (1) disruption of traditional channels of oral communication between older and young members of this community because in most cases children and adults now spend much more time outside the community then they used to do a few generations back; (2) migration of people to urban areas for service and business making them more dependent on the western medicine; (3) loss of biodiversity in the area hampering the traditional ethnobotanical knowledge to a great extent; (4) traditional medicinal practice being considerably affected by the rapid spreed of western medical system. Rural Meiteis still know and are aware of the efficacy of some traditional medicines which they use as home-made remedies, but urban Meiteis have lost that traditional knowledge and on some occasions show their almost total dependence on the traditional healers.

The findings of the study do not support a major difference in the health maintenance behaviors between urban and rural Meiteis. Whatever differences are noticeable could be attributed to the availability of resources in the area. Therefore, changes in the life style (due to adaptation in urban life) do not necessary change the overall health maintenance behaviors of the community as these are very much influenced by the culture of the specific community.The findings are partly corroborative with the study of Kar and Gogoi (1996), who worked among the Noctes of Arunachal Pradesh and opined that the treatment behaviours of the community are very much culture-specific.

FRAMEWORK

The present study is a very small step towards a bigger question to be tackled. From the above, an impressionistic framework can be developed to study the problem in a very brief manner. Health and illness are regarded as the two opposite states of life and one is defined by the absence of the other. Whether a person is in a healthy state or suffering from ill health is reflected in the perception of the community. It can also be judged in the context of the specific event (healthy or ill) and the tradition including beliefs, attitudes and customs of the community. Many of the peoples beliefs are the products of their direct experience and some are based on external authority (influence of elders and knowledge gained from other sources). Attitudes are likes and dislikes; favorable or unfavorable reactions to objects, people, situations, or any other aspect of the life world, including abstract ideas and social behavior pattern. Beliefs and attitudes often oversimplify the reality and lead to bias in the perception of events. The health of the members of a community or population is often maintained through a pattern of behaviours, which are a part of a large system called health maintenance system. In order to study the health maintenance system of any community, primarily four types of data are necessary: (1) different kinds of hygienic practices which help keep people healthy; (2) data on the concept and perception of health and illness of the individuals of the community; (3) data on behaviours and attitudes on health intervention especially at times of illness, and (4) data on health promoting behaviours.

Most of the studies conducted in the field of community health so far display a considerable lack of systematic information in the Indian context and the present study is also no exception to that. The data needed in this communication are related to the four areas mentioned previously. The concept of health and hygienic practices form the most vital part of the total health maintenance system of the community. The traditional system is fonned around cultural values and beliefs. The individuals of the community indulge in hygienic practices either knowingly or unknowingly (the effect of such a practice is not always known to them). These may be attributed to socialisation of the members of the community and their level of perception. Illness and sickness categories are also developed similarly. When hygienic practices are systematically correlated with cultural values and attitudes toward life, these carry an added meaning.

The health interventions are nothing but the use of various health care facilities (both traditional and modern) available in the accessible vicinity of the community. Health interventions are guided by several considerations, as and when people recognize the illness as health deteriorating factor, the severity of the illness (is it really worth to be treated in consultation with medical personnel) and sanctions of the culture (whether such consultations are permissible and their usefulness known to all) and tradition (beliefs and attitudes) of the society toward such illness. Actions toward health intervention also depend on socioeconomic condition, literacy level and awareness of the individual towards the treatment systems available in the locality. Then there is the question of the choice of appropriate medical personnel (sometimes multiple choice), which centers round the medical care facilities available in the area. All of these together may be recognized as health restoring behaviours provided that the beliefs and attitudes are in favour of consultation with other medical personnel and, of course, the socioeconomic condition of the individual which permits such consultation. The components of health restoring behaviours as described above are all connected with each other and should not be looked in isolation

There is also other planned health behaviours, which do not necessarily require any consultation with any medical personnel. These planned health behaviours are also a part of health maintenance system, which include three types of behaviours *e.g.*, self-regulation, precaution/ adoption and health promotion. People always try to keep themselves fit in order to face the challenges of rapidlly changing situations or circumstances. It has been observed that certain types of objects (food and drink), situations (environment), activities do not suit each and everyone. When people become aware of the fact that such objects, situations and activities are harmful for their health, they try to avoid those just as a person suffering from diabetes avoids carbohydrate rich food. Moreover, people also try to take some precautions and try to adopt such habits as may be responsible for causing illness/disease. Persons living in the malaria prone area will make it a habit to use mosquito nets. Thirdly, health promotion indicates some activities, which generally help people to stay healthy and the effects of such activities have been proved scientifically. Some of the physical exercises (walking, running, jogging, etc.) having positive effects on the health of an individual is well known; on the other hand, some of the abuses (excessive consumption of alcohol, smoking and taking other narcotic drugs, etc.) are known to have harmful effects on health. It is also true that most of the tribal populations are more or less physically active and do not require any physical exercise as described above but may have several abusing behaviours. Data on such health maintenance behaviours at the community level are particularly lacking.

However, generating information on a large number of regional, linguistic, socioeconomic, ethnic groups according to the broad framework presented above will hopefully help in assessing the state of knowledge and narrow down the gap in the existing knowledge system. The data will help policy makers and those who are engaged in health-related researches in unravelling the complexities of social and cultural determinants of health and health care utilization and solving health-related problems faced by the communities. More specifically, these will help to make suitable health policies for the communities concerned. The framework has no allowance for any particular population group and may be used at broader levels applicable for all societies/communities. All these may sound to be just general instructions to act upon, but one feels that at the present juncture of time these are badly needed. This is a huge task and young researchers, who are trained and sufficiently motivated to collect information in this specialized area, should come forward and use the framework of this nature more as the preliminary guideline for conducting a systematic study of community health. The present framework may appear impressionistic, but it is definitely community-specific. From that point of view, it may be worth considering, particularly in a region where community living comes above anything else.

REFERENCES

Akhtar, R. and N. Izhar. 1986. *The Spatial Distribution of Health Resources within Countries and Communities*. Examples from India and Zambia. *Social Science and Medicine* 22 (11). 1115-1129.

Ba...rji, D. 1981. *The Place of Indigenous and Western Systems of Medicine in the Health Service of India. Social Science and Medicine*. 15A : 109-114.

Bloom, J.R. 1990. *The Relationship of Social Support and Health. Social Science and Medicine* 39 : 635-37.

Calnan, M. 1987. *Health and Illness : The Lay Perspective*. London Tavistock Publication Ltd.

Evans, J.R., K.L. Hall and J. Warford, 1981. *Health Care in the Developing World : Problem of scarcity and choice. The New England Journal of Medicine* : 305 (19) : 1117-1127.

Grierson 1967. *Linguistic Survey of India* (Vol. I, part. 1; Vol. III, part III). Matilal Banarasidas, Delhi.

Johnstone 1971. *Manipur and The Naga Hills*. Vivek Publishing House, Delhi

Kar, R. K. & J. Gogoi 1996. *Health Culture and Tribal life : A case study the Noctes of Arunachal Pradesh*. In F. A. Das & I. Barua (Eds.) *Communities of North East India*, New Delhi Mittal Publication.

Lewis, G. A. 1979 *Beliefs and behaviour in disease*. In : *Health and Disease in Tribal Societies*, Ciba Foundation Symposium 49 (new series). Excerpta Medica, Amsterdam.

Roy S. K. 1991. Health Status of Oraon tea Garden Labourers. *Indian Journal of Social Work*, LII (3) : 369-377.

PART THREE

TRIBE AND ETHNICITY, CULTURE AND IDENTITY, DEVELOPMENT AND PROBLEMS OF CHANGE

8

Tribes Among Tribes: Progression in Interaction*

R. K. BHATTACHRYA

The situation in the heartland of India, from the perspective of tribes, can be described as one in which the tribes are more often neighbored by non-tribes, while in the north-east, till the recent past, the situation can be described as one of tribes among tribes. What differences or distinctions are expected to be imparted in these two situations? But before going into a discussion on distinctions, it is important to clearly understand the characteristics of each situation and its variants. From this kind of understanding will emerge a clear picture of the distinctions and based on generated inferences, insight may be gained on the ways we need to develop for research and intervention. This seems to be urgently called for in the north-east. My purpose of talking about research and intervention in the same breath needs to be clarified as usually these two are quite comfortably planted as discrete categories or activities in our minds, especially as we may like to believe that research and intervention are to be carried out by distinct groups of individuals or institutions. We also like to believe that as scientists, it is our academic requirement and commitment to concentrate on issues that would let us maintain our objectivity as well as having an appeal to our intelletnal capacity. The executing institutions are expected to

* The third Professor B Pakem Annual Memorial Lecture given in May, 2002 reproduced with the permission of North East India Council for Social Science Research, Shillong, Meghalaya.

cull from research which they can put to use. The results are often unfortunate; academe does not get its hand dirty and implementers are often dismissive of research being somewhat esoteric and abstract, if not abstruse. Thus, it is important that this impasse be resolved and an ambience of meaningful dialogue between the genres be encouraged, or else research will take its own tangential pathway in the course of development or intervention as this aspect cannot wait on and on. This is the reason why I speak of research and intervention in the same breath.

CONCEPT OF TRIBE

At the very outset I shall try to put forth in clear terms the concept of tribe as it is understood from different perspectives. In my attempt I shall look at it from an anthropological perspective. Tribe is a social category conceptualized by non-tribes when the latter came in contact with the former as colonizers. It is a description of 'otherness' and of differences; India has been no exception to this. In independent India, we have not really tried to redefine this concept in any way different from this 'encounter definition' that we accepted in toto from the British. No challenge has been posed to this definition or no attempt has been made to redefine this social category. Instead, what has been done is that the meaning of tribe has been constitutionally restricted resulting in highlighting their weaknesses and disadvantages. Of course, the overall aim was affirmative action and positive discrimination so that their general condition could be alleviated in the interest of the nation state. It must be remembered that the exercise of scheduling began during last leg of the British rule in India, *i.e.*, in the 30's. The academicians have been consistent in raising the issue of the need to redefine this social category, of the need to break out of stereotype, but it has been a weak challenge in the face of the widespread acceptance of the constitutional rationale for scheduling certain groups of people requiring special attention.

Let me now discuss the academic definition of tribe largely generated through sociological and anthropological data. From the perspectives of these disciplines, tribes are conceived as being segmentary societies distinguished from the organic nature of caste and class (for details see Durkheim 1993). The term segmentary has special implications – segmentary societies are homogeneous in terms of division of labour except gender differences in tasks. Caste and class are organic in nature as each part within the organic system along with its distinctive function is dependent on the other parts for their existence. This is how an organic system is understood as far as societies are concerned. Because of the availability of specialized functions, life experiences across the societies are not homogeneous. It is this interdependency between the sections that lends the binding to the organic whole.

It contrast, there is a commonness of life experiences among members of segmentary societies. It is not that there is no specialization among tribes, but the specialization being role specific, there is not enough scope of formation of guilds through generations. Anthropologists usually perceive tribes as territorial groups adhering to oral traditions, *i.e.*, groups that do not have scripts or written texts.

As an anthropologist it has time and again occurred to me that in our study of tribes, we have necessarily taken a cross-cultural perspective. The perspective has been offered to us when we, who have been socialized in a particular or more specifically, in a non-tribal ambience, study tribes. We often use, without being conscious of our cultural idioms, in order to probe into those of the studied groups and thereby we lose out on objectivity to some extent. We also take for granted certain 'givens' and proceed on those premises. We are often inclined to perceive them as being backward or more ancient in their practices as compared to ourselves. When we consider our own societies, we tend to gloss over those groups that do not match our stride and pace and claim that lack of opportunities is the responsible factor rather than cultural configurations. It is against this backdrop and with this consciousness in the forefront of my thinking that I shall discuss the concept of tribes as I have had experience of them.

I shall try to portray the various tribes that I have knowledge about, also keeping in mind the tribes of the north-east whom I have known from the secondary sources and through occasional personal interaction with them as individuals either in the hills in the north-east or in the plains away from it. Most of the tribes appear relatively non-inhibitive, non-acquisitive and have little status anxiety. They also seem not to consider the earth merely as expendable resources but of themselves being a part of nature. These are the broad categories of differences that I shall highlight here. For people who are oriented in such a way that the entire process of living does not focus on individual life span of birth and death but as the continuation of generations and their traditions, individual lives are events in the continuation of their living. There is a sense of peace, of inner well-being and a quiet belongingness to their surroundings. One should not consider this as romanticism; one gets a feel of this while one looks at them or studies them dispassionately without having stereotyped age-old nations about them as are prevalent among the people of the so-called mainstream (also see Nehru and Pandit Pant as quoted by Elwin, pp. 55 & 57).

Let me discuss the socialization among the tribes that I have encountered. A fact has always struck me is that children in a tribal society are not subjected to anxiety arousing pressures. They are not physically punished nor verbally assaulted for their misbehaviour. This is not to imply that children are not controlled or disciplined, rather to say that they are chided in a manner ensuring that their honour and dignity are not damaged. From a very young age they are found to comply with the norms laid down, or in other words, they seem to be cognizant of the social codes of conduct and the range of socially approved or accepted behaviour. There are always exceptions and in those cases, parents do not unduly pursue the cause of discipline. Parents seem conscious of how far they could go in their dealings with children. This honourable disposition of self makes them distinct even while they are found to be living in comparatively poor state of economy, health, or unfavourable ecology or environment.

The non-inhibitive nature of tribes in contrast to the inhibitions that one observes among the non-tribes, comes to the fore during the times of the festivals manifested in abundance with which they participate and savour each aspect and the ease with which they break effortlessly into song and dance. The use of the term non-inhibitive is from a Freudian perspective and has to be understood from the point of view of repression of natural impulses. Certainly, the tribes that I have encountered do not display behaviour-channeling tendencies as part of socialization. There is instead freedom in pursuing one's own proclivities. This is in contrast to what we encounter and experience in our own growing up during which time the agents of socialization (be they persons or institutions) devote much of their attention to directing the young in pre-chosen grooves in keeping with the social expectations and forces in existence. Here, the need for the use of anthropological discipline has to be emphasized. If we care to look at the tribes in this way, may be we shall be able to understand much of their behaviours that appear to be in sharp contrast to ours and often seem inexplicable, especially in the light of their indifference to efforts at enhancement of their condition in terms that we perceive as advantages (constitutionally) available to them.

From the above description it may appear that I am presenting a picture of contentment. However, the psychological aspects innately present in human beings, namely anxiety and aggression, are also manifested in tribes. There are, of course, incidences of aggression and violence among tribes in their interactions that may not be as marked as in our cultures; a reason for which may be the various means available to them for restore channeling aggression in their culture as inferred from their range of accepted behaviours need to be reassessed. Hunting, slaughtering of animals, animal sacrifice for ritual purposes including the erstwhile practice of head hunting among some group of the Nagas could be considered as instances of cultural channeling of aggression. Infringement of proprietary rights can lead to aggression or display of violence. Aggression can also be observed in the day to day killing of animals for meat for consumption. Expression of aggression under the influence of liquor among tribes, other than the hunter gatherers who are not known to indulge in liquor, is socially accepted behaviors and is seen as a means of letting off steam. Like the Naga head hunting, violent form of aggression is observed among a few tribes in the form of witch hunting. However, an important prerequisite for taking any such extreme measure requires strong social agreement and approval regarding the identity of witches and the means for their persecution. Defense of territory among hunter-gatherers can take a violent form of expression of aggression; trespass is not tolerated, it is combated with violence. In the case of the north-eastern tribes, this was applicable though they were not hunter-gatherers. It cannot be said that at present they are completely free from the hangover of a tradition.

A characteristic feature of the majority of the tribes is that they practise subsistence level economy. Maintaining a subsistence level economy in itself precludes generation of surplus and there is no tendency to store any surplus for future use or of ploughing it back into production. Instead any generated surplus is consumed through festivities and rites. Even among the tribes that have achieved some degree cf statehood in terms of either constituting royalty or of being affluent in term of ownership of the means of production do not show the accumulating tendencies of non-tribal royalty or the landed gentry (*e.g.* the Singphos). This helps in maintaining homogeneity and hinders the crystallization of strong class distinctions. However, serfdom practised among some tribes brought about the concept of living on others' labour (cf. Kar, 1993, p. 226).

Nature is perceived by the tribes as being bountiful and a provider, though there may be periodic failure of yield. However, they could consider nature to be their best custodian as long as they display prudence in its use and avoid over-exploitation. These are the reasons why they seem not to endeavour in generating surplus. It may be interesting to point out the similarity or parallel sentiments of Chief Seattle, who decried the greed of the White settlers for land that he and his tribe considered sacred and akin to them, knit with the memories of their forefathers (Chief Seattle's Great Speech, *Seattle Sunday Star* October 29, 1887). Tribes in the north-east are no exception to this notion of man-nature relation and this seems to be a major difference in the mindset between tribes and non-tribes. Most developmental measures are not nature friendly, rather nature is being construed as an expendable resource. Thus, the modern approach to development would not probably appeal to those who look at nature as a provider to them and their successive future generations.

Status in tribal societies is ascribed rather than acquired. Status depends on kinship, age and gender. Roles of importance played in village bodies do impart prestige but only as those of office bearers. The positions of office bearers are hereditary. However, if required, individuals for these positions can be decided on the basis of election or selection. The persons occupying these positions of prestige are not motivated or do not show any greed for accruing extra benefits of the trappings of power. It is important to note that this holds true when such roles are played out in the context of their social malice. The tribesmen in an alien miliers are often unable to be judicious in their greed and ambition and this creates a situation wherein they are evaluated in negative terms by the dominant social groups. However, there can also occur positive outcomes in cross cultural adaptations and adjustments. Similarity in life experiences through cohering to a world of which limits are well marked and within the ambit of the aspirations and expectations of individual members homogeneity is reinforced and strengthened.

Most of the tribes including those in the north-east have oral tradition in which cultures are transmitted from one generation to another orally. Oral tradition is usually the tradition of people who have no script and there is a large difference between those who can at any time refer to their texts and those who have no texts whatsoever to confirm their claims of any kind of authority if individuals opt to assume any specialized role(s). There is no script through which tradition could be recorded, substantiated and verified across generation. Myths, legends and tales thus transmitted are shared in their essentials with regional variations in their embellishments. There is instant recognition of such tales and myths and all versions appear right and true. It is remarkable to note the large areas of consistency in their accounts of genesis, *i.e.*, stories of origin, transmitted from one generation to another and even spread across regions, when/if they are spread over a large area. Absence of scripts does not encourage the rise of special agents, who could exercise authority in matters of tradition, though there are individuals who are looked up to as possessors of special knowledge, be it in matters of rites or in matters of treatment of illness. These individuals develop their special skills based on their personal initiative, learning and practice of such skills. An important consequence of this can be found in the blurred lines between priests and deity, in the absence of any religious fundamentalism or fanaticism and in the maintenance of homogeneity in social order. This is another way in which it could be demonstrated that status is ascribed rather than acquired.

A classless and non-stratified society with an oral tradition has in its favour the very forces of homogeneity, while the absence of scripts and texts obviates the streak of fundamentalism. Religion among the tribes derives from stories of origin and its practice makes use of simple means and articles available in most houses. Religious practices sometimes appear to give the impression of being magical. However, it is a realm that does not interfere with their secular life—the two worlds are so enmeshed that they are complementary to each other. Religion as such is not the sole moral arbiter, for which, society is otherwise adequately equipped. In the north-east, tribes experienced Christianity in a major way and in consequence, many of their traditions underwent change but the mindset of the majority among them and the ways in which they perceived the world did not go through the full cycle of transformation as might have been targeted by the missionaries. Though in the long run, Christianity has not been able to bring about solidarity among tribes inhabiting various territories, it at least helped to equip them to encounter the changed situation after independence.

The concept of world view has often been used in understanding the perceptions of different tribes about the world. But this seems to be a concept that is more meaningful in the context of people who have a textual/scriptual or a background of a system of education where knowledge or training can indirectly or through logical inference be imparted. In other words, there is a possible scope for training and learning through theory. Education among tribes occurs more through learning from primary sources based on direct practice and experience. The significance of role models cannot be overlooked here. Role models are used in practical life rather than in texts; these are manifested in persons, individuals, or groups within communities. The world view of the tribes can be thought of as being 'the world as perceived' and not 'as viewed'. Perception involves individual interaction with the world, range of personal experiences as well as consciousness of its significance in the individual life, whereas viewing involves many angles of vision; understanding, contending are not necessarily restricted to ones' proclivities.

It is common to perceive the tribes as being shy of encountering the 'other', of avoiding fluid boundaries with the 'other' and often this is interpreted as due to their general backwardness. Illiteracy and 'ancient' style of life. Could it be an expression of disinterestedness in what we have to offer to them, a feeling that is some ways, alien to their culture and values ? We have never thought of it in this way, instead we have taken for granted the 'wisdom' of our perceptions. May be they too have become accustomed to our views of them and do not want to make efforts to make us change our pre-set opinions. The problem seems to have been compounded in the case of the north-east by the carrying over of our pre-set ideas 'called' from our experience of the tribes of the plains. That the situation is different in the north-east, or the problems of the tribes require different approaches very often escapes our attention and eludes the notice of planners.

TRIBES IN A TRIBAL ENVIRON

The central theme of my deliberation in short is that as long as tribes are in non-tribal milieu we can observe two kinds of conditions—one, living close to non-tribal populations and two, living relatively isolated. These two conditions differ in the extent of interaction that is mainly economic. In the preceding section I have highlighted the self-sufficiency and self-containment of tribes with their characteristic strengths and it is in the light of this I shall discuss the condition of tribes within a dominantly tribal milieu. It is found that the tribes have the capacity to keep themselves separate from other tribes and sustain themselves and it is because of this they do not experience the pressure of forming federation of communities in order to survive. They do not seem to respond to the need to impose or persuade others in their milieu to join forces with them in generating surplus of any kind or for reasons of interdependence. This is in contrast to the situation that is observed in conditions of tribes in a situation dominated by the non-tribes. In the other or the former situation, tribes, among tribes, have is very little scope for building up clientele through service. For instance, whereas the tribes (the Bhils, Santals and Mundas) in the plains provided the labour to their neighbouring cultivating castes or communities, smaller tribes like the Birhors, Kadars and Banjaras (to mention a few) fulfilled their needs of forest produce and certain rare commodities by their own effort. Admittedly, there was no such scope for the tribes of north-east to remain engaged in an organic division of labour and service. From this perspective, it becomes clear that sufficient force was required to federally knit the north-east comprising of many tribes, who traditionally do not share much interaction, rather there existed revelry or enmity between certain tribes. In view of this, a certain amount of outside force must have been applied in nation state formation. It is obvious that goals other than purely cultural ones had to be set up and the consequent needs created in order to make people follow the goals of forging links among the inhabiting tribes of the region. The first thing that was affected was the territorial right of tribes by weakening the sovereignty of tribes. Extraneous forces in the form of government machinery replaced in various ways the autonomy of the people to a great extent. The disturbance in territorial right and control over environment, ecology and resource management and utilization led to psychological repercussion manifested in problems of identity. It was not just encroachment but exploitation of various kinds along with the changed mindset or values regarding surplus, environment resource and even ways of life. What was intended to be measures for welfare and development was not appreciated or perceived in the same light. One of the reasons for this might have been the initial hesitation of the tribes to exploit their natural habitat only for material benefits. The contrast in the mindset of the non-tribes and tribes resulted (forced) in the formation of federations of tribes inhabiting different regions in the north-east. This was mainly done to combat the extraneous forces and to exercise some form of 'autonomy'.

TRANSFORMATION OF CULTURALLY DISCRETE TRIBES

The first positive step that was introduced in order to transform the culturally discrete tribes to form nation state society was the exercise of adult franchise. Two other factors that aided the transformation were Christianity and persistent measures of the government for planned rural transformation mainly through agriculture and other means of production. Christianity for the last one and half century (Barch, 1967 p. 380) has slowly made sections of various tribes conscious of a world beyond their segmentary system. Along with the proselytizing process they were exposed to modern education, concepts of health and hygiene (*ibid.* pp .380-81) and practical training and incentive for saving. All these culminated in a tendency towards surplus generation and attitudinal changes towards private wealth. This is not to be considered at par with a simple change towards materialism but involved many complex mechanisms by which the basic mindset or ways of perception had to be reorganized with entirely new elements. From the fifties onwards, the Indian rural society has been experiencing induced developmental changes in area in areas like agriculture, animal husbandry and cottage industries through the creation of Block Development Offices. These also contributed significantly to the process of great transformation (cf. Bhattacharya, 1993).

This great transformation of the tribes when it occurred in the plains or even what can be considered mainland India had resulted in the processes of either assimilation with the dominant communities, in this case the non-tribes, or in the formation of states. These processes were triggered by emulation of the ready at—hand models available in the immediate neighbourhood. The nature of assimilation was through a well-known process of tribal absorption. (Risley, 1915, pp. 75-76; Radhakrishnan 1965, p, 29; Bose 1949, p, 22 & 153, pp, 156 – 70). Such a situation does not arise in any way in the north-east hills though in the plains of Assam there is the example of the Ahoms, in the context of state formation in plains, there are a number of examples that can be cited in support of this (Sinha 1962, pp, 35 – 80). It is interesting to note that this process too was ineffective among the tribes of the hills of the north-east as the knowledge of this was not available in the immediate socio-cultural milieu. What happened in the north-east was an initial effort towards establishing or claiming sovereignty keeping themselves away from any pan-Indian political and administrative machinery (Bhagbati 1993. p 168). In the course of years after independence, this effort was transformed from independent sovereignty to sovereignty as part of the larger nation, a sovereignty achieved through various programmes of development of the government. State formation in the perspective of nation state with political identity or identities was a result of this. This is the significant distinction in the pattern of progression in interaction of the tribes in the hills of north-east.

CONCLUSION

Tribe can be constitutionally defined as well as anthropologically explained. For the academics it is the latter that is thought to be more reasonable and logical as well as being of more interest though it is not possible to ignore the constitutional definition. It does serve a purpose, if at least in identifying initially the groups that are designated as tribes. For the executing institutions it is quite possible to ignore altogether the social science definition and consider only the constitutional one as it helps in targeting the central focus of intervention. There is no denying the fact that the implementation agencies experience conflict of interests when faced with the academics, however justified may be their shifting points of perception. Thus is born gaps in communication that could account for the lack of collaboration and communication between the executors and the academics. I am highlighting this fact as I would like to reiterate that there is urgent need to close these gaps because the mistrust that has been engendered in the tribes of the north-east with the larger nation state is becoming increasingly divisive. The anthropological way of looking at tribes, I can say with some confidence, would not have engendered mistrust or the creation of vested interests. Development measures become more effective when the people who are being targeted are considered or looked at as possessing strength in sectors that may be different from those of ours.

In the north-east one finds it is not just individual tribes which are in isolation (as socio-cultural discrete categories) as they were in the past, but tribes as part of constellations of tribes with their interest sometimes in conflict with each other and sometimes confederating among themselves against others for appropriating a bigger slice of the development pie. There is sufficient anxiety and concern for the situation in the north-east. What we fail to appreciate is the fact that the people of the region are trying to adjust to the situation of nation state and its dynamics. There is lack of understanding about the people and their mindset though there is no dearth of academic and other publications. What some lack is focussed research or being able to provide insight into the subtleties of situations through deep probing into the minds of people.

REFERENCES

Bareh, Hamlet 1967. *The History and Culture of the Khasi People* Calcutta, Manimala,

Bhagbati, Annada C, 1993, "*Social Formation in North-East India*" in S.B. Roy and Asok K. Ghosh (ed.) *People of India: Bio-Cultural Dimensions*, New Delhi, Inter-India Publications.

Bhattacharya R.K. 1993, "*Emerging Patterns of Indian Peasantry*" in S. B. Roy and Asok K. Ghosh (ed.) *People of India : Bio-Cultural Dimensions*. New Delhi, Inter-India Publications.

Bose, Nirmal Kumar 1949. *Hindu Samajer Gadan*, Calcutta, Visva-Bharati, 1953. *Cultural Anthropology and other Essays*, Calucutta, Indian Associated Publishing Company Limited.

Durkheim, Emile 1933. *The Division of Labor in Society*. New York, The Free Press.

Elwin, Verrier, 1960. *A Philosophy for NEFA* Shillong. Government of India.

Kar, R. R. 1993. "*A Small Tribe in the Eastern Himalayas*" in S. B. Roy and Asok K. Ghosh (ed.) *People of India : Bio-Cultural Dimensions*, New Delhi, Inter-India Publications.

Radhakrishnan, Sarvapalli 1965. *Hindu View of Life*, London, Unwin Books.

Risley, H. H. 1891. *The Tribes and Castes of Bengal* Calcutta, Bengal Secretariat Press – 1915. *The People of India*. Calcutta and Simla, Thacker, Spink and Company.

9

Communities of Modern Times: A Note on the Political Anthropology of Modern Assam

SAMIR KUMAR DAS

This paper seeks to reexamine the complex interconnection between ethnicity and modernity and makes a plea for using 'community' as one of the most important categories or analyzing the society in Assam. The task is necessary primarily because there are many amongst us who feel that contrary to what we are making a plea for here, "modern India has now lost most of the ideological and practical means of revolutionary community that might have been available"[1]. Recently, Professor Hiren Gohain in one of his addresses reaffirmed this position and underlined the necessity of building a 'common platform' cutting across the community lines as a means of resolving the ethnic conflicts in the northeast. Such a 'common platform' he argues, can be built around the 'common features' (rather than the differences) shared by the apparently conflicting communities and nationalities of the region. The visible and blatant strife between ethnic communities according to him often distracts our attention from these historically observed 'common features' shared by the conflicting ethnic communities.[2] Our plea for re-invoking community as a worthwhile analytical category therefore can be made only in polemics with such a position. The present paper hence is written in a somewhat polemical vein. Besides, my occasional references to it in a few of my early writings have already created some confusion.[3] In this paper I have taken the opportunity of clarifying the concept in order to dispel, if not wholly– at least in part, the confusion that has centred on my references to it.

Before I make any headway, it is necessary to start with a working definition of what we mean by the term 'community'. Community in this paper is taken to mean a body of people related to each other on the basis of certain enduring bonds that transcend their specific and temporary interests. The presence of such bonds implies first of all, that one adheres to one's community and continues to do so even when such adherence turns out to be detrimental to one's survival interests and instincts. In 1699 A. D. and on the occasion of a *Sharbat Khalsa* (religious congregation) held on the auspicious Vaisakhi day, five loved disciples (*panj piyaras*) expressed the readiness to sacrifice their lives at the call of their Guru Govind Singhji to the cause of the *Khalsa Panth*. Martyrdom for the community is by no means rare in Sikh history and usually celebrated as a noble virtue. Moreover, the presence of such bonds in this sense is very exhaustive. Since a community does not exist in order to fulfill this or that interest of its individual members, one's whole life can be lived within it: 'all of one's social relationships can be found in it' and one cannot withdraw from it at one's will. Its emergence presupposes as Sudhir Kaskar tells us, 'an assault on the sense of individuality'[4]. The point needs some clarification. While the articulation of community rules out the individual's right to dissent from it, the modern communities invest the individual members with the relative freedom of deliberating over 'the common good' of the community. The communities of modern times do not scuttle and prevent deliberations and debates on what constitutes 'common good' of the community. For, after all, the individual members participating in them share some degree of concern for their community; a community's articulation is premised on the members' common concern for their community. But, it implies, as Seyla Benhabib puts it, an individual's right to 'situate the self within the community[5]. The community seldom gives her the right to oppose it or even walk out of it. Both opposition and exit are anathema to the articulation of a community.

At the outset, it is necessary to mention that unl .ss otherwise stated all the arguments and conclusions of this paper have to do with the contemporary society and politics of Assam. We would do well to keep in mind that what holds true in the case of Assam may not mechanically apply to other parts of the northeast, let alone India. Northeast as a region is too internally heterogeneous to fit into any of the available schemata of Social Sciences. In this connection, it may be instructive for us to make a distinction between the *society in Assam and the Assamese society*. Society in Assam refers to veritable mosaic of people composed of both the Hindus and the non-Hindus (like, the tribals and the Muslims), not necessarily speaking the Assamese as their mother tongue (like, the Bengalis and the Bodos). Assamese society, on the other hand, is composed predominantly of the Assamese-speaking Varna-Hindu population—often referred to, as the 'mainstream' in Assam. Viewed in this light, society in Assam includes the Assamese society but is larger in its scope, though there are borderline cases that give rise to some amount of indeterminacy and confusion, their distinctions are much too serious to be overlooked. The distinction, if overlooked, has the dangerous consequence of steam rolling and chauvinistically bundling the veritable mosaic into the one and uniform Varna-Hindu Assamese mainstream of the Brahmaputra Valley.

CULTURAL RELATIVISM AND THE CRISIS OF MODERNITY

While 'rethinking' Modern Political Theory back in 1985, John Dunn observes that its 'epistemic status' is presently in 'doubt'.[6] There is nothing new in this argument for we know that the 'epistemic status' of Modern Political Theory has been in 'doubt' for a fairly long time particularly since the turn of the twentieth century when cultural relativism began to hold its sway on the anthropological scenario. It was in the wake of the ongoing anthropological researches of that time and most importantly, the anthropologists' expeditions to distant and faraway lands that our knowledge about the non-European societies was considerably widened and a distinct interest in alien and exotic cultures developed in these societies.[7] Initially, these researches conducted predominantly by the western anthropologists were issued from their keenness on not only differentiating the West from the Rest almost in absolute and blanket terms but vindicating and reiterating their cultural superiority to those that they had cared to survey. But as these researches gathered momentum, a section of anthropologists gradually began to realize the dangers involved in such cross-cultural exercises. In most cases, the scale and tools of comparison that they were working with seem to have been derived from the congnitive categories and frameworks of the Western cultural ethos. Their all too evident roots in the Western anthropological traditions often belied their universalist claims. We have only to recall that Edward Said's excellent study on Orientalism shows how the West established its cultural hegemony in the world of knowledge since the time of European Enlightenment.

As cultural relativism grew into a powerful intellectual movement, it assumed two rather conceptually distinct forms. We said 'conceptually' because in practice it might be impossible for us to make a clear distinction between them. In one form, cultural relativism is based on the premise that all cultures and communities embodying them are equal and of equal importance. In this sense, hierarchy of cultures and cultural communities is simply anathema to any cross-cultural comparison in anthropological circles. The argument is that since there is no way by which the superiority of one culture over another can be impeccably established, any attempt at organizing cultures within the same hierarchy is bound to be hazardous. In another, it is built on the assumption that "nothing that obstructs that which I recognize as my community's supreme goal can be allowed to have equal value with it".[8] Given this assumption, a community in ferment is necessarily driven by an overvalued sense of its self and perceives itself to be superior to anyone of its ilk. This assumption establishes a hierarchy in the sense that a community very like what Dunn talks about modernity, lays down the 'universalist claim to know better' than anyone else. It is by way of making the same claim that a community becomes modern. The modernity of a community in simple terms lies precisely in its eagerness to make the universalist claim and its urge to 'create a world after its own image'. A community that looks upon itself as an entity superior to anyone of its ilk also expects and more often than not forces others to emulate and follow it. The writings of such German Idealists as, Hegel, Herder and Fichte point to the presence of these hierarchies in the world of communities and nations.[9] Hegel for example asserted that 'the Spirit of the Age' *(zeitgeist)* is always embodied in only a few nations. The universalism of the community according to Isaiah Berlin is at odds with the very tenor of cultural relativism. For a community that makes 'the universalist claim to know better' spurns by definition the relativistic nature of cultural formations.

But it would be wrong to argue that the two universalisms – those of modernity and community are often qualitatively of the same kind. Universalism of modernity always makes a 'seductive' appeal so much so that its 'claim to know better' is almost uncritically acquiesced to, even by those who supposedly know *worse* – the pre-and the non-moderns amongst us. The most interesting thing about modernity is that it is capable of eliciting their acquiescence not by force but by establishing the superiority of its arguments. The otherwise voluntary acquiescence is what reiterates and validates its universalist claim. On the other hand, a community's universalist 'claim to know better' is likely to be contested by another community over whom it is made and to spark off negative reactions and animosities. The most obvious instance of this is that both the number and intensity of communal riots (like, those between the Nagas and the Kukis/Paites in Manipur Hills and between the Bodos and the Santhals/Bengali-speaking Muslims in Assam etc.) have considerably gone up in recent years. There is hardly any universally agreed-upon hierarchy amongst the culturally distinct communities. How many of us including the Sikhs themselves, would find plausibility in Bhindranwale's rather inflammable assertion that 'one-lakh-twenty-five (12.5 million) thousand Hindus are equal to a Sikh'?

Let us pause here a bit and look back closely into what John Dunn was saying. He seems to have been suggesting that modernity's universalist claim is 'flourished menacingly at identities – personal, cultural and political'.[10] In other words, modernity's claim to better knowledge gets easily translated into a monstrous claim to power. For it has disoriented and disarticulated smaller cultural communities and ethnic minorities in the name of ostensibly advancing universality and also in the name of castigating them as pre-or non-modern and hence on the ground that they know worse.[11] The claim to 'better' knowledge becomes synonymous with the claim to greater power. Modernists are so much fired by their sense of self-piety that they consider any dialoguing with the ethnic protagonists as 'sheer wastage of time'.[12]

MODERNITY AND COMMUNITY

The argument that modernity has epistemologically informed the entire ambit of Modern Political Theory has encouraged two very different—but not altogether unrelated perspectives on community. According to the first, modernity brings about a change that is so fast and rapid that it is difficult – if not impossible on our part to represent it. Representation demands a certain degree of stability of objects and in a world where rapidity of changes *continuously* makes 'everything something different from itself', our attempts of representation are definitely to end up in a failure. All our representations are preposterous for they are bound to freeze objects around us and are necessarily overtaken by the rate of changes in them. As a result, modernity is expected to sweep away the foundations of community. Many of Marx's writings on India are marked by this 'radical expectancy'. For instance, in one of his journalistic papers 1853, he observed : "Modern industry, resulting from the railway system will dissolve the hereditary divisions of labour, upon which rest the Indian castes, those decisive impediments to progress and Indian power". Marx was only too optimistic about the nature and pace of these changes. Consecutive field surveys – in most cases generously funded by American agencies during the 1960s and the 1970s came out with the nearly unmistakable conclusion that communities have not only survived the advent of modernity but become more potent and stronger than ever before. For instance, Melson and Wolpe summarized these surveys by way of saying that "modernization far from destroying communalism both reinforces communal conflict and creates the conditions for the foundation of entirely new communal groups".[13] They have taken the term 'communalism' in the broder sense of the term that also includes the ethnic communities.

This recognition has brought the second perspective into existence. According to it, community exists because it plays a useful role. The functionalist tenor of the argument should nor escape our attention. We know that modernity has perfected our knowledge of taming and mastering nature by way of bringing down the vagaries of our dependence on it. But it has nevertheless increased the risks caused by human behaviour and released uncertainties 'for which there is no insurance'.[14] The world now changes at a pace that it constantly makes out known ways of knowing and mastering it both inane and redundant. The sense of belonging to a community serves as the insurance, as an antidote to all risks and uncertainties that modernity has released but for which it has no insurance. Andrew Greely, for example, has argued :

> The ethnic group was created only when the peasant commune broke up, and was essentially an attempt to keep some of the values, some of the informality, some of the support, some of the intimacy of the communal life in the midst of an impersonal formalistic, rationalized, urban, industrial society.[15]

While Greely's conclusion by his own admission applies to the limited context of White ethnic communities of the US, more recent studies on northeastern India point to the functions the communities in this region seem to perform even now. Soumitra De, for instance, in one of his thought-provoking papers has shown how communities in the northeast (are made to) act more as "means of entitlement to power" than as vestiges and survivals of the past that are generally on their way out. Power devolves along community line and hardly along individual line. In simple terms, only the claims of the community stand higher chances of access to and retention and contestation of state power.

While the state lays down the rules of entertainability of the community claims, the individual claims to power are more often than not drastically ruled out. Since the communities are made to act in this manner the state seems to have 'adapted itself to the characteristic type of society in northeastern India'.[16]

COMMUNITY AS A CRITIQUE

In both these perspectives, modernity serves as a critique of community. The idea of community as a remainder does not in any way preempt modernity's inherently optimistic claim to devise an appropriate knowledge of social insurance in future and on its own terms, that is to say, without falling back upon community. Even if modernity cannot master the risks at present, it holds out the alluring promise of mastering them in future. The most interesting thing about modernity is that it promises the infinite possibilities of engineering individual and social life and never gives it up. Community certainly is not the way to resolve the problems associated with modernity. If people are seen to fall back on community, it is certainly not the best solution. It is only a palliative that people are to fall back on in the absence of any better alternative. Modernity's promise to deliver is as much important as its actual ability to deliver at any given point of time.

But nowadays tables are turned around and we seem to have moved away from a critique of community to community as critique. Modernity's critique of community seems to have given way to community as a critique. Community can provide as a critique of modernity in either of the two ways. First of all, what is made to serve as a critique of modernity, that is to say, community is assumed to preexist the age of modernity. A supposedly prexistent community untrammeled by the forces of modernity may be brought to the forefront and subsequently celebrated. But images of those preexistent communities are by no means uniform. At least two of them suggest themselves: on the one hand, communities may be thought of not only as isolated and separate entities but also perpetually condemned to a Hobbesian 'war of all against all'. The thesis that the Nagas and Kukis cannot mix up as simply as oil cannot mix with water is derived from this sort of argument. Jinnah's argument that the Hindus and the Muslims in the subcontinent constitute two separate and independent nations gives credence to the same argument. On the other hand, we have a more 'positive' image of communities evident in the writings of Rajni Kothari and his cohorts. According to them, community is not just a constellation of isolated individuals sealed off from each other and entering the community on the basis of some voluntary contract but is 'an interactive structure' both from within and from without. Kothari pleads for a 'regeneration' of community for it can become "a source of alternative people's security where people derive protection not from a militarized state but through the creation of structures of mutual nurturence and protection within and across community spaces."[17]

We have two objections to these notions of preexisting community. First, to think that community in the present-day world remains unperturbed by the forces of modernity is not only extravagant but also empirically erroneous. Community, as we argue, is not just an 'inherited tradition'– a deadweight from the past. It seems to re-articulate itself in an age of modernity. Secondly, the forces of modernity are not considered strong enough to decisively sweep away the foundations of community. "Community is nor easily appropriated within the narrative of capital (read, modernity, SKD)".[18] The forces of modernity or what Partha Chatterjee calls, 'the narrative of capital' are 'limited and conditioned' by the numerous instances of resistence to their hegemonic sway. Both these objections make it imperative that we appreciate the changing nature of community in our country in general and in the region under review. It has to be admitted that the celebration critique— whether negative or positive, denies historicity to community for it seeks to resusciate and rejuvenate community almost from the otherwise soiled pages of history. Community, as we see it is both 'a persistent identity' as well as 'an historical moment' for being a 'persistent identity' does not imply the repression of 'the new and the non-identical', but it in the words of Fredric Jameson means that "abstractions are wrested away from the primal flux".[19] In our pursuit for viewing community as a means of stability and insurance, we often forget that it too changes and takes various forms and shapes in accordance with the changing requirements of time.

The argument bears out two major implications for us. First, in this view, community exists as an 'abstraction', a representation or a construction or maybe a plurality of all of them. We would do well to remember that the objects that the community consists of do not automatically give birth to it. These objects available to us at a determinate historical epoch are to be welded together deliberately to form a community. Viewed in this light, abstraction involves two relevant social and political processes – *othering* and *supersession*. Othering is a process whereby a community imaginatively marks itself off from it considers as its other. The process is nowhere more sharply illustrated than in the case of the Bodos insofar as they made a critique of what the students of Assamese society and culture call, "the dominant Assamese nationalism".[20] Dominant Assamese nationalism asserted itself by way of raising two major demands: assimilation and expulsion. The demand for assimilation spurred off invariably by the universalistic aspirations of a community was made to create 'a world after its image'. The demand makes it mandatory that all the non-Assamese people living in Assam have to acquire the language and culture of the Assamese. The plea was so strong that even Nava Kanta Barooah, the famous poet and litterateur – widely known for his liberal frame of . mind, once argued that the immigrant other – whoever she is, should be assimilated into the Assamese culture as 'sugar melts in milk'. Assimilation we must remember also implies an antecedent de-culturation. The demand for complete de-culturation was aimed precisely at making others relinquish and abandon their own language and culture. Charu Chandra Bhandari reporting on the Assam disturbances of 1960 points out:

> In the northern part of the Darrang district and in the Uttar Lakhimpur subdivision, the special feature of the disturbances was to compel the Bengali-speaking girls and women to wear *mekhla* (a kind of long skirt worn by the Assamese women, SKD) or to create circumstances in which they would be compelled to wear *mekhla*. It is a decent dress no doubt... But when one has to wear a particular costume under compulsion it becomes a different matter altogether.[21]

The demand that the non-Assamese, especially women among them have to wear a particular dress has to be interpreted that way. The women everywhere are vested with the responsibility of embodying literally in their bodies the honour of their community.[22] More often than not, women accept the responsibility. But in some cases, they also voice their resentments against their being burdened with this extra-responsiblity unlike their male counterparts. The Khasi women's protest against the recent imposition of dress code on them by the Khasi Students' Union (KSU) serves as a case in point.

Dominant Assamese nationalism also asserted itself by raising the demand for expulsion of the non-Assamese outsiders – sometimes citizens from other parts of India, from Assam. 'Quit notices' were reportedly served to many of the non-Assamese who have been living in Assam for generations together as early as in 1979 and at a time when the erstwhile Assam movement (1979-1985, was yet to take off. Before we move over to an examination of the Bodo critique, it would be proper to point out that these two demands of assimilation and expulsion are not altogether mutually exclusive. There were instances of people who were under the threat of being driven out in spite of the fact that they had been living in Assam for generations together and had assimilated themselves successfully into the mainstream.

The preparation of the Bodo critique was by no means a unilinear process and the Bodos seemed to have adapted themselves 'overwhelmingly' to the central premises of the dominant Assamese nationalism down to the 1960s. They were, as Mukherjee and Mukherjee have pointed out, 'for a long time eager to be accommodated into the lower rungs of Hindu hierarchy'.[23] But by 1960s, the Bodo critique of dominant Assamese nationalism was beginning to assert itself. Its preparation can be traced back to the establishment of the Bodo Sahitya Sabha in 1952 and the first thing it did after its establishment was to demand for recognition of the Bodo language as a medium of instruction in primary and higher secondary schools. The use of Bodo language was officially recognized at the primary level in 1963 and at higher secondary level in Bodo-concentrated areas much later – only in 1968. Similarly in 1974, Plains Tribal Council of Assam (PTCA) launched an agitation with the demand for using Roman script in place of the Assamese script by Devanagari script two years later in 1976. The critique perhaps culminated in the final breach marked by the Gohpur riots of 1989. Not a single hapless Bodo amongst those who were rendered homeless and fled to the adjoining areas of Arunachal Pradesh took shelter in any of the relief camps of Assam on the ground that they, according to them, were run by the Assamese-dominated administration.[24] Besides, Rabi Ram Brahma, the then General Secretary of the All-Bodo Students' Union (ABSU), issued a warning that all the non-Bodos living in proposed Bodoland would be expelled if they did not vacate it on their own by 15 August, 1989. Besides, the ABSU-resolution entitled 'Divide Assam fifty-fifty' (1987) that forms the nucleus of contemporaty Bodo militancy, underscores the social and cultural distance in these terms:

> . . . the attitude of the Assamese people is anti-tribal; Assamese people are deporting Assamese colonialism in tribal areas and dominating the tribals; Assamese people are following the policy of Assamese expansionism and chauvinism; Assamese people feel that Assam is only for Assamese and not for tribals;

> Assam Government is nothing but only an Assamese Government and not the Government of the prople of Assam; Assamese people want to assimilate others.[25]

This, of course, implies a certain reversal of the earlier trend towards 'accommodation into Hindu hierarchy' and seeks interestingly to celebrate 'the tribal culture' as the mainstream within the proposed political unit of 'Bodoland'.

On the other hand, abstraction also means that the differences internal to the community are superseded *albeit* at the subjective level. That is to say, once the community takes its shape, its members seem to share the same 'consciousness of kind' irrespective of the classes or sections they hail from. This first of all, presupposes that the objective differences both of class and non-class nature exist within the community and its members do not belong to the same class as much as the members of a class are not drawn from the same community. Class differences in simple terms, are seen to cut across the differences among the communities. But, that a community exists as an 'abstraction' also means that members are infussed with a consciousness of belonging to it and also that this consciousness prevails over other forms of sectional or segmented consciousness.

Let us turn back to Jameson. By saying that "abstractions are wrested away from the primal flux" he did not in any way dispute that the abstractions themselves are apt to change. For instance, a community's perceptions of its collective self are never given and immutable. The notion of the Assamese identity as crystallized during the erstwhile Assam movement of 1979-1985 is remarkably divergent from the one articulated by the United Liberation Front of Assam (ULFA) during the 1980.[26] To cite an instance, we know that the erstwhile movement of 1979-1985 was directed against the foreigners – more particularly, the illegal Bangladeshi immigrants. On the other hand, they are regarded by the ULFA as 'integral part' of the Assamese identity and culture and as one of the indispensable building-blocs of the Assamese identity and culture.[27] The instance shows how the perceptions of collective self and other change their mutual positions in course of time.

Another way of appreciating the protean nature of community is to note that it may be constructed differently – not only by those who are outside it but by those who decidedly belong to it at any given point of time. A community thereby provides a site of contest with a plurality of modes of representation or construction competing with each other for laying siege over the community space sometimes to the exclusion of others. It goes to the credit of Clifford who has viewed a community's culture "as composed of seriously contested codes and representations".[28]

Community defined as a site of context bears two major implications for us: First, this definition sensitizes us to the politically constituted nature of a community. In its quest for gaining supremacy over a community's site of symbols and meanings, "each mode of representation is engaged with and elaborates a politics".[29] Politics thus amounts to a contest over the symbolic space of a community. We may note here that in real life situations, there is hardly any chronologically neat succession of one determinate mode of representation by equally determinate another. Indeterminacy and ambiguity in the modes of representation obviously mark the community space. We may also refer to two sources of such indeterminacy and ambiguity in this connection. First, we may conceive of a situation where no single mode is strong enough to wipe out the other that contends with it. Community in such a situation thrives on a juxtaposition of several modes. This juxtaposition, as we will see, does not tell upon the solidarity of a community. Secondly, we may also keep in mind that the contest we are talking about is hardly of zero-sum character. The appropriation can be mutual in the sense that approprition by one mode may not rule out the same by another. This springs from the ambiguities and equivocations that mark the symbolic site and the site holds itself available for mutural appropritions.

The argument that communities in modern times have lost much of their revolutionary potential is premised on the assumption that they are appropriated to the point where 'communities and their institutions are transformed into apparatuses of hegemony, often characterized by an amalgam of capitalist and pre-capitalist forms of exploitation'. Those who argue along these lines see appropriation by the All-Assam Students' Union and All-Assam Gana Sangram Parishad (AASU-AAGSP) combine, for example, did not stand in the way to the emergence of the one spearheaded and champigned by the ULFA. As I have argued elsewhere, there were and may be there are people who would hold on to the former while lending their political support to the latter.[30] The line dividing between the two organizations seems to disappear because of this. Thus, in spite of their ideological differences, the members of Asom Gana Parishad (AGP) were according to Sanjoy Hazarika, 'hand in glove with ULFA'.[31] Ambiguity of a community's symbols and meanings accounts for such a multiplicity as well as mutuality of appropriations. We may even take the point a step further in order to argue that this only helps in reinforcing and broadening the community's popular base. For the availability of alternative modes of representation offers to its members a freedon to choose from amongst them. Thus we may say albeit in somewhat Aristotelian vein that some may appreciate one, some another, but all together appreciate all. Community's life gathers momentum to the extent it widens its horizons of choice. This obviously is not possible when a single mode exhausts in an authoritarian manner the entire site of community. The availability of alternative modes and their mutural appropriations make the community boundaries porous and flexible. The illegal immigrants from Bangladesh settled in Assam in the recent past who were excluded in the formulations of AASU-AAGSP combine were sought to be accommodated in ULFA's formulation. Hence, their exclusion in the former was undone and compensated by the latter.It only shows how Assamese nationalism circulates within a range of mutually exclusive modes of representation and cannot simply be reduced to any one of them.Notwithstanding these mutual exclusion, people assemble together within the broad umbrella of the Assamese community and are unmindful of the mutually exclusive nature of the modes. The articulation makes them forget the mutually exclusive nature of these modes and bring a community into existence. Transcendence of these modes of representation harps on the amnesia of their differences. The articulation of nationalism everywhere is predicted on this complexity and diversity.

Secondly, alternative modes of representation have also historically negotiated certain modes of existence between themselves'. A site of contest should not be linkened to a Hobbesian "war of all against all". The alternative modes at times are concerned with thrashing out appropriate strategy of survival and mutual existence. Even the strategy of survival and mutual coexistence can be a matter of disagreement,dispute and contest among the alternative modes. The procedural question of consolidating the bond of Assamese community by way of levelling off differences internal to it set two political parties—Asom Jatiyatabadi Dal and Purbanchaliya Lok Parishad apart from the AGP in 1985. We may remind ourselves that both were constituents of AAGSP during the Assam movement of 1979-1985. Indeed, their rivalry was so serious that two consecutive National Conventions and one Jatiya Karmasuchi Pranayan Sala had to be organized under the aegis of AASU to settle it.[32] It is ironic that the issue of settlement brings in its wake multiple and often mutually exclusive modes of consolidation and common survival into existence. Contest in one word is all-pervasive and it touches upon everything including the issue of common survival. There is no sector in a community's life that is immune to contest and competition. To be indifferent to them entails an idyllic romanticization of the community not quite uncommon in scholarly circles.

NOTES

[All translations from original non-Assamese sources are mine. SKD]

1. Asok Sen, Subaltern Studies : Capital, Class and Community' in Ranajit Guha (ed), *Subaltern Studies* : Writings *on South Asian History and Society* (Delhi : OUP, 1987), p. 221.
2. Professor Hiren Gohain's Valedictory address to the National Seminar on 'Coming out of Violence: resolving ethnic conflict in northeast India' organized by the Department of Political science, Gauhati University in collaboration with the Indian Council of Social Science Research, North Eastern Regional Centre, Shillong in Guwahati on 11-12 November, 2002.
3. Especially my Agrarian Question and the Assamese Community : Towards a political framework' in K. Alam (ed.), *Agricultural Development in Northeast India* (New Delhi : Deep & Deep Publications, 1993) , pp. 236-49.
4. Sudhir Kakar, Some unconscious aspects of collective violence in India in Veena Das (ed.), *Mirrors of Violence* (Delhi : OUP, 1990), p. 143.
5. Seyla Benhabib, *Situating the Self : Gender, Community and Post-Modernism in contemporary Ethics* (Cambridge : Polity Press, 1992).
6. John Dunn, *Rethinking Modern Political Theory : Essays* 1979-83 (Cambridge: Clarendon Press, 1985), p. 343.
7. A review of how it grew in French Anthropological thought is available in Tzvetan Todorov, *On Human Diversity : Nationalism, Racism and Exoticism in French thought,* trans, by Catherine Porter (Cambridge, Mass : Harvard University Press, 1993).
8. Isaiah Berlin, *Against the Current : Essays in the History of Ideas* (Oxford: Clarendon Press, 1981), p. 343.
9. For an excellent review of these positions, see, Elie Kedourie, *Nationalism* (London : Hutchinson, 1966), pp. 51-61.
10. John Dunn, op. cit,
11. Manoranjan Mohanty, 'Secularism : Democratic and Hegemonic' in *Economic and Political Weekly,* XXIV (22), 3 June 1989, p. 1219.
12. While I made a plea for dialoge with the fundamentalists in one of my controversial Bengali essays, I was severely criticized by a number of 'rationalist secularists' for 'wasting my time'. See, Samir Kumar Das. 'Moulabad Baunam Moulabad' (in Bengali) [Fundamentalism versus

fundamentalism] in *Parichaya*, August-October, 1993, The severest rejoinder to my mind was sent by Amitabha Chandra, 'Moulabad baunam yuktibad' (in Bengali) [Fundamentalism versus rationalism] in *Parichaya*. November-December, 1993.

13. Robert Melson & Howard Wolpe, 'Moderization and the Politics of Communalism : A theoretical perspective' in *American Political Science Review*, December 1970, p. 113.
14. Amiya Kumar Bagchi, 'Communalism and the Limits of Enlightenment' in *Seminar*, 411, November 1993, p. 40.
15. Andrew Greely, *Why can't they be like us? – America's White Groups* (New Delhi Prentice Hall, 1976), p.40.
16. Soumitra De, 'Of Insurgency in Northeastern India : a note on theory and practice' (1995), mimeo.
17. Rajni Kothari, *Rethinking Development : In Search of Humane Governance* (Delhi : Ajanta, 1988). p. 223.
18. Partha Chatterjee, *The Nation and its Fragments : Colonial and Post-Colonial Histories* (New Delhi ; OUP, 1994), p. 236.
19. Fredric Jameson, *Late-Marxism : Adorno and the Persistence of the Dialectic* (London : Verso, 1990), p., 20
20. Apurba Kumar Baruah and Manora Sharma, 'Nationality Question in Assam: Some conceptual issues' in Udayon Misra (ed.), *Nation-Building and Development in Northeast India* (Guwahati : Purbanchal Prakash, 1991), p.20
21. Charu Chandra Bhandari, *Some thoughts on Assam Disturbances* (Rajghat: A. B. Sarva Seva Sangh, 1961), p.36.
22. See, my 'Ethnic Assertion and the Women's Question in north-east India' in Anil K. Jana (ed.), *Indian Politics at the Crossroads*, (New Delhi : Commonwealth, 1998), pp. 172-88.
23. D. P. Mukherjee & S. P. Mukherjee, 'Contemporaty Cultural and Political Movements among the Bodos of Assam' in K. S. Singh (ed.), *Ttribal Movements in India*, Vol. 1 (New Delhi : Manohar, 1982), p. 277.
24. Radhika Ramaseshan, 'Carnage in Gohpur' in *Sunday*, 27 August-2 September 1989, p. 101.
25. See, P. S. Datta (ed.), *Autonomy Movements in Assam : Documents* (New Delhi : Omsons, 1993), p. 240.
26. Samir Kumar Das, *ULFA – A Political Analysis* (Delhi : Ajanta, 1994). pp. 96-101.
27. Samir Kumar Das, 'Modernity, Self and the Question of Rights : The case of Assam in the 1990s' In *Rabindra Bharati Journal of Political Science*, 4, 2001, pp. 48-69.

28. James Clifford, 'Political truths' in James Clifford and George F. Marcus (eds.), *Writing Culture : The Politics and Poetics of Ethnography* (New Delhi : OUP, 1986), p. 2

30. Samir Kumar Das, op. cit. pp. 97-8.

31. Sanjoy Hazarika, *Strangers of the Mist : Tales of War and Peace from India's Northeast* (New Delhi: Viking,1994),p.189.

32. For a detailed account of this see, my 'On institutionalization: A reconsideration of the Assam movement (1983-1985)'in *Journal of Politics*(Dilbrugarh)Vol. V, December 1998,Pp.55-76.

10

Ethnicity and Social Transformation in North-East India*

AJIT K. DANDA

In a common parlance, ethnicity is ordinarily attributed with rather a negative connotation, since by and large it is presumed to have manifested mere narrow loyalty. Such a notion fails to receive unequivocal support, at least on two counts. First, ethnicity as such having plural usages, convey widely different meanings. Obviously, they cannot and are not in perfect consonance with one another. In other words, various phenomena or processes that have been referred to by ethnicity, do not necessarily imply narrow loyalty. Rather, if they are analysed taking the overall context in view, to a major extent such references are likely to appear as the sufficiently rational responses to the demand of the situations. Second, multiplicity in meanings apart, the negative sense in ethnicity seems to have been enforced upon the concept through a subjective choice, if not a prejudiced approach to the same. In a wider perspective, ethnicity may and generally should convey a value-neutral meaning highlighting the exact nature of the processes involved. Looking at it from a specific value-premise of questionable sense of neutrality, it should not and cannot be accepted as anything entirely objective. In the interest of science, therefore, there appears an urgent and important need for evaluating the ethnicity-related issue afresh for arriving at an agreeable consensus in this regard.

---

*First Published in *Man In India* (1992), 72(2): 131-140.

The aim of the present discussion is neither to record a plea, nor to elaborate a critique on either of the just-referred positions. Elsewhere I have already discussed at some length the nature of plurality in meanings of ethnicity, particularly highlighting how the concept has been variously referred to depending on the orientation and ideology of the concerned societies (Danda : 1988b and 19888c). To a limited extent, I have also commented upon the implicit nature of subjectivity in the somewhat over-used notion of ethnicity (Danda: 1988a). My present objective, in comparison, is rather too modest, as I propose to demonstrate here through illustration that an apparently negative concept, when adjudged afresh from a value-neutral position, is not only likely to look different but could very well appear as a major source for social transformation. In order to drive home my point, I would refer to selected case studies from among contemporary tribal movements of North-East India that, due to their apparently limited objectives, have by and large been perceived as the expressions of narrow loyalty. Since the exact character of a movement depends more on the perspective than on the subjective value-premise, the issue would receive eleboration in the appropriate context.

A note of clarification on my reference to social transformation seems important at this stage since the same would have a decisively limited connotation here. Changes in attitude, behaviour, customs, habits, manners, relations, and values of people, including change in the structure of social institutions would, for the purpose of this essay, stand for social transformation.

Examples of social and political processes that have contributed toward crystallisation of demand for autonomy of the tribes and their territories in India are several. Our reference to tribal movements implies such demands, quite a few among whom culminated into the formation of separate States or Autonomous Tribal Councils. Multiple of such movements are either on-going or still emerging. For the benefit of our discussion here, we would refer to only such movements that culminated into the formation of Meghalaya, Mizoram, and Nagaland as separate states as well as to those that involve all the tribes of Tripura and only the Bodo-speaking tribes of Assam. The latter, during the initial years of its emergence, was known as Udayachal movement which of late is often being referred to as Bodoland movement, by which I would designate it here.

It may be noted in this context that the case-studies incorporated in this discussion are neither exhaustive, nor fully representative of the overall tribal situation of North-East India, not to speak of India as a whole. They have rather been purposively chosen so as to indicate the broad trends of socio-political processes as become conspicuous among the tribes of North-East India.

BODOLAND

The movement that culminated into the demand for creation of a separate State for the Bodo-speaking tribes of Assam had a modest beginning, initially as a socio-cultural movement with implication for economic development. Started by the Bodo-Kachari tribes of Darrang, Goalpara, and Kamrup districts of Assam, where the people have a major concentration; the movement as well as its leadership were at the beginning somewhat diffused in character. Not until the involvement of Bodo Sahitya Sabha and the Bodo Students' Association, the objective thereof could be properly crystallised or spelt out and the movement assumed an definite direction.

Emergence of Brahma movement during the mid-nineteenth century and its influence upon a section of the Bodo people was perhaps one of the major factors to arouse a level of cultural consciousness hitherto unknown among them. Kalicharan Brahma, a Mech by birth, is believed to be the first convert who and his followers, being influenced by the ideas of one Sibnarayan Paramhangsa, propagated the need for education and social reforms like: changes in marriage customs, stoppage of dowry system, use of liquor, pig-rearing, and such others for the benefit of their people. Accordingly, the Brahma among the Bodo became culturally distinct and educationally advanced to be able to properly articulate their ideas and initiate steps toward bringing about socio-political changes within the neighbourhood.

During the early second quarter of the present century, the college-educated Bodo, particularly the Brahma, formed the Bodo Chhatra Sammelan with the explicit aim of uniting the Bodo-speaking tribes through conferences and to initiate social reforms, at first within the immediate neighbourhood and then around. Demand for facilities in education, health and economic development was their first priority.

With the establishment of Bodo Sahitya Sabha, the movement took a new turn as the people registered a demand for introduction of Bodo language as an optional subject along with Sanskrit and Pali in the schools of Assam. This was followed by the demand for use of Bodo language in the schools of Bodo-dominated areas which was conceded for the primary schools in 1963 and for the secondary schools in 1968. This initial success led to the demand for a separate script in 1975 and then for a separate State. Thus, out of a socio-cultural movement, through certain structural transformations, there emerged a political demand for creation of Bodoland.

On close scrutiny, the Bodo case speaks for major changes that the people have undergone over the decades, particularly with respect to behaviors, customs, habits, manners, and relations that together reflect transformation in attitudes as well as values. They have, in fact, demonstrated clear options in favour of change in the structure of social institutions as such through their endeavour for transforming the tradition-bound people by exposing them to various socio-cultural and political processes. Measured by any standard, the changes are bound to reflect integration of the people at a higher plane and their extension of horizon.

MEGHALAYA

Demand for creation of an autonomous hill state within India around what is now Meghalaya, grew under implicit British support during the last few decades of British rule in India. This was articulated in the move for creation of an Eastern Frontier State during States' Reorganisation in 1953. When that demand was rejected, hill leaders belonging to different tribes and denominations who used to operate rather independently, came forward together to form Eastern India Tribal Union.

The unity thus forged no doubt experienced periodic stress but the decision to recognise Assamese as the State language by the Government of Assam of which Meghalaya constituted a part, put them together again. At this, the tribal leaders agreed to bury their mutual differences to form the All Party Hill Leaders' Conference (APHLC) which took up creation of a separate hill state where English would be the official language as well as medium of instruction, as its primary objective. There was, of course, provisions to replace English by Hindi after a period of time. Improvement of the standard of living of their people was also within their agenda for positive action.

In September 1968, APHLC organised a non-violent *satyagraha* that resulted in the creation of the Autonomous State of Meghalaya within Assam comprising Khasi and Jaintiya Hills District and Garo Hills District. But by that time the demand for full State had already grown. With the creation of Nagaland as a separate State, the pressure became very much intensified. As a result, within a short while, on January 21, 1972, Meghalaya became a full State; since when APHLC assumed the status of a regional political party.

In the creation of Meghalaya as a separate State, the local people, particularly the Khasi, Garo, Jaintiya have clearly demonstrated their cagerness to go for a structural change within the framework of the Constitution of India, which in fact, is the culmination of their changes in values and attitudes. Due primarily to this reason, apparently disparate tribes could not only effectively communicate with those who really matter, they could achieve what they aspired for rather at relative case. In fact, their initial success in creating an Autonomous Hill State as such also became the source of impetus for subsequent achievements.

MIZORAM

Several ethno-culturally distinct peoples, on their own volition brought themselves together through adoption of a territorial identity. Mizoram or the land of the highlanders has been the home for a number of Kuki-Chin tribes among whom the position of a Chief is considered highly important. The chiefs traditionally had the exclusive territory and unrestricted powers. The British Government, through introduction of an intermediate tier of Chief's Council indirectly tried to weaken the authority of the chiefs. This was at that time strongly frowned upon by the people. But intensive drive of Christian missionaries to convert the people to Christianity helped them to achieve through cultural intervention, what appeared politically formidable.

Pan-Christian identity and adoption of the Western way of life subsided inter-tribal differences to a major extent and helped forging Mizo solidarity. Nevertheless, their deployment in the World War II and the extraordinary flow of cash that followed disturbed the traditional balance of power and the otherwise egalitarian base of the Mizo society. This resulted in the formation of sharp cleavage between the commoners and the chiefs. Formation of the Mizo Union by the District Superintendent around 1946 by involving chiefs and commoners together further sharpened the cleavage between them. The emergence of District Conference, where one-half of the members were commoners, further worsened the situation. After a period of flerce rivalry between the Mizo Union and the District Conference, the former declared itself a formal political party for whom forging political solidarity among various tribes around was the principal objective.

In the wake of independence of India, through favour of the British administrators, there grew the demand for creation of a Crown Colony in the Agency Area dominated by the Christian subjects. Being influenced by this spirit and for achieving this end, several Mizo clergymen started exaggerating ethnic and religious differences between the Mizo and the non-Mizo. They highlighted the separateness to such an extent that the spirit of inter-tribal distinction too, within the immediate neighbourhood became very conspicuous. At that phase of development, introduction of Assamese as the State language was interpreted as a direct threat to the Mizo cultural identity. This to a major extent contributed to the emergence of Mizo solidarity that was hitherto illusive.

The Mizo National Front established in 1961 renewed the demand for a separate State. After about a decade's insurgency, a peace accord was sighned in July, 1976 which culminated into the formation of Mizoram.

It is thus seen that despite intervention by the State and the Christian missionaries, traditional structural arrangement, particularly in the domain of politics, had a very important role to play in the Mizo life and in the formation of Mizoram. Major changes did take place only when the people questioned the validity of the traditional line of divide between the aristocrats and the commoners. Besides apparent changes in their material culture as well as manifestations, this also resulted in the transformation of attitude and value of the people.

NAGALAND

The inhabitants of the Naga Hills were referred to by the non-Naga population of the neighbourhood as the Naga, who otherwise had distinct identities like the Ao, Angami, Konyak, Lotha, Rengma. This, nevertheless, had very little impact on the pan-Naga solidarity movement. In contrast, Christiantly was undoubtedly a force to reckon with for consolidation of a common Naga identity. In fact, this initially helped the people to identify themselves as fellow believers of the rulers. Thus, they came together primarily due to their more or less equal proximity to British administrators.

Establishment of Naga Club at Kohima and Mokokchung in 1918 was perhaps the first conscious attempt to promote inter-tribal solidarity. The Naga elites, who became members of the Naga Club were mostly those who had been educated in institutions run by the Christian missionaries. From the Memorandum submitted by them to the Simon

Commission, the common design of the British Government and Christian missionaries of separating the Naga from the people of the plains of Assam became evident.

Formation of Lotha Council in 1923 and Ao Council in 1928, however, re-emphasised independent socio-cultural identities of the major Naga population. But formation of Naga Hills District Tribal Council in 1945, considerably reinforced the solidarity movement of the Naga tribes. In 1946, the Naga Hills District Council was renamed being influenced by the idea of pan-Naga nationhood, as Naga National Council.

The British design of creating a Trust Territory was, though outright rejected by the nationalist Indians, had caught the imagination of the Naga elites, who unilaterally declared formation of independent Nagaland on 14th August, 1947. This was followed by a series of disquite developments until 1957, when the Naga Peace Organising Committee and the chruch authorities gave a call for tranquility. Successive Naga Peoples' Conventions and negotiations with the Government of India that followed ultimately culminated into the creation of Nagaland as a separate State in 1963.

The major issues that led to the development of Nagaland were cultural distinctions of the Naga and plain dwellers, and discontent among the emerging elites while adjusting themselves to the changing socio-political situation in the country as a whole. The fear of losing privileges and newly acquired pan-Naga identity also had a crucial role in this respect.

TRIPURA

Among the 19 Scheduled Tribes of Tripura, the Tripuri, Reang, Jamatia, Noatia, and Halam are considered autochthones; the first having the largest population strength played important roles in the history of the region. The former rulers of Tripura, under whose patronage the tribal communities of the region became kshatriaised, belonged to the Tripuri community.

The king practised Shaivite Hindusim but the people in general was under strong influence of Vaishnavism of Bengal. The Tripuri and the Janatia also came under the influence of the Bengale Brahman priests and such contact influenced the Maharaja to follow an open-door policy so far as the Bengalee immigrants are concerned. This, nevertheless, soon resulted in a demographic imbalance, as the tribes who constituted the bulk of the populations became reduced to mere insignificance. This also resulted in an extraordinary pressure in their livelihood threatening their very social and cultural survival.

Political processes in Tripura, which got the status of Part C State in 1950, reflected ethnic tension resulting from economic and cultural imbalances between tribes and non-tribes.

Table 10.1: Trends of Response

Categories determining social trans formation	*Bodo-Speaking people of Assam*	*People of Meghalaya*	*People of Mizoram*	*People of Nagaland*	*People of Tripura*
Attitude	Positive	Positive	Uncertain	Uncertain	Uncertain
Behaviour	-do-	-do-	Negative	Negative	Negative
Customs	-do-	-do-	Positive	Positive	Positive
Habits	-do-	-do-	Positive	Positive	Positive
Manners	-do-	-do-	Negative	Negative	Positive
Relations	-do-	-do-	Negative	Negative	Uncertain
Change in value	-do-	-do-	Positive	Positive	Positive
Change in structure of social institution	Positive	Positive	Positive	Positive	Positive

Around 1961, a section of the tribes under the guidance of the Eastern India Tribal Union demanded the Fifth Schedule of the Constitution to be applied to Tripura. As this was not agreed to, the people became somewhat restive. However, following the success of APHLC in Meghalaya, the tribes of Tripura put their pressure for extension of the Sixth Schedule of the Constitution to Tripura and formation of Autonomous District for Tribes.

Emphasis on harmony of tribes and non-tribes by the national political parties acted as a deterrent in this respect. Nevertheless, with the decline of influence of national political parties and continuous exploitation of the former by the latter, the Tripura Upajati Juba Samity (TUJS) emerged in 1967 as the champion of the cause of tribes, who formulated a four-point programme for fulfilment of aspirations of tribes of Tripura. What is important to note down here is when the conventional political machinaries proved themselves inadequate to protect the interest of the people or fulfill their ambitions, the tribes of Tripura took initiative to articulate their demands drawing freely from modernity as well as tradition.

Table 10.2: Directions of Movements

Movement	*Inital phase*	*Intermediate phase*	*Ultimate phase*
Bodoland	Socio-cultural development	Solidarity through demand for language and script, economic upliftment	Separate State
Meghalaya	Autonomous Hill State	Inter-tribal solidarity	Separate State
Mizoram	Inter-tribal solidarity through territorial identity	Reinforcement of solidarity through pan Christian identity, perceived threat to cultural identity and demand for separate Hill State	Periodic insurgency leading to separate State
Nagaland	Establishment of Naga Club under British patronage to forge intertribal solidarity	Creation of Naga Hills District Coundil reinforces pan-Naga solidarity and demand for Trust Territory	Periodic insurgency leading to separate State
Tripura	Tribes with independent identity under a tribal feudal lord	Tripura Kshatriya movement under feudal influence, influx of Bengalee populations	Demand for languange, script, and Autonomous District Council

From the given description of movements, it becomes fairly evident that all the populations involved in them consciously opted for breakthroughs—some phasing them out for a gradual transformation and some other trying to radicalise their ideas and strategies for achieving the goal at the earliest opportunity. As for example, the Bodo initially aspired for socio-cultural reforms and over the decades of such exposure to such programmes they developed a base from where they could place their demand for fulfillment of political aspirations. Their approach, nevertheless, was all-through positive. The Naga and Mizo, instead, tried to force it out of the system and for achieving that end; they did not hesitate to strain their relationship with the existing establishment. Naturally, their behaviours and manners had sufficiently reflections of them. The people of Meghalaya, on the other hand, have demonstrated extreme patience in this respect. Adoptions of satyagraha as a tool for achieving their goal was rather unique in their of Tripura took time initially perhaps to comprehend what was going on around and then to articulate their aims and objectives. There were occasions when they were somewhat uncertain in their attitude and apparently negative in their behaviors. The overall trend of the five sets of populations, from the larges society's point of view could be broadly summarised as in Table 10.1.

Despite such differences between movements, there is a common denominator, since all of them aimed at articulating themselves at a relatively higher level. The details as enumerated in Table 10.2 will make the point explicit. If for the purpose of clarity in our understanding, we presume that the movements have passed through three as outlined in Table 10.2, then their trends of change and direction becomes conspicuous. It, of course, is admitted that while assigning values to both Tables 10.1 and 10.2, there remains scope for some amount of disagreement as well as modification. Still it is held that in the interest of generalisation it should be possible to arrive at an overall consensus in this regard.

The movements enumerated in this discussion reflect fringe peoples' aspirations and their mechanisms for fulfilling them. Although legitimacy of such developments cannot be outright questioned, there is a tendency to virtually relegate them more or less to a position by assuming them as the manifestation of ethnicity. This is particularly so when ethnicity is presumed to express mere narrow loyalty.

There is no denial of the fact that socio-political processes anywhere express periodic stress. The off-repeated tendency of centripetality and centrifugally generally finds expression through such stress. Under the circumstances, such outbursts appear only natural in any dynamic society. Since totally stagnant society is beyond anybody's comprehension, socio-political movements of this kind are sometimes bound to occur.

From the point of view of the existing order, such developments are likely to appear embarrassing, if not altogether negative. This is particularly so as ethnicity often creates pressure on the existing order and sometimes throws challenge to the validity of the same. Since such notions primarily depend on perspectives, it is only likely to have some amount of disagreements on this count. An embarrassing experience of the society at large may appear rewarding to a particular section thereof. In pluri-cultural societies like India, possibilities for such an occurrence is relatively more. In view of this fact, it will be rather short-sighted, if not unrealistic, if ethnicity is attributed with negative connotation alone.

The five movements narrated here have no doubt embarrassed the administration to a considerable degree. But how do a Bodo, Khasi, Mizo, Naga, or Tripuri analyse the phenomena? Illustrations are not infrequent when at least a section of each of these populations tied to brand any initiative to check such movements as oppressions needed out by the State. It, therefore, appears to be a matter of opinion dependent upon specific value premise.

If such movements are analysed from a value-neutral position, each of them speaks of transformation in terms of attitude, behaviors, custom, manner, habit, relation, value, as well as structure of social institutions. If we take the political boundary of the concerned nation-state as something sacrosanct, some of the responses are bound to appear negative or sometimes hesitant. But they undoubtedly speak for breakthrough and the overall pattern in this respect its more than obvious.

There could be a slightly different way of looking at the phenomena from specific society's point of view. There cannot be any doubt about the fact that the people involved in such movements could come out of their ethno-centric shell and forge unity across tribes and people. They have also demonstrated their preparedness for participating in the wider socio-political processes. As has been evident from some of the movements referred to here, the people not only expressed concern for adoption of local cultural attributes in order to equip themselves better to ensure solidarity several of them had definite economic implications as well as programmes. As it appears, the movements designated as ethnicity were as such responsible for forging unity among the people, preparing them for participation in wider arena, and undertaking greater responsibilities. In other words, ethnicity appears as the factor for bringing about socio-cultural transformations among the people. Therefore, unless prejudiced ethnicity cannot be associated with negative connotation as such.

REFERENCES

Danda, Ajit K. *1988a: Ethnicity and Nationality in India : Some Theoretical Issue. Human Science*, Vol. 37(2).

Danda, Ajit K. *1988b : Ethnicity in a Pluri-cultural Society, Journal of the Indian Anthropological Society*, Vol. 23(1).

Danda, Ajit K. *1988c : Process of Ethnic Integration : Some Theoretical and Methodological Problems, Human Science*, Vol. 37(4).

11

Ethnic Conflict and Self-Determination: Examples of North-East Indian Tribes

RAJAT KANTI DAS

Ethnic conflict is an age-old phenomenon, but today, with increasing nationalistic feelings pervading individual communities and mounting tension gripping national and international scenario, it has assumed a new significance. Looking at the political situation in the world after the end of the twentieth century, one gains the immediate impression that most of the serious armed conflicts have an ethnic dimension. The emergence of 'neo-tribes' with increasing emphasis on 'self-identification' and 'ethnic and geo-cultural allegiance' is also linked with it. The term 'ethnic' qualifies a people and the concept of ethnic group may be used in multiple senses. An ethnic group may sometimes be interchangeably used to refer to a nationality, a minority, a tribe, a community, a culture, a society, a race, a people, or a nation (Lewis, 1988). Conflict and competition between different ethnic groups regarding political sovereignty and control over territories have almost become regular features. Of course, ethnic conflicts does not always strictly follow institutional politics. Instead, they become parts of an interactional pattern, enacted as they are in day-to-day situations. Both assertion of indigenous rights and acquistion of rights by the immigrant groups lead to ethnic conflict. There are, however, noticeable differences between the two. While the aim of the former is to reinstate indigenous political order usually followed by the demand of their own state, to the latter it is more a question of ensuring cultural survival by demanding the right to equality with the majority.

Ethnic conflict is taken to be an expression of ethnicity. But ethnicity does not necessarily entail conflict. Even where ethnicity involves conflict, the phenomenon is a complex one. In any case, ethnicity, with or without conflict manifestation, refers to a type of relationship between groups placed in different situations and whose members consider each other culturally distinctive. Cultural distinctiveness ensures a strong collective identity, which is a manifestation of ethnicity. Anthropoligists like Fredrik Barth, Leach, Mitchell hold the view that 'cultural traits' do not entail ethnicity. Barth (1969) wants the focus of research to be the social boundaries between groups rather than the 'cultural stuff' they contain. The groups may change their identity, but the social boundaries or ethnic boundaries separating the groups remain in tact. So, following Barth, ethnicity may be seen as an aspect of a relationship, not as a property of a person or group. Leach's (1954) Kachin study deserves mention in this context. The Kachin could become Shan by adopting the way of living of the latter, but the ethnic boundary remains unaffected. Even at the political level, adoption of the Shan political system in the form of a state by the Kachin does not signal the end of Kachin political system functioning within an ethnic framework. Gunnar Haaland's study (1969) in the Sudan also confirms this. As Haaland has shown, in Sudan the sedentary Fur may become the nomadic Baggara by changing their way of life, which does not in any way affect the ethnic boundary separating the two groups. The same phenomenon could be observed in India's North East. Smaller tribes like the Anal, Aimol, Lamgang, Kom, Koireng, Moyon of Manipur have changed their identity from 'Kuki' to 'Naga' without changing their ethnic boundary. Of course, here the focus is more on the realignment of political forces.

Ethnicity's political importance leaves no one in doubt. Ethnic boundaries operate in relation to certain stereotyped power disparities. Abner Cohen, who has studied ethnicity in Nigeria, Sierra Leone and London (1969, 1981, 1993), holds the view that ethinic cohesion as well as we-feeling are actually created through social and political processes, especially in contexts of competition for scarce resources. Cohen considers ethnicity as an essentially political phenomenon. Studies of ethnicity concentrating on the maintenance of ethnic boundaries and negotiations over identity will remain incomplete unless we look more closely at the ways in which power disparities may be decisive for interethnic relationship. The political implication of the majority-minority group relationship needs to be understood. The majority does not only possess the political power, it also controls important parts of the economy and, perhaps most importantly, defines 'the terms of discourse in society enforcing the language, codes of conduct and mastering the relevant skills'.

There is also a close parallel between nationalism and ethnicity. As a matter of fact, some would regard nationalism as 'special cases of ethnic ideologies'. Nationalism tends to appear as 'traditionalist ideology', whose main concern is to glorify a presumably old cultural tradition. This, however, does not automatically lead us to the conclusion that the concept of nationalism is 'traditionalist' in itself. In anthropology, the cultural importance of nationalism has been given prominence. There were even attempts to describe it as a cultural phenomenon. From this perspective, nationalism is defined as an ideology which holds cultural boundaries corresponding to political boundaries. The state in that case ought to contain people 'of the same kind' (Gellner, 1983). On the other hand, the so-called cultural uniqueness has been utilised by a number of groups to strengthen unity at the political level. It has been observed that indigenous peoples all over the world are placed in a potentially conflictual relationship to the nation-state, more precisely, to the state as an institution.

The indigeous politics has also a bearing on ethnicity and nationalism. The indigenous politics is centered around the idea that as a culture-bearing group the indegenous people should have their own state which can only ensure preservation of their cultural identity. In this exercise some indigenous societies bring about important changes in culture and social organization in keeping with their cultural survival and preservation of cultural identity. There is a compromise between indigenization and modernity. Sahlins' argument that 'the indigenization of modernity', which frequently takes the form of 'traditionalist' movements and often presented as ethnic or nationalist ones, carries sense. The globalization of culture is not simply a concept now. It not only threatens to eradicate important cultural differences, but also triggers counter-reactions in the shape of ethnic or traditionalist movements. The spirit working behind these movements is the one which could be identified as the guiding force behind a national political programme. The programme envisages the right to exercise sovereign control over a continuous stretch of territory with a clear delimited border and inhabited by a homogeneous population or constituents of a population. In a pluralistic situation power disparities mark the relationship between majority and minority groups, who are, so to say, unequal partners. The continuous struggle for sovereignty of a number of ethnic groups, who are tribes, minority groups or territorially organized groups with linguistic or cultural homogeneity, may be viewed from this angle.

In this struggle for attaining sovereignty many of the ethnic groups have taken recourse to self-determination. Self-determination is a key concept today, which has gained popularly among minorities, peripheral sections and colonised and/or non-self-governing peoples of nation-states. Because of the magnitude of the concept and its ambiguous nature, self-determination has been given a manipulative meaning for subjective ends varying between social, cultural, economic and/or political cause.

The Webster's Encyclopaedic Unabridged Dictionary of the English language (1989) defines 'self-determination' as :

(i) determination by oneself or itself without outside influence;

(ii) freedom to live as one chooses, or to act or decide without consulting another or others;

(iii) the determination of the people of the form their government shall have, without reference to the wishes of any other nation, especially, by people of a territory or former colony.

The New Encyclopaedica Britannica (1999, Vol. 10) defines self-determination as "the process by which a group of people, usually possessing a certain degree of national consciousness, form their own state and choose their own government".

Though definitions given by individual scholars somewhat vary, the central focus of all of them veer round the sovereignty of a people as a nation which involves the 'right' of a 'people' to decide their own course without any interference from any quarters. Lung-Chu Chen (1976) goes as far as to suggest that 'the essence of self-determination is human dignity'. Whether or not self-determination is a human right, the concept has one moot point, that is, 'the determination of the self', which in other words, means 'the formulation of the criteria for belonging to a people'. 'Self' here represents the 'people', or more specifically, 'ethnic group'. Naturally, the type of self-determination involved here is 'ethnic self-determination'.

The purpose of this paper is to show, with the help of specific examples, that the determination of the self hardly follows a uniform pattern involving all members at a time. It encourages formation of pressure groups of factional nature, all vying for supremacy and trying to prove that they are the right ones in inculcating a set of attitudes related to a sense of ancestral identification with the 'people' they belong to. It is worthwhile to mention here that ethnicity is, after all, an attitude or a set of attitudes. In this respect it is different from an ethnic group, which is more a sociological concept. The point that emerges is, the composition of an ethnic group has a level of abstraction within it since the factional groups may not always agree on all issues pertaining to social, economic and political status. It then becomes a question of reaching a consensus by the constituent parties. In such a situation the different constituents create their own image of the 'self'. This is apparent from the independent course of action devised and followed by each one of them. By doing so, they may also be trying to prove that they are the true representatives of the 'Self', which qualifies 'peoplehood'. In the light of the above observations the Naga and Bodo examples are discussed here.

'Naga' is a generic term that includes tribes with different but more or less allied cultures. Each tribe has one or more dialects which are unintelligible to others. Diallectical differences apart, it is rather difficult to bring out common cultural factors of the Nagas for the simple reason that there is no exactly similar culture among the Naga tribes. Every Naga group has its own version of origin and pattern of migration and each has developed its own socio-political organization. Still, despite diversities, the Nagas have been successful in forging unity and developing a strong sense of ethnic and emotional solidarity among themselves, which may be directly or indirectly attributed to British colonialism. The British who conquered the Nagas and brought them under their control had also created in them a feeling of isolation and separateness from the Indians, which was in a way responsible for creating a sense of unity among the various Naga tribes.

The ongoing struggle by the hardcore Naga outfits for sovereignty has been termed by some as 'the Naga National Movement'. The so-called Naga National Movement is basically an ethnic one, launched and carried out with the idea to constitute an independent Naga nation-state. The movement could be traced back to the formation of the 'Naga National Council' (NNC) on February 1946 at Wokha. In its session here the 'Naga Hills District Tribal Council' formally launched the 'Naga National Council' with Maying Nokcha as its President. The organization received official patronage in its attempt to unify Naga tribes, which was seen by the British Government officials to have a modering influence on various Naga tribes. Though NNC did not speak of separation from British India at the beginning, its political programme actually laid the foundation of that. As Elwin (1961) observes:

> "Its [NNC's] original political objective was to achieve local autonomy for the hills within the province of Assam and to train the people for self-government. It encluraged the Tribal Councils already set up by individual tribes and started others to administer their own local affairs and consider possible reforms."

The Naga National Council made its political aim expressed on June 19, 1946, when it submitted 'Four Point Memorandum' to the visiting British Cabinet Mission who had come specifically with the purpose to prepare the ground for granting independence to India. The four points were related to:

1. promoting solidarity among Naga tribes including those in the unadministered areas;
2. protesting against any attempt to group Assam with Bengal;
3. favouring constitutional inclusion of the Naga Hills in the autonomous Assam;
4. preparing a separate electorate for the Naga tribes.

On February 20, 1947, the NMC sent a Memorandum to Lord Mountbettan, the then Viceroy of India, for setting up an 'Interim Government' for the Nagas for a period of ten years, after which it would be left to the Naga people to choose any form of government they would like to have. But the NMC's meeting with the Members of the Sub-Committee of the Advisory Committee's on the Aboriginal tribes on May 20, 1947 at Kohima did not bear fruit because of the Committee's reluctance to accommodate the NMC's terms for the formation of the Interim Government. This was almost immediately followed by what was called 'Hydari Agreement'reached between the Government of India represented by Sri Akbar Hydari, the then Government of Assam, and the Naga National Council. But the agreement, particularly the point nine, became a bone of contention between the Government of India and NMC in their future relationships. The question of self-determination was linked up here. As A. Z. Phizo, who led the extremist group after a virtual split in the NMC on this issue, admitted later that the point nine of the Hydari Agreement "was not a clear promise of self-determination" (Quoted in Nibedan, 1993). Nothing short of self-determination was acceptable to the minority group led by Phizo, who also took the stand that the Nagas should be left outside the Indian Union once the British completely withdrew from India. The Naga National Council moved quickly along the extreme line of action and declared Naga National Independence on August 14, 1947. The Declaration was, however, not signed by nine members of NMC. The NMC was never unanimous on the issue of Naga Independence at all stages of the Declaration. Elwin (1961) quoted a Naga leader to bring into focus the different stand taken by the Nagas at various levels on the question of independence:

> "While one group of Nagas favoured immediate independence some moderated favoured the continuance of governmental relations with India in some modified form until they were sufficiently schooled in the art of running a modern state. There was a third minority which wanted to bring Nagaland into the position of a mandatory State under the British Government for a specified period of time."

But gradually the extremists among the NMC led by Phizo gained more and more control over the Council. Phizo was elected President of the NMC on December 1950. After that the movement of the Naga people for self-determination became more intense. A series of events marked by violence, clashes, killings followed. On March 22, 1956, the NMC set up the Federal Government of Nagaland and its flag was hoisted at Phesinyu, a Rengma village. A Constitution of the newly formed Naga Government, called Yehzabo, was formed and the Naga Army with its wing, Naga Home Guards was inducted. But, side by side, assassinations of those who opposed the movement were carried out. There were those moderate Nagas, who had taken a middle path between the conflicting parties—the NMC and Government of India. An 'All Tribes Naga People's Convention' held at Kohima from August 22 to 26, 1957 took a resolution pleading for a negotiated settlement of the Naga problem and another resolution advocating the creation of a single administrative unit consisting of the Naga Hills District of Assam and the Tuensang Frontier Division of NEFA under the External Affairs Ministry (Elwin, 1961). The second Naga People's Convention held in Unkma village near Mokokchung on May 21 – 23, 1958 appointed a Liaison Committee to 'explore possibilities for an agreed solution of the Naga problems'. Later 16-Point Memorandum for the constitution of a separate state to be called 'Nagaland' within the Indian Union was drafted and passed with little modifications in the third Naga People's Convention held at Mokokchung from October 22 to 26, 1959. The NMC althrough opposed this agreement. But despite the creation of a Nagaland state, the incidences of violence and hostilities went on unabated. A Peace Mission was launched under the aegis of Naga Baptist Churches on February 24, 1964. The formation of the Peace Misson was agreed upon by both the Indian Government and the so-called Federal Government of Nagaland. A cease-fire was declared from September 6, 1964. Successive talks failed to break the deadlock. More assassinations and clashes followed, but efforts to work out a compromise formula also continued. All of these culminated into signing the Shillong Accord in 1975.The signing of the Accord also resulted in a split of the NMC into NNC and NSCN. The National Socialist Council of Nagaland (NSCN) was formally launched in 1980, which was also split into two – NSCN (Isac-Muivah) and NSCN (Khaplang). Although the NSCN (IM) has wider network and greater area of operation, the other unit is also successful in keeping its existence in tact, thereby complicating the Naga problem. The conflicts among the various Naga underground organization had a telling effect on the overground Naga populace, which had very little to get enthused over.

At present, the Naga nationalists representing different underground organizations have one goal, that is, national independence or sovereignty of Naga homeland (*Nagalim*, as it is called now). The Naga nationalists consider their movement to be essentially political in nature having socio-cultural, economic dimensions. Self-determination is only a step in the direction of attaining sovereignty. But in view of factional representation of nationalists, the main issue seems to be self-representation. Side by side, it has to be admitted that the Naga 'self' is a truncated one, its representation being different among different tribes. There was hardly anything like the Naga 'self' in the past. What they have today is an imposed one necessitating the creation of a strong nationalistic feeling, which could overshadow intertribal differences. There is, however, no surity that these differences would be completely obliterated in course of time. After all, the image of the 'self', when created and imposed on groups, each striving to maintain its separate identity, can generate internal counflicts of a greater intensity. Sometime back, Vihuto Yepthomi, Secretary of the Naga Ho Ho, the apex body of the Nagas, predicted the worst if "unification among the different underground facilities do not come soon" (The Statesman, 18 August, 1999). It needs to be mentioned here that the Naga Ho Ho has been trying to unite all Naga underground organizations. The killing of Dathy Mungro, the NSCN-Khaplang General Secretary and 'Prime Minister' of the so called 'Governement of the People's Republic of Nagaland' (Khaplang group), was indicative of the fact that Yepthemi's fear was not unfounded. No doubt, with Mungro's killing the Naga Ho Ho's move to unify the Naga underground outfits had received a jolt. Even Yepthemi himself was said to have been roughed up by the cadres of the 'Federal Government of Nagaland' (NSCN-IN group) a day after the killing of Mungro. The bitter struggle for gaining political control with the purpose of creating a new 'ethnic category' could lead to a situation when the process of restoration of the 'self' takes a backseat. The purpose of individuals at the helm of power structure and different factional groups may be one—to create new institutions and set up new normative values to give expression to their identity. But it is difficult to bring in uniformity in this endeavour since those who dictate terms are hardly in a position to combine meaningfully the aggregations of lived and living experience with terminal identities cutting across all social contexts and situations. It is too early to revise the opinion even after the latest round of talks of the Government of India representatives with the NSCN leaders Muivah and Isac Su in Delhi and Bangkok. The underground outfits have now come to realise the need for all of them to stand united. They have started voicing their opinion in this regard with more conviction and sense of purpose. However, the differences still remain, which surface at the slightest provocation. Beside the two factions of NSCN, three more Naga underground outfits are also active. There are 'Federal Government of Nagaland', 'Naga National Council' and 'Naga National League for Democracy', which is based in Delhi and which, of late, has decided to merge with 'Naga youth Organization' of Myanmar. But the Myanmar-based organization is more concerned with lack of democratic rights in Myanmar than with the problems of Nagaland. There has also been reports of the formation of a new outfit in the name of 'Reformation Army of Nagaland' by the Naga youth.

Like the 'Naga', 'Bodo' or 'Boro' is a generic term referring to the plains-dwelling tribals of Assam, mainly concentrated on the north bank of the Brahmaputra. For quite some time, different Bodo organizations have been trying for an upgraded political status either in the form of a full-fledged state or an independent Bodoland. While the moderate groups are prepared to settle for statehood, the hardcore extremist groups would not accept anything less than sovereignty. The first political organization–the Plains Tribal Council of Assam, was set up in 1967 with regional autonomy as its main demand. Seven years later the demand was upgraded with union territory status. The movement was ultimately shelved. The PTCA leaders later forged an alliance with the Janata Party, which helped two of its leaders, Vice President Samar Brahma Chaudhury and General Secretary Charan Narzary to make it to the Assam Assembly and Lok Sabha respectively. This, however, affected the movement in as much as the demand for union territory status was withdrawn and the leaders reverted to the regional autonomy. Another organization, the Plains Tribal Council of Assam (Progressive) was formed in 1979. Two years before that, the All Bodo Students Union parted company with the PTCA. Initially, it made attempts to unify the PTCA and PTCA (P). In 1984, the PTCA (P) was dissolved and a new body called 'the United Tribal Nationalist Liberation' came into being demanding creation of tribal land with union territory status. Meanwhile, ABSU came out with a charter of demands which included, among other things, creation of a separate homeland for the Bodos on the north bank of Brahmaputra, creation of autonomous district councils for Rabhas and Lalungs in the tribal areas on the south bank and inclusion of Bodo Kacharis of Karbi Anglong district in the list of scheduled tribes (hills). Obviously, ABSU was trying to play the tribal card and extend its operational area by bringing other allied tribal groups within its fold. During that time the Bodo political movement started showing signs of aggressive militancy. At one stage the ABSU leadership passed into the hands of the militant group. But it is only with the formation of 'the Bodo People's Action Committee' that the homeland movement of the Bodos started gaining momentum. In mid-eighties the Bodo extremist youths formed an underground organization and named it 'Bodo Security Force'. Soon the Bodo militancy reached its height with 'the National Defence Force of Bodoland' (NDFB) spearheading the movement. The NDFB has been struggling to establish a sovereign Bodo nation outside the Indian Union. It was at loggerheads with the 'People's Democratic Front' (PDF), which was in favour of Bodoland within the framework of Indian Constitution. Sometime back the outfits had decided to temporarily bury the hatchet to work together to achieve their goals. But with goals remaining different, it is still doubtful whether such an arrangement could ensure a lasting impact. Moreover, the Bodo movement has created chain reactions among the neighbouring smaller tribal groups striking discordant note in the present situation. The recently formed *'Sanmilito Janaghostiy Sangram Samiti'* representing eighteen non-Bodo groups has expressed its opposition to the creation of the Bodo Territorial Council (BTC) for which the Bodo Liberation Tigers, the extremist Bodo group were involved in negotiations with the Centre (The Telegraph, August 13, 2002). Subsequently, an agreement was reached with the Government of Assam for granting full autonomus status to Bodo-inhabited areas. The agreement on Bodo autonomy notwithstanding, one cannot but remember the fact that the Bodo Liberation Tigers, a constituent of the NDFB, were engaged in carrying out subversive activities and making daring raids into government installations and human targets for more than a decade. The two groups have now fallen apart, with the NDFB stiking to the position of complete sovereignty. A section of the Bodo leadership still maintains that the Bodo problem is not a socio-economic but a political one. In reality, Bodo leadership, which is more factional than unified in nature, has always been on a quandary on the question of the exact nature of devolution of power to be brought into effect. It cannot be said that the present agreement is a foolproof one. One is also not sure whether there is enough room for the Bodo 'self' to get fully expressed here. Moreover, merely making changes in the political equation and power-based structure without seriously addressing to socio-economic ills will hardly be able to bring real benefits to the people. As it appears, operationalising a power structure with greater political control at the regional level may not have equal impact on all sections of the population.

While dealing with concrete case of self-determination involving tribal and indigenous groups, one gathers the impression that self-determination carries with it a lot of clout in the form of factional power groups competing for politiical control and domination. In such a situation it is probably necessary to look into the 'self' as it is perceived and projected at the basic group level and not as it is manipulated and imposed by the hardcore on the common people. The task is, however, far from easy. Another point of significance is the working of a long-term moral allegiance in the tribal system which transcends changing political developments. The power game of politics is centered around short-term gainful ties, whereas a long-term social relationship involves a moral commitment. But there is no guarantee that 'the roles of the polity' will always remain clearly differentiated from the social roles. Already there are indications that in North-East Indian situation pertaining to some tribes and other communities, 'the pattern of individual attitudes and orientations toward politics is increasingly taking the form of a long-term moral commitment. The people have started relying more on their 'political culture' where 'the attainment of power' is given a social expression. In that case, the gap between perceived and projected self may sound more unreal than hitherto thought to be. Self-determination will then appear to be a more meaningful exercise to the people in question. Even then, it is doubtful whether it will really be possible for the leaders of such movements to avoid altogether internal crisis situations likely to be created as a result of their rather uncertain support base at present and imperfect nature of the political institutional guarantees – the guarantees which are required to assuage security fears of the common people.

Only when a movement gets the wholehearted support of the common people, the question of security may be overshadowed by the depth of emotion involved in the issue. The agitation launched by the working committee of 32 organizations of Manipur against the Indian Army on the alleged custodial rape and killing of Th. Manorama and the killing of paster Khongsai may be an example of such an emotional outburst. But no people can draw sustenance from such on event for an unlimited period of time, unless it invokes concrete issues of substance of far-reaching consequence.

REFERENCES

Barth, Fredrik, 1969. "*Introduction.*" In Fredrik Barth (ed.). *Ethnic Groups and Boundaries: The Social Organisation of Culture Difference. London:* Allen & Unwin.

Campbell, John R & Rew, Allan (eds.) 1999. *Identity and Affect: Experiences of Identity in a Globalising World.* London: Pluto Press.

Chen, Lung-Chu. 1976. "*Self-determination as a Human Right*". In M. Reisman and B. Weston (eds.) *Toward World Order and Human Dignity.* New York: Free Press.

Cohen, Abner. 1974. *Two-dimensional Man: An Eassy on the Anthropology of Power and Symbolism in Complex Societies.* London: Routledge & Kegan Paul.

Cohen, Abner. 1981. *The Politics of Elite Culture.* Burkeley. University of California Press.

Danda, A.K. *et al* (eds.). 1998, *North-East India: Ethno-cultural Perspectives and Process.* Calcutta: The Indian Anthropological Society.

Elwin, Vernien. 1961. *Nagaland.* Shillong: Research Deptt., Advisor's Secretariat.

Eriksen, Thomas Hylland. 1995. *Small Places, Large Issues.* London: Pluto Press.

Eriksen, Thomas Hylland. 1993. *Ethnicity and Nationalism : Anthropological Perspectives,* London: Pluto Press.

Gellner, Ernet. 1983. *Nations and Nationalism.* Oxford: Blackwell.

Haaland, Gunnar. *1969. Economic Determinants in Ethnic Processes.* In Fredrik Barth (ed). *Ethnic Groups and Boundaries: The Social Organisation of Culture Difference,* Oslo : Scandinavian University Press.

Lama, I. B. 1999. *One step forward, two steps back. In The Statesman.* April 16, Calcutta.

Lewis, I. M. 1988 (1976). *Social Anthropology in Perspective : The Relevance of Social Anthropology :* Cambridge et al: Cambridge University Press.

Raha, M. K. & Ghosh, A. K. (eds.) 1998. *North-East India: The Human Interface.* New Delhi: Gyan Publishing House.

Roy, Ajoy. 1995. *The Boro Imbroglio.* Guwahati, Spectrum Publications.

Sahlins, Marshall D. 1976. *Culture and Practical Reason.* Chicago. Aldine.

Vashum, R. 1996a. "*Self-determination: Principles, Meanings and Practices*". *Indian Anthropologist.* Vol. 26:1; June 1996. Delhi: Indian Anthropological Association.

Vashum, R. 1998. *Nagas and the Question of Self-Determination : An Anthropological Historical Perspective.* A Ph.D. Thesis submitted to the University of Delhi (unpublished).

12

On the Movements for Autonomy and Statehood in North-East India

DEBNARAYAN MODAK

North-East India was always in the throes of tension and turmoil and the demands for statehood and/or autonomy were and are being raised every now and then by the different sections of the people living in the region. A closer scrutiny would reveal that although the demands for statehood and even the urge for separation were there in certain parts of the north-east region at the time of independence, the major parts of it were incorporated in the state of Assam while giving different degrees of autonomy to some areas. When the States Reorganisation Commission was formed in 1950s in view of the widespread demand for linguistic states, several memoranda were placed before the Commission, particularly by the hill peoples, for consideration of their demand for statehood. However, the Commission did not favour those, and as a result, the demand for separate statehood got intensified in certain areas which gradually paved the way for the emergence of 'seven sisters' in the region. Even after carving out of four states, *viz*, Nagaland, Arunachal Pradesh, Meghalaya and Mizoram, which formed parts of Assam at the time of independence, Assam still remained 'a museum of nationalities' and the demand for statehood and autonomy continued to rock the state over the years.

The present paper seeks to analyse the developments that led to the reorganisation of North-East India and formation of some small/ hill states in the region. In this connection, it deals with the experience relating to the implementation of the *Sixth Schedule* of the Constitution, which includes different kinds of institutional innovations like autonomous councils and the creation of a 'state within a state' for meeting half-way the aspirations for autonomy of different sections of people in the area. Besides the demand for statehood which were sanctioned over the years, the paper also summarises those that remained unfulfilled and particularly those which are very prominent today, to understand the very nature of the identity crisis being faced by the people of the region. Hence an overview of the movements for autonomy and statehood in the North-East region of the country may help one to go into the roots of the problem that rocks not only the North-East but the different parts of the country every now and then, and also to find out the clues towards its solution.

The consideration of the colonial rule in North-East India took a long time, especially since different areas came under British rule at different times. The Assam plains were acquired in 1826, Cachar plains in 1830, Khasi Hill in 1833, Jaintia plains in 1835, Karbi Anglong in 1838, North Cachar in 1854, the Naga Hill during 1866—1904, Garo Hills in 1872-73, and the Lushai Hills in 1890. Assam itself had to go through a lengthy granulating period before emerging as a nodel point in the administration of North-East India. However, the British always treated the area around Assam that were brought under their administration on a separate footing at different points of time. And for the purpose, one after another, legal and administrative decisions were taken between 1974 and 1935 recognising the separate and distinct identities of various areas in the North-East.[1]

Initially, the different areas of the North-East region, including Assam, which were annexed by the British authorities, formed parts of the Bengal Presidency and this was continued till 1874 when Assam was carved out of it. Assam was again merged with the newly created province of 'East Bengal' in 1905 after the 'partition' of Bengal to form the province of "East Bengal and Assam". The state of Assam as a separate province was, however, restored after the annulment of 'partition' in 1911. Although the tribal areas occupied by the British rulers in the region, formed parts of the province of Assam, those were accorded special administrative status by the British authorities.

The British efforts to isolate the hills from the plains was first made in the Bengal Eastern Frontier Regulations 1873, (better known as Inner Line Regulations) which prohibited entry of all British subjects in the area within *Inner Line* without proper permits issued by a competent authority. The inhabitants of the areas living outside the *Inner Line* could not have property rights or business interests without the sanction of the government. The regulation was applicable to the districts of Kamrup, Darrang, Nowgong, Sibsagar, Lakhimpur, Garo Hills, Khasi and Jaintia Hills, Cachar and Chittagong Hills.[2] The policy was pursued with such rigidity that even the national independence movement could not reach into those areas. Subsequently, a considerable part of the North-East was declared backward area as per Government of India Act, 1919. This was advised by Montague-Chelmsford Report of 1917. The Government of India Act of 1935 and the declaration of *Excluded* and *Partially Excluded Areas* were the result of the report of the Simon Commission. The *Excluded Areas* included Naga Hills, Lushi Hills, North Cachar Hills and North-East Frontier (Sadiya, Balipara and Lakhimpur) Tracts; and *Partially Excluded Areas* covered Garo Hills, Mikir Hills and British portion of Khasi Jaintia Hills.[3]

The attempts of isolating the hills from the plains of North-East was further made by certain British officials like Robert Neil Reid, the Governor of Assam, to get a Crown Colony to be carved out of the hill areas including the North-East Frontier Tracts, Naga Hills, Mizo Hills, Chittagong Hill Tracts etc. J. H. Hutton, Deputy Commissioner of Naga Hill District, J.P. Mills, Advisor to the Governor, and others subscribed to the idea. The plan of separation was again revised in 1941 when some British officials wanted to carve out *North-East Frontier Province* comprising the hill areas of North-East India and Burma under British protection. Andrew Clow, Governor of Assam and Sir Reginald Coupland favoured the formation of *Crown Colony* comprising hills of North-East India and Burma. Coupland took pains to point out the similarities in race and culture of the hill peoples and emphasised their differences with the Indians.[4] In fact, the British authorities did their utmost to protect their interests in the region and to keep the nationalist influence out of the tribal areas by encouraging their isolation from the rest.

It was in the mid-1940s, when India was approaching her independence, the future of the region was debated afresh. The Cabinet Mission suggested the formation of an Advisory Committee on the rights of citizens, minorities and tribals and *Excluded Areas*. Accordingly, the Constituent Assembly formed a committee under the chairmanship of

Vallabhbhai Patel on 24 January 1947 to look into the matter. The committee appointed a subcommittee known as *North East Frontier Tribal and Excluded Areas Committeee* with Gopinath Bordoloi, the Chief Minister of Assam (then called the Prime Minister), as its chairman. It co-opted two members from each hill district except the Frontier Tracts.[5]

At the time of transfer of power in 1947, the region consisted of: (1) the province of Assam comprising (a) Brahmaputra Valley districts: Goalpara, Kamrup, Nowgong, Darrang, Sibsagar, Lakhimpur; (b) Surma Valley districts: Cachar, Sylhet; (c) Hill districts: Garo Hills, United Khasi and Jaintia Hills, Naga Hills, Lushai Hills; (2) the North-East Frontier Tracts comprising: (a) Balipara frontier tract later divided into Kameng Frontier Division and Subansiri Frontier Division; (b) Abhor Hills District later renamed Siang Frontier Division; (c) Mishmi Frontier District later renamed Lohit Frontier Division; (d) Tirap Frontier Division; (e) Tuensang Frontier Division, and (3) the Princely states of (a) Manipur; (b) Tripura, and (c) Khasi states.[6]

The Muslim—dominated areas of the Sylhet district were, however, transferred to erstwhile East Pakistan (now Bangladesh). The remaining eight thanas of the district, which formed the Karimganj district now, were merged with the Cachar district. A portion of the Dooars area, which was taken away from Bhutan after the Bhutanese war by the British, was transferred back to that country as per decision of the Assam Legislative Assembly and Parliament.[7]

The issue of the administrative reorganisation of North-East India was debated in the Constituent Assembly particularly after the submission of the *Bordoloi Committee Report.* The Committee, after visiting the tribal areas, noted that, unlike other parts of India where tribals had assimilated themselves to a great extent with the life and culture of plainsmen, the process of assimilation was minimal in the interior of the Assam hills, particularly in the Naga and Lushai hills; that the tribesmen in North-East were very sensitive about their land, forests, system of judiciary and that they should be left free from any fear of exploitation or domination by the advanced sections of the people. The Committee recommended *Autonomous Districts and Regional Councils* providing adequate safeguards to the tribals in respect of their land, social customs and usages, language and culture.[8]

After much debates and discussions, however, special provisions were made under the *Sixth Schedule* of the Constitution for the administration of hill triabal areas. Accordingly, the tribal areas were no longer termed as *Excluded* and *Partially Excluded Areas*, but were specified in two parts, A and B, in the *Table* appended to the Sixth Schedule of the Constitution. The United Khasi-Jaintia Hills district (which included 18 tiny Khasi states which acceded to India), the Garo Hills District, the Lushai Hills district, the Naga Hills district, the North Cachar Hills and the Mikir Hills were placed in *Part A* and the North-East Frontier Tracts including Balipara Frontier Tract, Tirap Frontier Tract, Abhor Hills district and Mishmi Hills district and Naga Tribal Area in *Part B*. While *Part A* areas formed the *Autonomous Districts* and their *District Councils* and were administered by the Government of Assam, the *Part B* areas were administered by the Government of Assam acting at his discretion as an *agent* to the President. The *Autonomous districts* had representation in the Assam legislature and also in the Parliament.[9]

A closer study of the *Sixth Schedule* of the Constitution reveals that at virtually re-enacted the provisions of the Government of India Act 1935, as they applied to *Excluded* and *Partially Excluded Areas* and granted the latter even greater degree of autonomy. During the reading of the draft Constitution, the *Sixth Schedule* attracted stringent criticism. Some members complained that the hill areas of Assam were given "too much"; a few others, the Rev. J. J. M. Nichols Roy, a Khasi leader and a member of the Bordoloi panel being among them, thought that they were not given "enough". As the chairman of the subcommittee, Gopinath Bordoloi strongly justified the introduction of the *Sixth Schedule* in the hill areas. Two influential members of the Constituent Assembly from Assam, Rohini Kumar Chaudhuri and Kuladhar Chaliha, however, strongly opposed the *Schedule*. In Chandhmi's opinion, "the autonomous district was a weapon whereby steps were taken to keep the tribal people away from the non-tribals", while Chaliha saw "the British mind" behind the proposal to maintain the separatist tendency and warned that "you will be thus creating a *tribalsthan* as you have created a Pakistan".[10]

The debates thus reflected mutual distrust and suspicion among the tribal ans non-tribal population, the seeds of which were sown by the British rulers through their policy of isolation that made interaction of the tribals and non-tribals impossible. This was compounded by the activities of foreign missionaries who have fuelled anti-Indian feelings among the tribes, though they have also contributed to the spread of education and health-care in those areas. The Constituent Assembly was aware of the special needs of the tribal people arising out of their relative isolation from the mainstream and provided for the *Sixth Schedule*, as mentioned above, to meet their urge for autonomy. But, it is to be remembered that the Sixth Schedule was framed at a time when politics in the tribal areas was still evolving and it was being manifested through the formation of Mizo Union (1946), Garo National Council (1946) etc. with varying demands from autonomous statehood to independence. Hence, the provisions of the *Sixth Schedule* could not satisfy their urge for *autonomy* and ominous signs were visible from the very day the *District Councils* were inaugurated. Although the *District Councils* were formed in all other hill districts, it could not be constituted for the Naga Hills as the Nagas boycotted the election to the Council. While a section of them demanded full statehood, several others stood for independence of Nagaland.

In 1947, the Naga National Council (NNC) leader, A. Z. Phizo, proclaimed an independent Nagaland and organised an insurgency which assumed menacing proportions in the late 1950s. Meanwhile, on 20 February 1950 the NNC decided to hold a plebiscite on the question of being independent or remaining in India. On 16 May 1951 it was ultimately held. The NNC showed a remarkable organising ability through a total boycott of the general elections of 1952 in which the Naga district was allotted three seats in the Assam Assembly. On 22 March 1956 the NNC founded the Naga Federal Government and proclaimed *inter alia* the 'Nagaland' as people's sovereign republic.[11]

Although the situation was not so grave in any other parts of the North-East, it was very much apparent that the scheme for autonomy as envisaged in the *Sixth Schedule* as the process of its impkementation, was not acceptable to many of the hill tribes.The appointment of States Reorganisation Commission (SRC) in the wake of the growing demand for linguistic states in the other parts of the country in 1953, gave them an impetus to rise to the occasion and the regional aspirations in different areas of the North-East thus gathered momentum. In early 1954, a Cachar States Reorganisation Committee was formed, and in a strongly worded memorandum to the SRC, it declared :

> With the Cachar and Lushai Hills districts in despair under Assam, with the Nagas in revolt and effectively defying Assam's authority in every sphere, with Manipur and Tripura refusing to be the *Cinderallas* in a state...the only positive course left open to the Commission is, in our view, to suggest a separate administrative unit for these areas.[12]

The *Purbachal state*—as the proposed state was called—would also cover the North-East Frontier Agency (NEFA) and be a 'heterogenous one' with two divisions : (i) Cachar, Tripura, the Lushai Hills and Manipur in one, and (ii) NEFA and Nagaland in the other. However, the idea, smacking of a kind of Bengali dominance, could not appeal to the hill peoples. Tripura and Manipur also demanded full statehood.[13]

Attempts were also made to work out a new proposal for a separate hill state for the 'Autonomous Districts of Assam' through negotiations among the representatives of *Autonomous Districts* held in Shillong on 16-17 June 1954 and also in Assam Hill Tribal Leaders' Conference held at Tura in the Garo Hills on 6-8 October 1954.[14] SRC, however, rejected all those demands and was very categorical in its observation:

> . . . we have come to the conclusion that the formation of a hill state in this region is neither feasible nor in the interest of the tribal peoples themselves. The hill districts, therefore, should continue to form part of Assam and no major changes should be made in their present constitutional pattern.[15]

As regards the deman for a *Purbachal State*, the SRC was of opinion that the formation of such a state could not be an appropriate remedy for the grievances of the minorities, if any, and it might mean only that 'one set of problem is exchanged for another'.[16] The Commission further suggested the merger of Tripura with Assam by providing adequate safeguards in respect of language and culture of the Bengalees living there.[17] It favoured Manipur to continue 'to be a centrally administered territory for the time being' and foresaw its merger with the adjoining State of Assam. The States Reorganisation Act 1956, which was adopted after detailed discussion in Parliament, made no change in the boundary of the State of Assam. It, however, accorded Manipuir and Tripura the status of Union Territories.[18]

Being disappointed at the outcome of the exercises of the SRC, the movements for autonomy and statehood and even separation were intensified in different parts of the region, of which Nagas remained in the forefront. They went ahead with their insurgent activities, with their demand for independence. However, sober Naga voices started being heard very soon and a section of Naga population realized that the campaign by violence might prove futile for paving the path of indepencdence. It facilitated negotiations at the political levels, and, as a result, a Union Territory, named *Naga Hills and Tuensung Area (NHTA)* was formed on 1 August 1957 by merging the Naga Hills district of Assam—Tuensung division of NEFA. The advancement of the Nagas emboldened others who were aspirants for autonomy and separation, and the fuel was further added to the fire with the attempt to impose Assamese language on the non-Assamese-speaking peoples.

Indeed, the 1960 autumn session of the Assam Legislative Assembly provides a clue to understanding the dynamics of the North-East politics in the 1960s and 1970s that ultimately led to the political amputations of Assam. On 10 October 1960 when the Assam Official Language Bill was moved, there was an unprecedented polarisation of diverse non-Assamese communities both inside and outside the Assembly. Along with the MLAs from the Khasi-Jaintia-Garo-Mizo Hills and Cachar, the MLAs from the North Cachar Hills too opposed the spirit and contents of the Bill.[19] Nowhere in India had the language been so contentious a political issue as was in Assam. In fact, the single-most notable feature of the entire history of twentieth century Assam has been the fear of the Assamese community of the Bengal domination. The attempt to make the Assamese as the sole official language reflected this sentiment. But such feelings caused not only the lingual riots in different parts of Assam, but also accounted for many other serious developments in this multi-ethnic state. Besides the protests of the Bengalis, it also alienated the already estranged hill people who had also apprehended the suppression of their languages and cultures in Assam. The Bodos and other plains-tribes also joined the protest and Assam became turbulent in early 1960s.

While the Nagas were preparing themselves for complete statehood, Mizos were consolidating their strength through philanthropic activities among the victims of a great famine or *mautam* that engulfed the Mizo Hills during 1956-61. The Mizo National Famine Front, which was initially a voluntary organisation, having changed its name to the Mizo National Front (MNF) in 1961 after the famine was over, now came forward with the object of attaining independence for the Mizo Hills. Again, the formation of All Party Hill Leaders' Conference (APHLC) on 2 November, 1960 to fight for a hill state by peaceful and constitutional means, added a new dimension to the history of Assam at that critical juncture. It demanded the creation of a *North East Frontier State* comprising the tribal areas of Assam, Manipur and Tripura. It rejected the Scottish Plan—a loose federation with some autonomy—offered by the Government of India on the basis of its discussion with the APHLC leaders during 1960-62. The proposed statutory council which was just like the earlier Advisory Council, could not satisfy them. A revised proposeal, called the *Nehru Plan* was also mooted to dissuade the feelings of the tribal people. The Pataskar commission was appointed to work out the details in this regard. But when the demand for complete statehood was granted to the Nagas and Nagaland became the sixteenth State of the Indian Union on 1 December 1963 the floodgates of the demands for formation of smaller states were opened wide and the Government at the centre had to come forward with its proposal for reorganisation of the North-East India. The development, again, led to the attempts by various groups to assert their socio-economic identities by demanding the formation of separate states not only in the hills but also in the Brahmaputra Valley.

The most striking reaction of the development was that of the Ahoms in upper Assam, who ruled Assam for nearly 600 years and accepted the Assamese language. On 28 May, 1967, in a meeting of the representatives of the Ahoms held at Gargaon, the capital of the Ahom King, a resolution was adopted demanding 'a separate autonomous unit of upper Assam'; and a year later the demand was converted into one of separate state. Besides such a demand for *Ahomland* or the like, there was also a demand for *Udayachal State* by the Bodo-Kachari tribes in Assam. Geographically it was expected to comprise the northern parts of the Lakhimpur, Goalpara, Kamrup and Darrang districts of Assam. The leadership of the movement was in the hands of a tribal political organisation, called the 'Plains Tribal Council of Assam' (PTCA).[20]

As regards the development of the APHLC, it can be said that it represented somewhat a pack of a loose movement for the creation of a hill state comprising most of the hill areas of Assam. However, the ethnic, religious and cultural differences even among the hill peoples proved too strong to keep the movement together and in a few years what was left of it, was a common platform of Khasi and Garo leadership. The Mizos were the first to leave the APHLC which also lost its following in the Mikir and North Cachar Hills.[21] Manipur and Tripura were very keen to get the status of a full-fledged state. While the APHLC opted for peaceful and constitutional means to achieve their goals, the Mizos preferred violent activities. On 28 February 1966, the MNF organised a revolt and attacked the government treasury and other establishments in the district. However, the disturbances were quelled with the help of the security forces. Thus,the North-East was in a state of flux when the Government of India was going ahead with its plan for administrative reorganisation of the region.

Before accomplishing the task of reorganisation, the government at the centre, however, made an experiment with the idea of creation of sub-states to meet halfway the autonomy urges of the hill people without disintegrating the State of Assam. This idea of a "State within the State" envisaged the formation of Federated States of Assam including hill states, Manipur, Tripura and, if possible, NEFA, guaranteeing equal status for the fedrating units. Although this plan was abandoned shortly, the Government of India went ahead with the idea to implement it in a limited sphere by constituting and autonomous State of Meghalaya within the State of Assam comprising the districts of Garo Hills and United Khasi and Jaintia Hills. Parliament enacted the Assam Reorganization (Meghalaya) Act 1969 following the 22nd Amendment of the Constitution of India and it was brought into force on 2 April 1970. The most important feature of the Meghalaya Act (Act 55 of 1969) was that it created a new tier in India's state structure—'a State within a State'—similar to the autonomous republics of the former USSR.[22]

The formation of 'a State within the State' in Meghalaya, did not, however, settle the problems of the North-East, and the Government of India had undertaken a fresh scheme of the reorganisation of the entire region. Accordingly, the North-Eastern Areas (Reorganisation) Act 1971 was adopted, which provided for the establishment of the States of Manipur and Tripura and formation of the State of Meghalaya and of the Union Territories of Mizoram and Arunachal Pradesh.[23] The formation of these States and Union Territories was also followed by the creation of the *North Eastern Council* (NEC) to co-ordinate and expedite the developmental activities in the entire region, Subsequently, Mizoram and Arunachal Pradesh too attained statehood in 1986 and 1987 respectively. The fact of the promotion of Lushai Hill district to the State of Mizoram had elements common to the formation of Nagaland in the sense that in both cases carving out of the States were followed by insurgent activities, demands for secession and complete independence. Contrarily, the transition of NEFA to the State of Arunachal Pradesh was peaceful and guided by, among other reasons, the strategic necessity as it borders with the sensitive boundary of China.

The administrative reorganisation of the North-East India along with the formation of NEC as its regional planning and development organisation, is often regarded as an advance towards political settlement of the unrest in the hills and their integration with the polity although the NEC could not bring about permanent peace thereby. Apart from the border disputes between differnt states in the region, the movements for autonomy and/or separarte statehood or the assertions of different cultutal-linguistic and tribal identy continued to rock the region even after its reconstitution. The Karbi-Dimasa movement for an autonomous statehood since 1973 and the renewal of the movement for Bodoland from 1980s onward are very pertinent examples in this regard. Again, the Assam movement of 1979—85, which primarily aimed at ensuring the cultural-linguistic identy of the Assamese people in the face of the massive influx of immigrants from neighbouring Indian states and Bangladesh as well as the fall-out effects of it in its aftermath, though not strictly fall within the scope of the present essay, may be cited as the other instance.

When the proposal for reorganisation of Assam and the granting of statehood to Meghalaya was in the process, four MLAs from the North Cachar and Mikir Hills jointly issued a statement demanding separate statehood for the people of the area. They refused the proposal for inclusion of the area in the proposed State of Meghalaya due to inter-ethnic differences. However, the prople of the area could be persuaded at that time to accept the formation of a separate *Autonomous* District for them along with the assurance of providing proper facilities for development. But with the decision of the Guwahati and Dibrugarh Universities in 1972 to make the Assamese language as the sole medium of instruction at college education, the inhabitants of Mikir and North Cachar Hills gradullay became estranged and felt that the separation from Assam was the only solution. They formed an Action Committee of the *Mikir and North Cachar Hill Leadrs' Conference* and submitted a memorandum to the Prime Minister on 9 June 1973, in which, besides the issue of language, they raised economic issues to establish the point that the assurances given to them earlier were not being implemented. Again, on 24 November 1980 the Action Committee of the newly formed *Karbi-Anglong and North Cachar Hills Separate State Demands Committee* submitted another memorandum to the Prime Minister reiterating their earlier stand. In January 1982 another memorandum was submitted by yet another *Karbi-Anglong and North Cachar Hill State Demands Committee* asking for a full fledged separate state. But the emergence or the *Peoples 'Democratic Front'* which gave rise to the *Autonomous State Demand Committee* (ASDC) in May 1986 was the turning point as it was for the first time that a mass-based prolonged movement was attempted to realise the demand for statehood. The massive victory of ASDC securing 22 out of 26 seats in the election to the *Autonomous District Council* held on 7 January 1989 reflected the victory of the movement.[24] This trend continued even in the 1991 elections to the Lok Sabha and Assam Legislative Assembly. Being strengthened with the popular mandate, the ASDC tried to exert more autonomy in the *Autonomous District Council* and the conflict between the State government and the Council became inevitable. Although in July 1992 greater autonomy was given to the Council, soon it was superseded on the charges of 'gross financial irregularities'. The ASDC, again, got involved into a prolonged movement till a Tripartite Agreement was made in April, 1995. Subsquently, however, the movement was diffused with the growing inter-ethnic differences as well as the emergence of several organisations having different viewpoints, and the prospect of peace thus became a remote possibility in these two districts.[25]

As regards the movement of the Bodos, it can be said that the Plains Tribals Council of Assam (PTCA) since it inception in 1967, as already stated, has been demanding the state of *Udayachal* which was to be carved out of Assam to cover the area of the north of the Brahmaputra. The demand, however, was pushed under the carpet when the PTCA joined the Janata Government in Assam. Later on, the initiative was taken by the *All Bodo Students' Union* (ABSU) with the slogan of sharing Assam 50:50 and creation of a new state of Bodoland for them, particularly during the tenure of the AGP government in the State (1986-90). The movement initially followed the moderate menthods like *bandhs, dharnas* etc., but from 1989 onwards it took a violent turn and invited severe government repression. Very soon differences cropped up in its ranks and fatricidal strife took place in different areas. Added to this was the clashes between the Bodos and non-Bodos that arose during the course of the movement. The differences among various Bodo groups and those between Bodos and non-Bodos gave rise to different organisational set-ups highlighting some of the basic problems of the Bodo people.[26] However, the signing of the *Bodo Accord* on 20 February 1993, paved the way for the formation of Bodoland Autonomous Council (BAC). But the future of the BAC remained uncertain due to the controversy over its jurisdiction and consequent differences of opinion between and among the various Bodos and non-Bodo groups.

A close scrutiny of the movements for autonomy/statehood in the North-East area under study would reveal that there are significant differences in their goals and strategies. While some of the movements like those of the Nagas and the Mizos demanded complete sovereignty, others were organised for attaining different degrees of autonomy up to the level of separate statehood within the Indian Union. Again, when sections of the Naga and the Mizo people resorted to violent struggles against the Indian state to achieve their goals, some others, particularly the movements in the hill state of Karbi-Anglong, distinguished themselves by their exemplary use of peaceful means. Of course, there were movements which were more or less peaceful at the initial stage but took violent turn afterwards. The common feature, however, in all these movements was the assertion of identity by different ethnic and cultural linguistic groups motivated by the fear of socio-economic and cultural domination and guided by the urge for security and development for themselves through carving out autonomous structures and/or separation.

Although different socio-economic, political and cultural-linguistic reasons, specific to respective movements, may be attributed to the growing sense of mutual distrust and consequent expression of separatism, the 'development synodrome' has been proved to be the single-most important reason for the eruption of ethnic troubles in the region. Indeed, the region not only lags far behind some of the other Indian states both industrially and commercially, it also lacks the basic infrastructural facilities needed for the development of trade and commerce. Apart from continued economic stagnation which given rise to large scale unemployment in both urban and rural sectors, a continuous and massive influx of 'land-hungry' peasants from the erstwhile East Pakistan and, now Bangladesh, has resulted in serious pressure on the cultivable land in the Brahmaputra and Barak valleys. This has made the situation worse and provided a very fertile soil for assertions of ethnic identities.[27]

The 'quest for identity' particularly among the hill peoples and tribals may be understood with reference to the emergence of middle class elements in the community, who acquired western education in greater numbers than many or their plains neighbours. They now come to put forward their claim of equality both in the sphere of economic opportunities in respect to employment and enterprise, and in that of political status. What is very much interesting to note in this connection is that, although this class has adopted a modern life-style and has often been at odds with the traditional power structure prevalent in tribal society, it assumes the leadership of the autonomy movements and has become the spokesperson for the protection of tribal culture. Such an attitude of the tribal middle class can be explained only in terms of their feeling that they are being exploited economically, culturally and linguistically over the years by the non-tribals. This prompted the middle class elements among different tribal groups to raise the banner of cultural identity leading to fatricidal strifes. '*Bhumiputra*-enigma' is also the natural outcome of it. Economic grievances against the government at the centre are often mixed with the feelings of being culturally exploited by the non-tribals. The lack of proper handling of their problems by the government and the bureaucracy both at the state and the central levels have made the situation only more complex.[28]

Apart from the reasons which are specific to the region, one may also find certain root causes common to all such movements in other parts of the country too. The very nature of the capitalist development in this country, which has created unevenness both region-wise and community-wise, has given rise to mutual suspicions and ethnic discontents in almost every part of the country today. As the very nature of capitalist development is uneven and the growth of democratic consciousness is equally so, the assertions of ethnic and national awareness also take place at different times and in different forms. The smaller ethnic groups and particularly the hill peoples and tribals suffered most from the uneven development and regional disparities fostered by capitalist development. They are being denied of their basic legitimate rights and suppressed by force or by doing out some concessions to the top layers. The 'over-centralisation' of the state-structure and the lack of any clear-cut language and cultural policy of the State have only added to the growing sense of deception. It is important to note that the problems of regional disparities and resultant backwardness are not new; what is new is the perception of it and the generation of a new kind of awareness that has given birth to numerous ethnic conflicts throughout the country.

Uuless the problems are tackled at their socio-economic and cultural roots, neither state repression nor the 'politics of accords' and nor even granting of statehood in extreme cases, can provide any lasting solution to the problems as we face today in the North-East and elsewhere in India. It is now very much apparent that the creation of several new states out of composite Assam has not solved the problem of the region. Of course, the carving out of some new autonomous structure along with proper guarantee for devolution of power and their effective implementation may prove helpful as interim solution to some of the problems of the North-East. What are, however, needed most are the balanced and speedy economic development, the removal of social disparities and overall democratisation of the polity through the empowerment of the people up to the grassroots level. It presupposes not simply the amendment of the *Sixth Schedule* of the Indian Constitution but also a new vision towards the restructuring of the power relations in this country of diverse social formations and regional disparities.

REFERENCES

1. P. S. Datta, "*Autonomy in Assam : A Tale of Two hills*". *The Statesman*, Calcutta, 4 January 1990.
2. Subir Ghosh, *Frontier Travails : North East : The Polics of a Mess;* Macmillan, New Delhi 2001, p.3.
3. H. K. Barpujari, *India's North-East : Problems, Policies and Prospects: Since Independence*, Spectrum Publication, Guwahati & Delhi 1998, pp. 6-7.
4. B. B. Kumar, *Small States Syndrome in India,* Concept Publishing Company, New Delhi 1998, pp. 59-60.
5. Phawani Singh, *Politics of Alienation in Assam,* Ajanta Publications, Delhi 1984, pp. 8-9.
6. Subir Ghosh, op. cit., pp. 40-41. Also see B. B. Kumar, *Reorganisation of North East India,* Thomson Publications, New Delhi, p. 7.
7. ibid., p. 41.
8. Barpujari, op. cit, pp. 10-12.
9. S. K. Agnihotri, "*Constitutional Development in North-East India since 1947*" in b. Datta Roy and S. P. Agarwal (eds), *Reorganisation of North-East India since 1947, Concept Publishing Company*, New Delhi 1996, p. 59. Also see, Subir Ghosh, op. cit., p. 42.
10. Satic C. Kakati, "*The Sixth Schedule : Need to Review Its Working*", *The Statesman*, Calcutta, 31 August 1988. Also see, S. K. Chaube, *Hill Polities in North-East India,* Orient Longman, Patna 1999, pp. 93-114.
11. S. K. Chaube, op. cit., pp. 117-19. Also see, B. Datta Roy and S. P. Agarwal, op. cit., pp. 60-62.
12. Quoted in Chaube, op. cit., p. 12.
13. ibid, p. 121.
14. ibid., pp. 121-24.
15. Government of India, Report of the States Reorganisation Commission, 1955, Govt. of India Press, Delhi 1955, p. 188.
16. ibid., pp. 191-192.
17. ibid., p. 192.
18. ibid., pp. 196-98.
19. P. S. Datta, op. cit.

20 B. P. Sigh, *The Problem of Change : A Study of North East India,* Oxford University Press, New Delhi (pb), Second Impression. 1997, pp.100-01.

21. Baren Roy, *Socialism and Democracy with a Human Face,* Gyan Sagar Publications, New Delhi 1997, pp. 229-30.

22. B. B. Kumar, op. cit., pp. 66-73. Also see, S. K. Chaube, op. cit., p. 145.

23. "*The North Eastern Areas (Recognisation Act), 1971*" in Manilal Bose (ed.) *Historical and Constitutional Documents of North-East India,* Concept publishing Company, Delhi 1979, p. 262.

24. P. S. Datta, op. cit.

25. See for details, Tilottama Mista and Udayan Mista, "Movements for Autonomy in India's North-East" in T. V. Sathyamurthy (ed), Region, *Religion, Caste, Gender in Contemporary India* (vol. 3), Oxford University Press, New Delhi 1996, pp. 130-36. Also see, Barpujari, op. cit., pp. 101-03.

26. ibid., pp. 123-30.

27. ibid., pp. 108-09.

28. ibid., pp. 112-13. Also see, Chaube, op.cit., pp. 244-46.

13

All for a Buffalo: Events, Nature and Historiography of a Tribal Insurgency in Colonial India (1982-83)

SAJAL NAG

On 12th January 1882, a complaint was received at the newly established sub-divisional office's court at Gunjong (North Cachar, Assam).[1] The complaint was about an assault made on the plaintiff by a group of people led by one Sambhudhan for resisting the expropriation of his buffalo. The Sub-Divisional Officer C.A. Sopitt immediately issued a summon to Sambhudhan to appear before the court. But then the trouble started. It came as a surprise to the administration that no one, either from the administration or from the area, was willing to carry the summon to Sambhudhan. The Sub-Divisional Officer then sought the assistance of the Deputy Commissioner Major M.O. Boyd, who rushed to the help of the Sub-Divisional Officer. Major Boyd reached Gunjong and from there marched to Maibong, where Sambhudhan was based with a force of thirty armed policemen (15th January). Maibong was 20 miles away from Gunjong requiring six to seven hours of march, but on reaching the place, Boyd found Sambhudhan's camp deserted. Boyd decided to spend the night at Maibong before returning to Gunjong next morning. Early in the morning of the next day the police party was rudely awakened by war shouts and drum beats. It was an attack launched by Sambhudhan and his party. In the battle that followed there were causalities on both the sides. A total of eleven followers of Sambhudhan fell to the police bullets. Major Boyd himself received serious injury from a sharp weapon. He was carried to Silchar where he succumbed to his injury on 30th January 1882. It also came to light that on hearing the information of Boyd marching from Gunjong to Maibong, Sambhudhan and his followers marched in opposite direction to Gunjong where he attacked the administrative constructions, buru the homes, destroyed the property and killed three men—two British servants and a sick policeman. It was also found that the Kuki militia, raised by the British to defend the British, ran away at the sight of Sambhudhan and his party. The British then launched a massive man-hunt for Sambhudhan who remained in the hiding for about a year. He was eventually captured, but in the skirmish that followed Sambhudhan died on 12th February 1883.

This was a small event of two days in the history of one hundred and fifty years of colonial rule in South Assam. It occupies less than a para in the report of Shakespeare, B.C. Allen, Compiler of District Gazetteer and about a page in Alexander Mackenzie's report. In the administrative proceedings it was reported in a serial in a few files. If the entire sequence of events are not placed chronologically and if these are not seen in proper perspective, it would appear from the reports that only a minor battle was fought just for a buffalo, in which so many lives were lost including that of a British in the rank of a Deputy Commissioner. It would also appear that Sambhudhan's capture was sought only as an *outlaw*, a *criminal* and a *murderer*. What was more astonishing that after the destruction of the offices by Sambhudhan, the British never returned to Gunjong and they subsequently shifted the sub-divisional headquarters to a nearby location called Haflong. The subsequent reports described the events as *rising* and an *insurrection*[2] and revealed more details asserting that the Sambhudhan event was in reality a major uprising in the area which attempted to usurp the colonial rule. These also brought to light the fact that in conformity with the all-India trend of the period, this tribal uprising had a millenarian character.[3]

REPORTS AS HISTORY

The Annual Administrative Report prepared by the Government in 1882-83 described the events related to Sambhudhan as a 'rising' which was "contemptible in its origin but was lamentable in its conclusion".[4]

The report prepared by Alexander Mackenzie in 1884 entitled "History of the relations of the Government with the Hill Tribes of North East Frontier of Bengal" described the event as an "insurrection" and an "insane and murderous revolt".[5]

The British compiler of District Gazetteers in Eastern India, B.C. Allen followed the same structure of the events and characterization. The essentially anti-colonial character and its restorative orientation was revealed by another colonial chronicle by L.H. Shakespeare, "In 1882 Sambhudhan, a religious fanatic started a minor insurrection to try to restore the old Cachar Kingdom .... detachments of Frontier Police from Silchar and Kohima were sent up at once, who scoured the district, hunting down the gangs until at last Sambhudhan's main body of adherents were surrounded and he was shot down which ended the insurrection".[6]

Following these reports, few attempts were made to reconstruct the story of Sambhudhan from the nationalistic point of view. In doing so one school retained the colonialist structure including their perspective, while the other resorted to glorification of the event and attributing Sambhudhan elements of heroism and even an incarnation.[7] Thus to J. B. Bhattacharjee it was a 'curious outbreak'[8] and a 'sporadic rising'[9] but remained non-commital in characterising the event : "Sambhudhan is still a legendary name in Cachar and many considered his movement as a mission to revive the old institutions and reaction to British rule".[10] Bhattacharjee's was a reproduction of the British administrative report without adding much or raising many questions. It accepts the colonial reports as *history*. A report is not just a recording of the events for official purpose, but it is also a justification of the actions and measures taken by government, in this case colonial government. Hence, exclusive reliability on them for reproduction of the past would render it biased, partial and reflect only administrator's point of mind. Moreover, it is ironical indeed to write about anti-colonial movements on the basis of colonial reports only.

Amit Kumar Nag stated that Sambhudhan's uprising constituted a significant backdrop to the Jadonang-Guindinliu movement of the Zeliangrong group people of the twentieth century. [11] This was also an overzealous presentation of facts. After all, Nag's account had no addition to the details provided by the colonial report. In his attempts to glorify the 'main actor' and the events of a region where he belonged, he wrongly linked the two similar movements. Jadonang-Guindinliu's movement broke out among Zeliangrong Nagas in the 1930s in Manipur and Sambhudhan's was a uprising of the Dimasa tribe in North Cachar in the 1880s. There is no evidence to suggest that the latter was even remotely influenced by the former. In fact, it has been found that the Zeliangrongs were not aware of Sambhudhan's uprising. Sumit Sarkar correctly located Sambhudhan's uprising as part of the all India trend of the period.[12] But a gross inaccuracy was observed in his widely read textbook wherein he wrote "Millenarianism could also take violent form as when...... the Kacha Nagas of Cachar in 1882 attacked the Whites under a miracle worker named Shambhudhan".[13] While Sarkar's characterisation was appropriate, the reference to Kacha Nagas was wrong. Sambhudhan and his followers who attacked the Whites in 1882 belonged to the Dimasa tribe, who inhabit the North Cachar hills of North-east India. So the event should have been described as a Dimasa uprising. It should be mentioned here that the Kacha Naga appellation is given to the Zeliangrong Nagas who inhabit the hills of Manipur. A section of them have also settled in the North Cachar hills along with the Dimasas. 'Zeliangrong' is a collective name given to a conglomeration of three Naga tribes—the Zemi, Liangmei and Rongmei. The name 'Kacha' is given to these three tribes by other Nagas which has a derogatory connotation. It comes from the word *Ketsa* which meant people living in an area where no human habitation is possible.[14] However, the revolt of Sambhudhan against the Whites has already converted him into a demi-god in the local folklore and the search for local heroes comparable to such characters in other parts of India by the regional historiography elevated Sambhudhan to a *Hero*. S. K. Barpujari writes, "The Dimasas of North Cachar who have imbibed the courage and patriotism of their past heroes like Rangadao, Dehgadao, Dehmaloo and heroines like Waibangma and Wairingma's fame wanted some one to come to their rescue. They discovered such a leader in the person of Sambhudhan Phonglo".[15] This historiography casts no doubt that "Sambhudhan was a charismatic leader with prophetic power".[16] Another example of such eulozisation can be found in "Vir Sambhudhan died a martyr in 1883. His place in the history of freedom fighters may be evaluated from the fact that late M.K. Gandhi (1869—1948), the father of Nation, was a boy of thirteen at the time when Vir Sambhudhan revolted against and defeated the British soldiers at Maibong in 1882. Jawaharlal Nehru was born in 1889, six years after the death of Vir Sambhudhan and Subhas Chandra Bose in 1897, about 15 years later".[17]

Thus the state of historiography on Sambhudhan can be categorised as colonial, nationalist and regionalist. The colonial historiography consisted essentially of reports prepared by the administration denigrating the uprising and legitimising the official handling of the situation. The nationalists misconstrued these reports as history and since they reproduced the same version, it retained its original colonial tone. The regional historiography in north-east India in general is often insular and shy of viewing the regional development against a national backdrop. At the same time, it is constantly looking for local heroes, whose achievements are equal, if not greater than the heroes of other regions. A prominent historian of the region H.K. Barpujari had observed that "there has been a tendency in our local studies to magnify regional achievements, to enact local heroes and to glorify local languages, customs and usages out of all proportions to their intrinsic value".[18] As against this, the nationalist historiography generally excludes the history of north-east from its purview and when it does it tries to view the developments quite lightly as part of an all-India phenomenon. But those who have followed such a course are often handicapped by their ignorance about the factual details of the region resulting in inaccuracies as seen in the case of Sumit Sarkar.

MILLENARIANISM

As the colonial grip on India's economy and society was tightening, the various social groups began to react sharply to the colonialists. These rebellions took three broad forms : (1) civil rebellion, (2) tribal resistance and (3) peasant uprising. In fact, the tribal revelled more often and more violently than any other community. in India.[19] The period 1860 to 1920 was characterised by a number of tribal movements of essentially millenarian character, "borrowing elements from Christianity or Hinduism and promising a sudden miraculous entry into a golden age".[20] The word millenarianism comes from the word *Millennium* meaning a thousand years span, originated in the Bible. It was used to describe that Christ would return to govern the earth after 1000 years. The millennial kingdom will begin with the reappearing of Christ.[21] Such millennium concepts are aplenty in Hindu mythology also. The concept of *Yugas* (*Satya, Treta, Dwapar* and *Kali* in a cyclical order) and the *Avatara's* (that God incarnates himself in a human/non-human form to annihilate the evil and usher the rule of propriety or *Dharma*) have influenced and inspired most of the Sanskritised tribals of India in their revolt against the mighty colonial state. In these revolts millenarianism was an attempt to liberate a region or a community under a new form of authority. Although Gandhi was also viewed through millenarian [22] eyes by the subaltern classes in India, more often than not it was the tribal movement which could assume this character. In these movements a leader emerged to declare himself as a prophet and started a new cult. He preached that it was God's advice that the people should fight to usurp the ruling power, that God himself will assist in this combat and ensure their victory. Subsequent to this, it will be a period of ideal peace where everyone will be happy and content.[23]

THE EVENTS IN NORTH CACHAR

The rising in North Cachar had little to do with a buffalo. In fact in 1881 itself the colonial administration had reports that "a Cachari named Sambhudhan who first set up as a worker of miraculous cures and presently went on to claim Divine inspiration and took the title of a Deo"—the God (Incarnate).[24] The oral sources certify that Sambhudhan Fonglo, son of Deprondao and Kasaidi was born in 1850 in the tiny village of Longkor at Maibong.[25] There are stories woven around the person of Sambhudhan—how he became a devotee of Siva from his childhood and often immersed in mediation, how he cured fatally ill villagers through herbs.[26] In fact, this was corroborated by the British reports that Sambhudhan had opened a clinic for treating sick people where the herbarium was under the charge of his lieutenant Desain Kemrai. His cure through 'miraculous plantain' was so famous that it is still practised in the rural areas by the Dimasas. As Sambhudhan's fame as a miracle worker and *Deo* spread far and wide, he began to attract a large number of followers who came to attend him in his abode at Maibong with fowls, goats, buffaloes and other offerings. The administration had reports that Sambhudhan had set himself up at Maibong and assumed the title of 'Deo' with a lot of young disciples staying with him also called deos. "Among the credulous population of the hills, followers were soon attracted to him. The afflatus of his inspiration extended to them and they too became dose, though Sambudhan was still the principal God".[27] The report also stated that "He took up his abode at Maibong, the ancient capital of the Cacharis and lived on free quarters, on the forced contributions of his neighbours".[28] Another report complained that "He terrorised people into following him".[29]

The indigenous recording based on folk tale and oral history states that Sambhudhan had already decided on launching an attack on the colonial administration. It was with this aim in view that he established his base at Maibong where he recruited young men and used his abode as the training centre for the youths. He selected Man Singh and Molongthong, from among his followers as principal advisor and commander for the purpose. As far as appropriation of taxes were concerned. Sambhudhan did impose levy, mostly in kind, like labour on his people to meet the expenses of his establishment and except a few, the Dimasas did not object to such contributions".[30]

It cannot be established whether Sambhudhan had actually conspired to attack the British in Cachar; what is axiomatic however is that Sambhudhan had established himself as an alternative centre of power with a large number of followers who paid taxes to him and the British were alarmed by this development.

The transformation of Sambhudhan from curer of ills to God incarnate, inspiring people to revolt against the mighty colonial State had a lot to do with the assumption of power by the British from the Dimasas.

THE BACKDROP

The Dimasa are one of the major tribes of North East India who had evolved a state of their own and transformed chieftainship to kingship.[31] Its capital was located at Maibong, but due to the constant attempt at its absorption by the neighbouring Ahom power shifted its capital to Khaspur near Silchar. From them on the Cachar valley or South Cachar became the core area of the Dimasa State. The rulers adopted Hinduism as the state religion. Sanskritisation led to the renaming of the state as *Heramba Raja* referring to the connection with *Hidimba*—the Mahabharata princess belonging to the *Rakshasha* clan whom *Bhim* married and had a son named *Ghatotkoch*. The area was divided into hills and plains. Hills being inhabited by Karbis, Jaintias, Zemi Nagas beside the dominant Dimasas,[32] while in the plains there was concentration of the overflowing population of Bengal. A good section of the Dimasas preferred their traditional animist faith to Hinduism and to escape Hinduisation returned to Maibong, where, it being the old capital of the Dimasas, there was already a settled Dimasa population.

As part of the process of absorption of North-East India, the Dimasa State was also annexed by the British in two installments (1832 and 1854 AD). North Cachar was then placed under a British officer, with its headquarters at Asalu. But when Naga Hills were annexed and combined into a new British District (1866), Asalu was transferred to Cachar district. Since then no British officer was posted at Asalu and the Dimasas were left to themselves. By the end of 1879 Sir Stuart Bayley, the Chief Commissioner of Assam, recommended and the Government of India approved of a scheme for the establishment of a sub-division in North Cachar with Gunjong as its headquarters "to give direct attention to the development of the territory and improvement of the general condition of the people".[33] The advent of British rule no doubt brought tranquility to the region which was experiencing bloody internecine power rivalry and experienced violent trespass during the Burmese invasion. But the colonial rule also brought fundamental changes in administration, revenue, executive and judicial system.[34] The tribals resented being taxed, resented the transfer of judicial authority from the chiefs to the district authority. Above all, the advent of the new regime meant opening up of the tribal area to the plainsmen, merchants and speculators. The British settled the Kuki migrants and introduced opium in the area whose evil effects were soon evident. A local chronicler writes,

> Before the advent of automatic arms and weapons, the Europeans had one infallible armoury, that was opium. No where in the length and breadth of India, the weapon had such lavishly and effectively been used as it was in the case of Assam and particularly Cachar. The rude (martial) tribes as held by Captain Fisher, emasculated and neutralised under the miracle of that dosing potion, and within a few decades of British subjugation the Dimasa nation as a whole were enslaved and were placed under economic and political bondage. They were helpless, since unlike the Chinese, they were under a firm alien rule.[35]

The Dimasas therefore viewed the British rule as a "danger to their very survival".[36] Sambhudhan was one of those Dimasas who resented the presence of the White in the Dimasa area. As he established himself as a messianic leader with large followers, he declared himself as a prophet (*Deo*) and assured his followers that he would bring back the good old days, the proverbial Golden Age, secure justice and drive away the oppressors.[37] Sambhudhan's intentions were clear from the fact that he had raised a band of youth and imparted them martial training. Initially he toured the village to inspire the youths in his creed but when his *ashram* was set up at Maibong, these youths were encouraged to live with him. The oral sources testify that he had trained them in martial arts in a batch of thirty to forty each. After the ritualistic initiation, these youths were declared to have become deos themselves a repository or divine power.[38] After the training, while inspiring them against the Whites, Sambhudhan claimed that his power had made his followers immune to bullets.[39] Therefore, in their fight against the British they had nothing to fear about. Moreover, by his power during the battle, hailstorm would fall from heaven to overwhelm their opponents.[40] There was an old prophecy among the Dimasas that a Raja would appear to unite all who eat from the wooden platters. The Raja would then lead the highlanders (Dimasa) to freedom and greatness.[41] Sambhudhan was believed to be that Raja whom the crisis-ridden Dimasas easily accepted in the hope of their suffering to be over.

The British establishment was still very weak in North Cachar hills during that time. No elaborate offices were set up yet. Although major changes were being introduced, the physical presence of the 'whites' in the area was still very negligible. In fact, sirce 1866 when Asalu, the Sub-divisional headquarters was made over from North Cachar Hills to Cachar district, no British officer was posted in the hills of North Cachar. Except for occasional tours of the Deputy Commissioner, the Dimasas were left to themselves.[42] In 1868, John Edgar, the Deputy Commissioner of Cachar visited North Cachar and proposed a plan for the improvement of communication and development of the area. Mac William, who succeeded Edgar, had to return from North Cachar Hills to Silchar merely after a week due to the Lushai raids on the Cachar-Lushai hills frontier. In 1877, Johnson, the succeeding Deputy Commissioner, toured the hills and reported that the hills were "very peaceful and the inhabitants behaved very well".[43] The Deputy Commissioner had obviously misread the situation as discontent against the British rule was growing and Sambhudhan was already very active. Sambhudhan was a product of this growing discontent who could contemplate driving away the British mainly because in the absence of many Whites and any elaborate military arrangement in the area, he did not develop any high regard for the might of the colonial state. The British had organised a militia of about two-hundred indigenous Kuki tribals to defend the administration. But not only did the Dimasas have no regard for the Kuki with whom they co-habited in the area, the militia also was made to move from place to place. True to the Dimasa anticipation, Sambhudhan actually attacked the Whites and the Kuki millitia fled the scene without offering any resistance.[44]

THE COLONIAL COUNTER

The British had reports about the activity of Sambhudhan in which they had sensed danger. So when the opportunity appeared, they quickly seized it. A summon was issued to Sambhudhan to appear before the Sub-divisional Court. The apprehensions of the British and the hold Sambhudhan had over the masses were confirmed when no one was found willing to carry the summon to the 'Deo'. The alarmed administration immediately issued a warrant of arrest which was sent through a party of six constables. The police party was "really bewildered to see the size and strength that Sambhudhan had acquired and that he had already built a large village of his followers" at Maibong. On being served the warrant, Sambhudhan reportedly stated that he would not appear before any illegal authority and asked the party to leave the place immediately carrying his letter addressed to the concerned authorities wherein he had asked the British to quit the Dimasa land immediately and not to contemplate any offensive against Sambhudhan. The original letter is not available and the content survives only in oral testimony. But the fact that an offensive against Sambhudhan was launched immediately on the return of the police party, proves that the party must have presented a report suggesting danger. As described in the beginning, the attack not only failed, it led to the death of Major Boyd.

THE EYE-WITNESS ACCOUNT OF THE EVENT

"In January 1882, the Deputy Commissioner of Cachar, Major Boyd accompanied by the writer, who then held charge of North Cachar and a party of twenty-five Frontier Police marched to Maibong for the purpose of arresting Sambhudhan and his followers. Nothing occurred during the night but early in the following morning alarm was given by the Sentries and the Kacharis were seen rushing in a body from the neighbouring jungles on the camp. Orders had been issued forbidding the Sepoys not to fire until hard pressed, as it was desirable, if possible, to avoid bloodshed. The Kacharis were armed with long double edged swords and were preceeded by two men beating tom-toms. No attempt was made by them to seek cover but they rushed on in a compact body. One Sepoy was struck by a word which glanced off his rifle and Major Boyd at the same moment received a cut on his hand, which subsequently resulted fatally. As soon as the firing commenced....They broke and fled leaving seven dead on the ground. Four bodies were afterwards found in the jungle bringing the total to eleven".[45] Although Sambhudhan went the shoes of either the traditional institutions or the British authorities did not bring any improvement in the power position of the traditional chiefs (that is, the *Syiems*). On many occasions, there have been tussles between the traditional elite represented by the Chiefs and Headmen and the modern political elite of popular elected representatives.[25]

In 1959, the United Khasi Jaintia Hills Autonomous District Council passed the Appointment and Succession of Chiefs and Headman Act, 1959[26]. This Act was followed by six subsequent amendments between 1969—1995. The Act constitutionally empowers the District Council of a firm control over the mode of appointment, conduct, suspension and even removal of the traditional Chiefs and Headmen. On a number of occasions the Khasi Hills Autonomous District Council has been criticized for deviating from customary laws and practices in this regard. On the part of the District Council, it may be said that there appears to be genuine feeling that the Chief and their councils want to act on their own and do not like to toe the line with the District Councils to grow along with the time shedding all that which is out-dated[27]. The case of the Khasi Hills Autonomous District Council (hereinafter KHADC) versus the *Syiem* of Mylliem (Mr. Laborious Manik Syiem) may be cited here[28]. The KHADC had received complaints against the *Syiem* of Mylliem and had issued summons to him to appear before it to answer to the charges levelled against him. The *Syiem* failing to appear before the District Council was suspended by an order dated 20.03.01 and an Acting *Syiem* was appointed in his place. The suspended *Syiem* filed a petition in the Gauhati Court against the suspension order citing many reasons for his failure to appear before the KHADC. The suspension order was struck down by the Gauhati High Court on the ground that 'no opportunity of hearing was given before the suspension order'[29]. The matter was taken up to the Supreme Court by the KHADC. The Supreme Court allowed the appeal of the KHADC and upheld the suspension of the *Syiem* of Mylliem. A division bench of the Supreme Court on interpreting section 6 of the United Khasi-Jaintia Hills Autonomous District (Appointment and Succession of Chiefs And Headmen) Act 1959, held that no opportunity of hearing was required to be given in case where suspension was pending inquiry.[30]

Thus, the District Councils and these traditional institutions continue to be at loggerheads over power sharing and existence under the Sixth Schedule of the Constitution. The Khasi States under their umbrella organization, the Federation of Khasi States, have been making various representations to the Union Government to highlight their cause. In their appeal for constitutional recognition, the demand of the Khasi States is that special provisions should be included in the Constitution to recognize, restore and empower these traditional political organizations as guardians of local customs, usages and practices. This demand for constitutional recognition received a fillip with the setting up of a national commission to review the working of the Constitution (January 2000). The Khasi States have rejected the proposal of accommodating them in the District Council and instead placed their demands in the 13th Schedule, Article 244(3). Some of the demands include the creation of a Federal Council, right of the Federal Council to exercise legislative, executive and judicial functions; power of this Council to frame its own rules of procedure and conduct of business; creation of a centrally assisted Federal Fund[31].

CONCLUSION

Of late, analysis of the relations between District Council and traditional institutions has generated considerable interest among scholars, local institutions and non-governmental organizations. The Khasi States have their roots in the past when they could exercise independent control over their respective areas. These traditional political institutions are themselves undergoing a metamorphosis, the socio-political conditions under which they first merged and evolved and the position in which they are placed today are entirely different. An important question that arises today is if these Khasi States are given constitutional recognition, how well will they adjust and adapt themselves to the changing political environment? Before any concrete steps are taken to empower them and accord them constitutional status, a further debate on the issue will truly reflect and elicit the desired response of *Ki Khun Ki Hajar*, that is, the citizens of the Khasi States.

NOTES

1. The name Meghalaya which literally means 'abode of the clouds' was given by Suniti Kumar Chatterjee to the plateau in the 1930s.
2. Kharkongor, F.R: '*Scotland of the East*' in *India Today Plus*, Vol. III No. 1, New Delhi, 2002.
3. District Level Statistics 2002, Directorate of Economics and Statistics, Government of Meghalaya, Shillong, 2002.
4. *Basic Facts of Meeghalaya*, Directorate of Information and Public Relations, Meghalaya, Shillong.
5. Singh, K. S. (ed) : *People of India, Meghalaya*, Vol. XXXII, Seagull

Books, Calcutta, 1994.

6. Chatterjii, S.K.: *Kirata-Jana-Krti. The Indo-Mongoloids: Their contribution to the History and Culture of India*, The Asiatic Society, Calcutta, 1974.

7. Singh K : 'Syiems and Durbars in Khasi Polity', in S.K. Chattopadhyay, (ed), *Tribal Institutions of Meghalaya*, Spectrum Publications, Guwahati, 1985.

8. Costa, G. : *Ka Riti Jong Ka Ri Laiphew Syiem: Ka Bynta ka Ba-Ar*, Don Bosco Publication, Shillong, 1999.

9. Bareh, H : *The History and Culture of the Khasi People*, (2nd ed), Spectrum Publications, Guwahati, 1985.

10. Evans-Pritchard, E.E.: *The Nuer:A Descriptionof the Modes of Livelihood and Political Institutions of a Nilotic People*, Oxford University Press, London, 1968.

11. Bareh, H. : *op. cit.*

12. National Commission to Review the Working of the Constitution Consultation Paper, *Empowering and Strenthening of Panchayati Raj Institutions/Autonomous District Councils/Traditional Tribal governing institution in North East India*, 2001, downloaded from the interest, http:/ncrwc.nic.in.

13. Syiemlieh, D.R. : *British Administration in Meghalaya: Policy and Pattern*, Heritage Publishers, New Delhi, 1988.

14. Bareh, H.: *op.cit.*

15. Gassah, L.S. : *'Traditional Self Governing Institutions Among the Hill Population Groups of Meghalays', in A. Goswami, (ed), Traditional Self-Governing Institutions Among the Hill Tribes of North-East India*, Akansha Publishing House, New Delhi, 2002.

16. Claessen, H.J.M. and P. Skalnik (eds); *The Early State*, Mouton, The Hague, 1978.

17. Gassah, L.S.; op. cit.

18. *Ibid.*

19. *The Telegraph , 23rd August, 2002, U Mawphor, 30th October, 2002.*

20. Gassah, L.S: *op. cit.*

21. Syiemlieh, D.R.: *op. cit.*

22. *Ibid.*

23. Syiemlieh, D.R. :'*The Political Integration of the Khasi States into the Indian Union'*, in B. Pakem, (ed). *Regionalism in India*, Har Anand Publications, New Delhi, 1993.

24. Gassah, L.S.(ed). : *Autonomous District Councils, Omsons Publications,*

New Delhi, 1997.

25. Gassah, L.S. 'Effects of District Councils on Traditional Institutions', in L.S. Gassah, (ed). *Autonomous District Councils,* Omsons Publications, New Delhi, 1997.

26. *United Khasi-Jaintia Hills Autonomous District (Appointment And Succession of Chiefs And Headmen) Act,* 1959, (As Amended), Khasi Hills Autonomous District Council, 1995.

27. Gassah, L.S. : *Ibid*

28. *The Shillong Times,* April 3rd , 2001.

29. *The Shillong Times,* Augustl 11 , 2002

30. *Ibid*

31. National Commission To Review the Working of the Constitution *op. cit.*

refuse to go about and hunt for the insurgents except in parties of ten or twelve. They are of no use in getting information. Neither before the outbreak did they bring any news nor after it have then done anything towards catching any of the fugitives. They may be disbanded from the First of April; Foreign Political Proceedings (A) May 1882.

44. C.A. Sopitt op. cit
45. U.C. Barman op. cit
46. *Ibid;* Also. A. Mackenzie op. cit, L. W. Shakespear op. cit.
47. U. C. Barman op. cit., B.C. Allen, Assam District Gazeteers. Vol. I Cachar) Allahabad 1905, pp 35-36
48. See note 44 above
49. Foreign Political Proceedings (A) May 1882
50. *Idid.*
51. *Idid.*
52. *Idid.*
53. *Idid.*

14

Traditional Tribal Self-Governing Institutions of Meghalaya: The Khasi Syiem

C. REUBEN LYNGDOH, L.S. GASSAH

Meghalaya[1], 'the abode of the clouds', is a member of the family of seven states of the north-east that stretches out from mainland India. Meghalaya may be coy and silent but it has incredible secrets waiting to be spilled[2]. The state of Meghalaya was carved out of erstwhile Assam and it became a full-fledged state on January 21, 1972. The state has a total area of 22,429 square kilometers and a population of 2306069[3]. It is now divided into seven administrative districts comprising :

(a) Jaintia Hills District created on February 22, 1972;

(b) East Garo Hills District;

(c) West Garo Hills District created on October 22, 1976;

(d) East Khasi Hills District;

(e) West Khasi Hills District created on October 28, 1976;

(f) Ri-Bhoi District created on June 4, 1992 and;

(g) South Garo Hills District created on June 18, 1992[4].

Meghalaya is predominantly inhabited by the three tribal communities namely, the Khasis, the Jaintias and the Garos. These three tribes practice matriliny with minor variations from each other. These tribes belong to the "Indo-Chinese Linguistic Family", of which two important sub-families are the Mon-Khmer and the Tibeto-Burman[5]. The Mon-Khmer includes among other communities, the Khasis and the Jaintias, while the Tibeto-Burman includes the Garos. The Khasis have been classified into four main sub-divisions corresponding to certain geographical areas of Meghalaya:

(a) Khynriam, that is, the Khasis who inhabit the central plateau;

(b) Pnar or Synteng, that is, the Jaintias who inhabit the eastern area;

(c) Bhoi, who are concentrated in the northern area; and

(d) War, who inhabit the southern area.

While trying to ascertain the origin of the Khasi people, scholars have presented a number of views. These views range from the cultural and linguistic affinities that the Khasis share with other communities in South East Asia (as noted by Gurdon, Griesson amongst others) to the views that rest purely on mythical and oral tradition (as noted by Rymbai, Bareh amongst others). Speaking on the origin of the Khasis, Suniti Kumar Chatterjii makes an important observation, "they are said to be descended from the earliest Mongoloid immigrants into India who changed their language through contact with Austric speakers, either in Burma or on the soil of India, in prehistoric times"[6].

EVOLUTION OF THE OFFICE OF THE SYIEM

It is generally believed that the first waves of migration of the Khasis into the hills occurred in batches. Each batch comprised of a clan (*kur*), which settled in a particular area and paved way for the establishment of a village (*shnong*). The clan was headed by the eldest male member called a *Lyngdoh* (priest), who was chosen by a council of adult males of the clan. The *Lyngdoh* enjoyed both spiritual as well as temporal powers[7]. A second view draws attention to the existence of two types of *Lyngdohs*, while the first was vested with spiritual and religious powers, the second performed political and administrative functions[8]. As clans grew in numbers and size often accommodating new clans into their fold, the villages slowly came into existence. The head of the village was chosen from among the members of the original or founding clans of the village. In certain instances two centers of authority emerged during this early phase of socio-political development. The temporal powers were vested into a new authority, the *Basan* (an elder) who was the leader and representative of the founding clan which had first claimed possession and ownership of the land; the spiritual powers were vested with the *Lyngdoh*; who was chosen from the priestly clan[9]. This phase of socio-political development may be linked to what Evans-Pritchard terms as a 'stateless society' where there is the absence of a central institutional authority[10].

As the villages grew in size and the art of governance became comples, many villages merged to form a *Raid* or commune. The *Raid* would administer subjects of common concern of the constituent villages. The administration of the *Raid* was carried on by the *Basan* and the *Lyngdoh* with the assistance of a *Durbar* or council comprising of such councillors as *Matabors*, *Majis*, *Pators* and *Malehangots*. These councillors were appointed by the *Basan* or the *Lyngdoh* subject to the approval of the *Raid* comprising all adult male citizens[11].

In course of time, as the *Raids* grew in size and population, new developments emerged which necessitated the creation of a central and common authority to manage state affairs of a larger magnitude, which the existing socio-political authorities could not execute. It is under these circumstances that the clans, villages and communes federated to create the *Hima*, that is, a state. Thus the *Hima* is a "territorial conglomeration of communes and independent villages falling under the jurisdiction of administrative heads known as *Syiem* or *Lyngdoh* or *Sordar* or *Wahadadar*"[12]. A new political entity called the Syiemship emerged, which was administered by a ruler called a *Syiem*. Thus, the institution of *Syiemship* had emerged as the apex political organization of the Khasis. The *Syiem* was appointed only from the Syiem clan and heirship to the office of the *Syiem* is in all cases traced through the female side. Syimlieh observes that "this rudimentary stage of state formation evolved into the institution of *Syiemship* which probably arose out of the voluntary association of clans, villages, communes when new developments took place".[13] To these new developments are attributed the opening of markets, execution of marriage laws, appointment of judicial authority, maintenance of police power and so on[14]. Thus the office of the *Syiem* "arose out of an impulse for amalgamating identical pursuits, interests and necessities of the clan residents and villagers. It was instituted on the spirit of reciprocity along with a consolidation of their intimate relations which had grown amongst the different sections of people who made up their units"[15].

Today there exist 25 Khasi States, *Ki Hima Khasi*, each of which is under a ruler called a *Syiem, Lyngdoh, Sirdar* or *Wahadadar*. The mode of election of a *Syiem* may be direct or indirect. In states like

Langrin all adult males of the state have the right to vote in the election of a *Syiem*. However, in States like Khyrim, Mylliem, Cherra, the *Syiem* is elected by an electoral college comprising of the representatives of founding clans of the respective state, who have been in turn elected by all the adult males of their respective clans.

The *Syiem* in exercising his functions of the state is assisted by a council, *Durbar*. There are two types of *Durbars*, (a) *Durbar Hima* or state council which is a popular assembly comprising of all adult male citizens of the *Hima*, (b) *Durbar Synshar* or executive council comprising of a smaller group of councillors, *Ki Bakhraw* designated as *Basans, Lyngdoh, Myntris* who are vested with executive powers.

Thus the *Hima* represents the rudiments of what Claessen describes as an early state. It manifests a sizeable population that makes social categorization; society is stratified and specialization emerges; the emerging classes of people can be distinguished; governmental authority is centralized and has the power to maintain law and other. Finally, a common ideology exist which gives legitimacy to the ruling stratum[16].

POWERS AND FUNCTIONS OF THE SYIEM

Though a Khasi *Syiem* is the head of his state, he exercises his powers in accordance with "ethical instructions, prescribed by customary rules, laws and regulations, as well as customs, traditions and usages".[17] . He has to lay down his policy in conformity with the resolution of the *Durbar* of the people. In reality, it is the *Durbars* that transact both political and judicial functions and their decision is final. The acts or decisions of a *Syiem* can be vetoed by the Durbar if they are contrary to the usages and traditions of the community[18] . Similarly, the *Durbars* have also come to the rescue of their *Syiems*, when they felt that his position as a traditional authority was threatended. Thus has often been seen in the impasse between the *Syiems* and the District Council[19] .

In all acts of legislation, the *Syiem* and his *Durbar Synshar* are guided by customary practices and laws of the land. In executive matters, his authority principally extends to the management of markets, arrest of wrong'doers and criminals and the collection of fines and imposts of various quarters in the state. He also approves the appointment of subordinate officials of the state[20]. If necessity arises, the *Syiem* may also appoint a *Syiem Khynnath* or junior *Syiem* to assist him in managing the affairs of state if he is temporarily indisposed or to even succeed him if he is deposed or removed from office. In judicial matters, the

Syiem has the power to try cases and pass sentences in consultation with the *Durbar Synshar*[21]. In the past, the *Syiem's* court was the highest court of appeal within the *Hima*. It was often contended that in the trial and execution of cases, while the *Syiem* acted as a judge, his *Durbar* acted as the jury.

The *Syiem* is also vested with the authority to collect, "the material wealth of a citizen of the state whose lineage has become extinct and perform the cremation rights of those who had died without relatives"[22]. As a rular, the *Syiem* does not enjoy any entitlement to land holdings as land belongs to the clan and to the people. Hence he cannot claim land revenue. Nevertheless, a certain amount of *Raid* or commune land may be apportioned to him for his personal use. His revenue is derived from fines collected on settling cases, tolls or *khrong*, collected from the markets within his jurisdiction and from the issue and renewal of *patta* for land holdings.

RELATIONSHIP WITH THE CONSTITUTIONAL AUTHORITY

On account of various events the Khasi States came to be under the political control of the British between 1829—1947. When India became independent in 1947, the Khasi States were brought within the ambit of the new Dominion through the Instrument of Accession. The Khasi States signed the instrument of Accession in 1948 expecting to achieve some kind of autonomy within the Indian political framework. However, the expectations were short-lived as the Indian Constitution (1950) did not accommodate any special provisions for them. Instead, the Khasi States were merged with the State of Assam without any agreement of merger and disregarding the provisions of the Standstill Agreement[23]. The provisions of the Sixth Schedule were implemented in the hill areas of Assam. The Khasi States came to be a part of the United Khasi and Jaintia Hills District Council (inaugurated on 20th January, 1950) and continue as functionaries of the Khasi Hills Autonomous District Council till today.

The Sixth Schedule empowers the Autonomous District Councils to make laws and regulations in all matters relating to the customs, traditions and practices of the tribal people while also providing a compact mechanism for self-government[24]. However, the relations between the traditional authorities and the constitutional authority (that is the District Council) have often been strained and far from what the Sixth Schedule had envisaged. The stepping of the District Council into the shoes of either the traditional institutions or the British authorities did not bring any improvement in the power position of the traditional chiefs (that is, the *Syiems*). On many occasions, there have been tussles between the traditional elite represented by the Chiefs and Headmen and the modern political elite of popular elected representatives.[25]

In 1959, the United Khasi Jaintia Hills Autonomous District Council passed the Appointment and Succession of Chiefs and Headman Act, 1959[26]. This Act was followed by six subsequent amendments between 1969—1995. The Act constitutionally empowers the District Council of a firm control over the mode of appointment, conduct, suspension and even removal of the traditional Chiefs and Headmen. On a number of occasions the Khasi Hills Autonomous District Council has been criticized for deviating from customary laws and practices in this regard. On the part of the District Council, it may be said that there appears to be genuine feeling that the Chief and their councils want to act on their own and do not like to toe the line with the District Councils to grow along with the time shedding all that which is out-dated[27]. The case of the Khasi Hills Autonomous District Council (hereinafter KHADC) versus the *Syiem* of Mylliem (Mr. Laborious Manik Syiem) may be cited here[28]. The KHADC had received complaints against the *Syiem* of Mylliem and had issued summons to him to appear before it to answer to the charges levelled against him. The *Syiem* failing to appear before the District Council was suspended by an order dated 20.03.01 and an Acting *Syiem* was appointed in his place. The suspended *Syiem* filed a petition in the Gauhati Court against the suspension order citing many reasons for his failure to appear before the KHADC. The suspension order was struck down by the Gauhati High Court on the ground that 'no opportunity of hearing was given before the suspension order'[29]. The matter was taken up to the Supreme Court by the KHADC. The Supreme Court allowed the appeal of the KHADC and upheld the suspension of the *Syiem* of Mylliem. A division bench of the Supreme Court on interpreting section 6 of the United Khasi-Jaintia Hills Autonomous District (Appointment and Succession of Chiefs And Headmen) Act 1959, held that no opportunity of hearing was required to be given in case where suspension was pending inquiry.[30]

Thus, the District Councils and these traditional institutions continue to be at loggerheads over power sharing and existence under the Sixth Schedule of the Constitution. The Khasi States under their umbrella organization, the Federation of Khasi States, have been making various representations to the Union Government to highlight their cause. In their appeal for constitutional recognition, the demand of the Khasi States is that special provisions should be included in the Constitution to recognize, restore and empower these traditional political organizations as guardians of local customs, usages and practices. This demand for constitutional recognition received a fillip with the setting up of a national commission to review the working of the Constitution (January 2000). The Khasi States have rejected the proposal of accommodating them in the District Council and instead placed their demands in the 13th Schedule, Article 244(3). Some of the demands include the creation of a Federal Council, right of the Federal Council to exercise legislative, executive and judicial functions; power of this Council to frame its own rules of procedure and conduct of business; creation of a centrally assisted Federal Fund[31].

CONCLUSION

Of late, analysis of the relations between District Council and traditional institutions has generated considerable interest among scholars, local institutions and non-governmental organizations. The Khasi States have their roots in the past when they could exercise independent control over their respective areas. These traditional political institutions are themselves undergoing a metamorphosis, the socio-political conditions under which they first merged and evolved and the position in which they are placed today are entirely different. An important question that arises today is if these Khasi States are given constitutional recognition, how well will they adjust and adapt themselves to the changing political environment? Before any concrete steps are taken to empower them and accord them constitutional status, a further debate on the issue will truly reflect and elicit the desired response of *Ki Khun Ki Hajar*, that is, the citizens of the Khasi States.

NOTES

1. The name Meghalaya which literally means 'abode of the clouds' was given by Suniti Kumar Chatterjee to the plateau in the 1930s.
2. Kharkongor, F.R: '*Scotland of the East*' in *India Today Plus*, Vol. III No. 1, New Delhi, 2002.
3. District Level Statistics 2002, Directorate of Economics and Statistics, Government of Meghalaya, Shillong, 2002.
4. *Basic Facts of Meeghalaya*, Directorate of Information and Public Relations, Meghalaya, Shillong.
5. Singh. K. S. (ed) : *People of India, Meghalaya*, Vol. XXXII. Seagull

Books, Calcutta, 1994.

6. Chatterjii, S.K.: *Kirata-Jana-Krti. The Indo-Mongoloids: Their contribution to the History and Culture of India*, The Asiatic Society, Calcutta, 1974.

7. Singh K : 'Syiems and Durbars in Khasi Polity', in S.K. Chattopadhyay, (ed), *Tribal Institutions of Meghalaya*, Spectrum Publications, Guwahati, 1985.

8. Costa, G. : *Ka Riti Jong Ka Ri Laiphew Syiem: Ka Bynta ka Ba-Ar*, Don Bosco Publication, Shillong, 1999.

9. Bareh, H : *The History and Culture of the Khasi People*, (2nd ed), Spectrum Publications, Guwahati, 1985.

10. Evans-Pritchard, E.E.: *The Nuer:A Descriptionof the Modes of Livelihood and Political Institutions of a Nilotic People*, Oxford University Press, London, 1968.

11. Bareh, H. : *op. cit.*

12. National Commission to Review the Working of the Constitution Consultation Paper, *Empowering and Strenthening of Panchayati Raj Institutions/Autonomous District Councils/Traditional Tribal governing institution in North East India*, 2001, downloaded from the interest, http:/ncrwc.nic.in.

13. Syiemlieh, D.R. : *British Administration in Meghalaya: Policy and Pattern*, Heritage Publishers, New Delhi, 1988.

14. Bareh, H.: *op.cit.*

15. Gassah, L.S. : *'Traditional Self Governing Institutions Among the Hill Population Groups of Meghalays', in A. Goswami, (ed), Traditional Self-Governing Institutions Among the Hill Tribes of North-East India*, Akansha Publishing House, New Delhi, 2002.

16. Claessen, H.J.M. and P. Skalnik (eds); *The Early State*, Mouton, The Hague, 1978.

17. Gassah, L.S.; op. cit.

18. *Ibid.*

19. *The Telegraph , 23rd August, 2002, U Mawphor, 30th October, 2002.*

20. Gassah, L.S: *op. cit.*

21. Syiemlieh, D.R.: *op. cit.*

22. *Ibid.*

23. Syiemlieh, D.R. :*'The Political Integration of the Khasi States into the Indian Union'*, in B. Pakem, (ed). *Regionalism in India*, Har Anand Publications, New Delhi, 1993.

24. Gassah, L.S.(ed). : *Autonomous District Councils, Omsons Publications,*

New Delhi, 1997.

25. Gassah, L.S. 'Effects of District Councils on Traditional Institutions', in L.S. Gassah, (ed). *Autonomous District Councils,* Omsons Publications, New Delhi, 1997.
26. *United Khasi-Jaintia Hills Autonomous District (Appointment And Succession of Chiefs And Headmen) Act,* 1959, (As Amended), Khasi Hills Autonomous District Council, 1995.
27. Gassah, L.S. : *Ibid*
28. *The Shillong Times,* April 3rd , 2001.
29. *The Shillong Times,* Augustl 11 , 2002
30. *Ibid*
31. National Commission To Review the Working of the Constitution *op. cit.*

4. Certain values got discarded in course of time as they had lost their utility in the society.
5. The incoming culture mainfested certain vested interests which had actually encouraged the retention of traditonal beliefs of the receiving culture.

On the basis of the above generalizations, we may draw the inference that the Ahoms in course of their long history have been successful in synthesising a new culture based on the process of acceptence, rejection, and persistence. The new form that has been synthesized shows the persistence of old values to a remarkable degree and thereby helps in maintaining a "dynamic equilibrium".

REFERENCES

Barua, I. 1978 : *Social Relations In an Ahom Village*. New Delhi : Starling Publishers.

Borgohain, R. 1988. : *Ahom State Formation: an Inquiry into the Factors of Polity Formation in Mediaeval North-east India*. Unpublished Ph.D. thesis, NEHU : Shillong.

Bhuyan, S.K. 1962 : *Deodhari Assam Buraji Guwahati* : Deptt. of Historical and Antiquarian Studies.

Firth, R. 1954 : *Social organization and social change*. The Journal of the Royal Anthropolotical Institute of Great Britain and Ireland. Vol. 84, part-1.

Gogei, P. 1968 : *The Tai and the Tai kingdoms*. Guwahati : Deptt. of History, publication Gauhati University.

Gait, E. 1926/1984 : *A History of Assam*. Delhi : Cine Tarika Publications.

Heesterman, J. C. 1972 : *India and the Inner Conflict of Tradition*. S. N. Fisenstadt (ed). Post traditional societies. New York : W. W. North & Company, INC.

Kane, P. V. 1974 : *History of Dharmasastra : Ancient and Medieaval Religions and Civil lawa*. Vol. II, Part-1, 2nd edition. Poona : Bhandarkar Oriental Research Institute.

Nandelboum, D. G. 1970 : *Society in India. Bombay* : Popular Prakashan.

Person, T. 1961 : *An outline of the social system. Person* et. al. (eds.), *Theories of society*. Vol. 1. New York : Free Press of Glencoe.

Phukan, J. N. 1968 : *Lik-Phan-Tai*. Gauhati : Congress Press.

Sen, D. 1982: *Early History of the Tai Ahoms, Proceedings of NEIHA*, 3rd session. Shillong. Deptt. of History, NEHU.

16

Social Offences and Penalties Imposed on Garo Offenders

JULIUS L. R. MARAK

At the very outset, it may be pointed out that in the Garo society the punishment and penalties imposed on the social offenders during the pre-British days was nothing short of death. The acts of *Botril dinga* and *Garo dinga* were common practice during those days. But with the annexation of the Garo Hills by the British in the year 1867, the usual practice of killing in the form of death penalty came to an end. And just to compensate the harm done to the person and to give a healing touch to it, the system of payment of *dai* to the complainant was introduced. The word '*dai*' in the real sense of the term means, *an' chi mitipa pari u'sita* (blocking the flow of blood and wiping the wound). The rampant killings of persons for minor offences were stopped forthwith and the payment of *dai* and fines were gradually introduced into the Garo tribal custom. The implication of *dai* is more civil than criminal, while fines have only criminal overtones. Implementation of the Garo customary laws regarding the offences committed is linked with these deterrents. Some specific laws or rules in existence relating to the nature of offences committed by the individual and the punishment imposed in the form of penalties, fines bearing a stamp of traditional control are discussed below.

It has, however, to be acknowledged that the moral standards of the Garos are high and such social evils as prostitution are almost unknown in the Garo society. Still, adultery is not uncommon, though it is considered a social evil. It is considered a social offence and a fine is imposed on the person committing such an offence with the idea that he or she has caused harm to the society. The fine imposed is a token one; what is more important is the question of individual shame and social disapproval involved with it.

'*TILEKANI*' (ADULTERY) COMMITTED BY A MARRIED PERSON

(i) If a man having a wife commits adultery with another, the offender shall have to pay a sum of Rs. 30/- as *dai* and a sum of Rs. 6/- as *gitok* (token compensation) to his wife. Likewise, the woman also shall have to pay the same amount of money to her husband and the wife of the man with whom she had relation. Thus, each offending person shall have to pay to the claimant or his/her *mahari* (reference group) , as the case may be.

(ii) If a married man commits adultery with a spinster, he will be required to pay a sum of Rs. 30/- as *dai* and an additional sum of Rs. 6/- as *gitok* to his wife or the *mahari*. In the same way, the spinster will have to pay the same amount of *dai* to the wife of the man with whom she had the relation. However, the payment of *dai* depends on the decision of the *chra* (kin group) and her *mahari*.

(iii) If a woman having a husband commits adultery with a bachelor, she will pay the sum of Rs. 30/- as *dai* and a sum of Rs. 6/- as *gitok* to her husband. The same amount of *dai* is to be paid by the man to the husband of the woman or as decided by the *chra* and the *mahari*.

ADULTERY COMMITTED BY A BACHELOR AND A SPINSTER:

A bachelor can under no circumstances commit adultery with a spinster. There are some restrictions on committing the act. In case a bachelor commits adultery with a spinster, he will have to marry that particular girl. If the bachelor refuses to take her as his wife after committing such an act, he shall have to pay the *dai* of Rs. 60/- to Rs. 120/- to the *mahari* of the girl. Likewise, if the spinster also refuses to marry the boy, she too shall have to pay the same amount of *dai* to the bachelor. The payment of *dai* shall have to be made even if the bachelor and the spinster consummated the act with mutual agreement. The act of committing adultery between a bachelor and the spinster is called *tilek nagandea, an.cha soldarenga*. The act of polluting an innocent girl is far worse than seducing an already married woman. In all cases of adultery, the *chra* and the *mahari* of both sides come together in *Melaa* (Council meeting) and decide the case. The decisions of the *chra* and the *mahari* in all cases are final and binding on both the offenders.

'DRANE TILEKANI' (RAPE)

Acts of *drane tileka* (rape) are very rare among tribes. The Garo are also no exception to this. Among the Garo, the penalties imposed on those people committing such social crimes are decided according to the damage done in terms of social status and on such consideration whether one is free from *akim* (claims or payments) or not.

(i) If a man commits or attempts to commit rape on a woman or a girl and sufficient number of witnesses are available to confirm the act, then he must pay a sum of Rs. 60/- and an additional sum of Rs. 120/- as *dai* to the girl or to the *mahari*, as the case may be.

(ii) If a man having a wife commits rape on another women or girl, he will be required to pay a sum of Rs. 60/- as *dai* to his wife. In addition, he will pay the same amount of money to the girl or to the *mahari* she belongs to.

RAPE OF A MINOR GIRL

If a man commits rape on a minor girl, who has not attained the age of puberty, he shall have to pay a sum of Rs. 1000/- to the girl and in addition, a sum of Rs. 50/- to the *jat* (tribe).

If the girl is found to have consented to the act, she too will pay a sum of Rs. 50/- to the *jat* (tribe) and a sum of Rs. 30/-as *dai* plus Rs. 6/- to be paid as *gitok* to the wife of the man, in case he is having a wife. The man also pays to his wife the same amount of money as paid by the girl. In such cases, the concerned *chra* and *mahari* should come together in a *Melaa* and decide the case, which is binding on both the offending parties. But in all such cases, the future of the girl becomes the foremost consideration.

'TILEKRAMRAM GIPANI DAI'

If a man or a woman commits adultery with someone who has a wife or a husband, then he or she shall have to pay a sum of Rs. 30/- as *dai* to the persons offended. Over and above, the person, who had committed such an act, must pay a sum of Rs. 100/- to the *jat* (tribe) for creating a public offence (*jatko kratchaatani*).

Saraighat War canons were fired only at the time stipulated by the Hindu astrologers (Gogoi,1985:99). Hindu influence got more intensified during the reign of Pratap Singha (1603—1641). He came to be known as Buddhi-Svarga-Narayan Pratap Singha. It was Pratap Singha who brought about a revolutionary change in the Ahom diplomatic structure by installing 13 Brahmin families as diplomats.

So far we have observed that religious affiliation of the kings coupled with the installation of non-Ahoms to certain key posts in administrative structure did not apparently influence the social life of the Ahom commoners, but at the same time it had, for sure, an impact on traditional Ahom social structure. For instance, official rank, responsibilities, were mostly according to one's birth in a particular Ahom clan. The entry of non-Ahoms to these posts which were hereditary, further stratified the Ahom society. This also paved the way for the dilution of clan-based Ahom society to the lineage—based one. The strength of this statement lies on the 'assumption' that perhaps the hierarchical and functional interdependence that operated within the seven clans of the Ahoms was gradually becoming weak. Moreover, the establishment of new *khels* and reorganization of villages along with other non-Ahoms resulted in a heterogeneous village community.

By then, the Neo-Vaishnavism of Sankaradeva was gaining much strength and popularity among the masses in spite of much restrictions imposed by the Ahom court. Yet another contact situation emerged when Sankardeva's Neo-Vaisnavism under four *Samhatis* (Sects) started getting royal patronage. Likewise, from Udayaditya Singh (1669—1673) to Sulikpha (1678—1681), all the Kings were the disciples of one Satra or the other. Gradually, besides the royal clans, the Ahom commoners started getting initiated into Vaishavism. This marked the begining of a conscious change in traditional Tai-Ahom beliefs and practices. Although until the reign of Gadadhar Singh (1684—1696), both the royal families and commoners openly followed dual religious practices—the traditional Tai-Ahom practices and Neo-Vaisnavism. This further divided the Ahoms into four endogamous groups based on their religious affiliation as *Brahma, Kala, Nika* and *Purusha-samhatis*.

THE CONTEMPORATY AHOM SITUATION AS REVEALED IN THE VILLAGE STUDY

So far we have examined the possible historical contact situations that brought about the process of acculturation among the Tai-Ahoms of Assam in a wider perspective. Now we shall examine the contemporaty Ahom situation in an Ahom village.

Within the village, a villager relates himself to several classes of kinsmen beyound his immediate families. His most frequent interaction is usually with those families close to him in patrilineal descent and in residence—a group that may be called a 'localized lineage' (Mandelbaum, 1970:134). The men are brothers who have set up separate households or the sons of brothers or patrilateral cousins.

Due to the wide dispersal of the erstwhile clans throughout Assam today, this localized lineage remains as the source of strength of the group. The role played by the localized lineage brings about a functional integration within the group and also helps to define the boundaries of the group. Interestingly enough, in such a group even certain rituals reinforce the sense of common feeling and that definitely stabilizes the identity of the group within a changed environment. This suggests that among any group, no matter how much a group undergoes changes, there is at a certain level a set limit to such changes thereby maintaining a functional integrity within itself. In a society individuals are mainly organized around its social structure. Both social structure and social organization are complementary to each other. Praxis do not necessarily tally the ideal and within the social organization activities are thus regulated according to the need of the society. Any departure from the ideal does not affect the structure as long as it is within the limit. Only those departures that exceed the limit set by the structure and become permanent, can bring about a structural change (Firth, 1954:4).

In case of the Ahoms, 'assimilation' of the autocthones enlarged the scope of Ahom social organization (through regulated marriage, selective adoption/diffusion of cultural traits, etc.). It was necessary for a definite purpose relating to production relation system and administration (administration of the people with varied culture) and it also consolidated the strength of the Ahom social structure in terms of social, economic and political power. Secondly, owing to the spatial dispersal of the clans, formation of the 'localized lineage' replaced the role of clans to a large extent, *Sapinda* rule gave a similar recognition to the 'localized lineage' as enjoyed by the erstwhile clans. Thirdly, all these changes occurred in conformation, not in deviance to the Ahom traditional social structure which actually gave a stability to the structure.

On examining the traditional Tai-Ahom and the present day Hinduized beliefs and practices, we find similarity in a number of cases.

Differences may occur in the way of performing the associated rituals, *i.e.* the forms. Presence of such similarity may suggest a much early exposure of the group to Hinduism. This aspect of 'exposure' to Hinduism can not be ruled out totally because "...in South-East-Asia Hinduism was predominant in those days. This was partly due to the efforts of Hindu colonists and partly due to commercial intercourse between India and the South-East-Asian countries (The Imperial Gazettee of India Vol. IX. 1908:107, cited in Sen 1982:53). As a proof of this interaction, it may be mentioned here that "...Indian alphabet *Dev Nagri* was used in Tai-language up to the thirteenth century A.D. in Thailand and its neighbourhood (Mazumdar, 1968:261, cited in Sen 1982:53).

If this is so, then Hinduism and later impact of Buddhism in South-East-Asia had undoubtedly set on the process of acculturation of the Ahoms even before they had migrated to Assam. Later influence of Buddhism in South-East-Asia is very much evident from their Tai-script and other philanthropic activities which they undertook like construction of roads, digging of large ponds and building of temples on the banks of these ponds (Gogoi, 1985:58).

Acculturation is a historically established phenomenon. It is also well established that one of the ways that cultures have grown is through borrowing. But the most interesting and at the same time challenging aspect is the selective borrowing and converting the borrowed items in such a manner that they fit into the culture of the borrower. It may continuously go through a process of fine tuning . On this we may superimpose the economic and political compulsions a group has to confront. The acculturation process thus becomes highly complex showing diverse trends.

The contemporary beliefs and practices in an Ahom village appear to be dominated by Hinduism. This is not surprising because the people claim themselves to be Hindus. But they are Hindus with a difference. They have a non-Hindu history which is pretty well known through a variety of popular texts. They have a history of which the people are proud. It is not something which they would discard or erase from their memory. It could be that a group like the Tai-Ahoms would be very selective in adaptation. Our data support this hypothesis. The data suggest that those beliefs which have similar connotation in other cultures get readily accepted. So is the case with the practices which the receiving culture finds of similar utility and value. Even myths which are similar get superimposed on the myths of other culture. For instance, the origin myth of the Ahoms that they are the descendants of *Lengdon,* the lord of heaven, has led to the creation of a new myth that facilitated the acceptance of *Indra* as synonymous to *Lengdon* and thereby accepting the Kshatriya status with a lineage of *Indra vamsiya* (Gogoi, 1968) and the titles, *svarga-narayana* and *svargadeva.*

Coming back to the beliefs and practices, the Ahoms readily accepted those Hindu *samaskaras*, which are similar to their own. They accepted some to emulate or to achieve certain goals—upward mobility on caste hierarchy. But in course of time, some were discarded when their purpose was fulfilled and their utility value had diminished. The Vaishnavas in Assam perform *Smarta* rites in accordance with the prescription of *Dharmasastra.*The Vaisnavas belonging to backward classes and tribes, however, do not uniformly perform these *samaskaras* (Sarma, 1966:119).The Hindu scripture *Jatukaranya* (as quoted in Sam. Pr. , P.135) enumerates sixteen *samaskaras as garbhadhana, pumsavana, caula, maurji (upanayana), vratas (four), godana, samavartans, vivaha, and antyesti* (cited in Kane, 1974 : 194). Gait (VIII.14-24) speaks of forty *samaskaras* (Kane, 1974 : 193)

To begin with, we present our data related to the life cycle rituals of a man as observed in an Ahom village. Birth is not simply a biological phenomenon of conception, pregnancy and delivery. These are enveloped in sociological process that entails a series of socio-religious beliefs and practices.

The prescribed traditional Hindu *samaskaras* like *garbhadharana* and *pumsavana* are visibly absent among the group as they are meant specially for the *dvija* or the twice-born caste Hindus. *Samaskaras* after conception like *garbharaksana anulobhana* can be equated with *panchamrit-khowa.* It is perhaps an extension of *garbharaksana* or may be equated to *sasyantikarma* which among the traditional Hindus is performed on the 10th month of pregnancy. In an Ahom village it is performed in the wife's natal home on the 5th or 7th month to gain strength and vitality for the growing foetus, *Sasyantikarma,* otherwise, is a rite for a woman who is about to deliver a child (Kane 1974:227).

Jatakarma, the Hindu ritual performed in the case of birth of a son is formally absent among the Ahoms of the village. But there is a pratice of distributing fish, especially large scaled fish when a couple is blessed with a son. Even this ritual seems to be an adaptation from the local niche, and can be seen only among those who can afford it. In the village the practice under question has become completely redundant today.

Homasutikagni is established near the door of the lying-in chamber of the lady who has delivered a child. White mustard seeds and rice chaff are to be offered in the fire for ten days whenever anybody enters there. Similar practice of establishing a fire near the bed of the mother and child after delivery is seen in the village. This practice is known to the Tai as *unfai* and is devoid of any ritual, it is meant for 'drying-up' of the abdomen of the woman who has delivered the child. There is no stipulated number of days for the fire to be kept on. *Niskramana* is a ritual of taking the child out of the house or in the open for the first time. A number of rituals are associated with it. A strong resemblance of this traditional Hindu ritual can be drawn with similar objective of introducing the child to the world, from the traditional Tai ritual called *aw-cook-can* or *bajj ulua* (in Assamese) as found in the village Lakhimipukhuri. It has also been adopted by other Assamese groups at large.

Cudakarma or the first hair shaving ritual is prominent among the western Tai groups and is believed to be due to 'Indianization' of the groups by the 'Indianized' people with whom the Tai who trekked westwards, came into contact, which, however, does not belong to the ancient Tai culture of the first millennium A.D. (Terwiel, 1980:39). Therefore, it can be seen as a continuation of that 'Indianized' practice (*ibid*) which has found a similar meaning among the Hinduized Ahoms. The ritual again has become redundant and is seen completely out of practice in Ahom villages.

Nua-tuloni-biya is a ritual which is typical of and unique to the Hinduized Tai Ahoms and many other Assamese groups. The very nature and the objective of this ritual seem to be contradictory to the prescription of *vivaha* in the *Dharmasastra.* According to the prescription of *Dharmasastra,* unmarried daughters at their natal home, after attaining menarchy, incur sin to their parents and brothers (Kane, 1974:444); while in *nua-tuloni-biya,* it is an open exhibition of their daughters at the age at menarche. Perhaps the ritual of mock marriage is a symbolic atonement achieved by the parents by marrying off the daughters when the actual marriages take place much later when suitable grooms are found. This is an example of innovation of culture trait to fit into the central theme of the religion that they have adopted.

As far as the ceremonial aspect of marriage is concerned, the *Vaisnavas* in Assam (including the Ahoms) follow the practice of *sampradan. Agnisthapana* and *homa* are completely absent in this ritual, while there are present amongst other Assamese groups. But in *chaklang*, the traditional Tai-Ahom marriage ritual, *agnisthapana* or *homa* is represented by lighting 101 earthen lamps which symbolise 101 deities witnessing the ritual.

Besides these special life-cycle rituals, there is another important ritual *snana,* which is prescribed in the *Dharmasastra* (Kane, 1974:664-67). This ritual bathing or *snana* has been selectively accepted by the Ahoms although they do have a similar concept of *aptang* (ceremonial bath) within a larger purview of *rik-khvan-mung-khvan performed* with the primary objective of gaining strength and vitality. This ritual can be seen in the light of *kamya-snana* (bath for some desired object) as prescribed in *Dharmasastra* (Kane, 1974:666).

AN OVERVIEW

Some 700 years back, in the year 1228, a small group of adventurous people, with their chief Sukapha entered Assam little knowing that they would be arrested forever by the banks of the mighty Brahmaputra. In course of time, they set the foundation of a nation called Assam and a new nationality called Assamese had emerged. While doing so, the group ungrudgingly accepted the ethos and values of the soil, leaving "some of their own" and equally contributing "some of theirs" to the local population. Now, 700 years after their first entry into Assam the group stands proudly as the genitor of the Assamese culture. Even when they have undergone a tremendous change in every sphere of life, they seem to have set a limit to the forces of change and zealously guard their identity of being an Ahom within the greater Assamese identity. Consequenty, certain new elements are incorporated into the group by a selective elimination process with a definite purpose of maintaining their identity. The historical forces that opearated on the Ahoms of the Lakhimipukhuri village were similar to all the Ahoms of Assam. Therefore, from our discourse on the acculturation of the Ahoms, we may venture a few generalizations to show how the process of selection-elimination opearated under a number of contact situations the Ahoms had to face, while undergoing acculturation. They are as follows :

1. Certain forms were borrowed and incorporated to achieve a higher status in a wider social framework.
2. Those values which were similar to theirs got incorporated without much change in the original form.
3. New forms with similar values showed considerable ability to persist.

4. Certain values got discarded in course of time as they had lost their utility in the society.
5. The incoming culture mainfested certain vested interests which had actually encouraged the retention of traditonal beliefs of the receiving culture.

On the basis of the above generalizations, we may draw the inference that the Ahoms in course of their long history have been successful in synthesising a new culture based on the process of acceptence, rejection, and persistence. The new form that has been synthesized shows the persistence of old values to a remarkable degree and thereby helps in maintaining a "dynamic equilibrium".

REFERENCES

Barua, I. 1978 : *Social Relations In an Ahom Village*. New Delhi : Starling Publishers.

Borgohain, R. 1988. : *Ahom State Formation: an Inquiry into the Factors of Polity Formation in Mediaeval North-east India*. Unpublished Ph.D. thesis, NEHU : Shillong.

Bhuyan, S.K. 1962 : *Deodhari Assam Buraji Guwahati* : Deptt. of Historical and Antiquarian Studies.

Firth, R. 1954 : *Social organization and social change*. The Journal of the Royal Anthropolotical Institute of Great Britain and Ireland. Vol. 84, part-1.

Gogei, P. 1968 : *The Tai and the Tai kingdoms*. Guwahati : Deptt. of History, publication Gauhati University.

Gait, E. 1926/1984 : *A History of Assam*. Delhi : Cine Tarika Publications.

Heesterman, J. C. 1972 : *India and the Inner Conflict of Tradition*. S. N. Fisenstadt (ed). Post traditional societies. New York : W. W. North & Company, INC.

Kane, P. V. 1974 : *History of Dharmasastra : Ancient and Medieaval Religions and Civil lawa*. Vol. II, Part-1, 2nd edition. Poona : Bhandarkar Oriental Research Institute.

Nandelboum, D. G. 1970 : *Society in India. Bombay* : Popular Prakashan.

Person, T. 1961 : *An outline of the social system. Person* et. al. (eds.), *Theories of society*. Vol. 1. New York : Free Press of Glencoe.

Phukan, J. N. 1968 : *Lik-Phan-Tai*. Gauhati : Congress Press.

Sen, D. 1982: *Early History of the Tai Ahoms, Proceedings of NEIHA*, 3rd session. Shillong. Deptt. of History, NEHU.

16

Social Offences and Penalties Imposed on Garo Offenders

JULIUS L. R. MARAK

At the very outset, it may be pointed out that in the Garo society the punishment and penalties imposed on the social offenders during the pre-British days was nothing short of death. The acts of *Botril dinga* and *Garo dinga* were common practice during those days. But with the annexation of the Garo Hills by the British in the year 1867, the usual practice of killing in the form of death penalty came to an end. And just to compensate the harm done to the person and to give a healing touch to it, the system of payment of *dai* to the complainant was introduced. The word '*dai*' in the real sense of the term means, *an' chi mitipa pari u'sita* (blocking the flow of blood and wiping the wound). The rampant killings of persons for minor offences were stopped forthwith and the payment of *dai* and fines were gradually introduced into the Garo tribal custom. The implication of *dai* is more civil than criminal, while fines have only criminal overtones. Implementation of the Garo customary laws regarding the offences committed is linked with these deterrents. Some specific laws or rules in existence relating to the nature of offences committed by the individual and the punishment imposed in the form of penalties, fines bearing a stamp of traditional control are discussed below.

It has, however, to be acknowledged that the moral standards of the Garos are high and such social evils as prostitution are almost unknown in the Garo society. Still, adultery is not uncommon, though it is considered a social evil. It is considered a social offence and a fine is imposed on the person committing such an offence with the idea that he or she has caused harm to the society. The fine imposed is a token one; what is more important is the question of individual shame and social disapproval involved with it.

'*TILEKANI*' (ADULTERY) COMMITTED BY A MARRIED PERSON

(i) If a man having a wife commits adultery with another, the offender shall have to pay a sum of Rs. 30/- as *dai* and a sum of Rs. 6/- as *gitok* (token compensation) to his wife. Likewise, the woman also shall have to pay the same amount of money to her husband and the wife of the man with whom she had relation. Thus, each offending person shall have to pay to the claimant or his/her *mahari* (reference group) , as the case may be.

(ii) If a married man commits adultery with a spinster, he will be required to pay a sum of Rs. 30/- as *dai* and an additional sum of Rs. 6/- as *gitok* to his wife or the *mahari*. In the same way, the spinster will have to pay the same amount of *dai* to the wife of the man with whom she had the relation. However, the payment of *dai* depends on the decision of the *chra* (kin group) and her *mahari*.

(iii) If a woman having a husband commits adultery with a bachelor, she will pay the sum of Rs. 30/- as *dai* and a sum of Rs. 6/- as *gitok* to her husband. The same amount of *dai* is to be paid by the man to the husband of the woman or as decided by the *chra* and the *mahari*.

ADULTERY COMMITTED BY A BACHELOR AND A SPINSTER:

A bachelor can under no circumstances commit adultery with a spinster. There are some restrictions on committing the act. In case a bachelor commits adultery with a spinster, he will have to marry that particular girl. If the bachelor refuses to take her as his wife after committing such an act, he shall have to pay the *dai* of Rs. 60/- to Rs. 120/- to the *mahari* of the girl. Likewise, if the spinster also refuses to marry the boy, she too shall have to pay the same amount of *dai* to the bachelor. The payment of *dai* shall have to be made even if the bachelor and the spinster consummated the act with mutual agreement. The act of committing adultery between a bachelor and the spinster is called *tilek nagandea, an.cha soldarenga*. The act of polluting an innocent girl is far worse than seducing an already married woman. In all cases of adultery, the *chra* and the *mahari* of both sides come together in *Melaa* (Council meeting) and decide the case. The decisions of the *chra* and the *mahari* in all cases are final and binding on both the offenders.

'DRANE TILEKANI' (RAPE)

Acts of *drane tileka* (rape) are very rare among tribes. The Garo are also no exception to this. Among the Garo, the penalties imposed on those people committing such social crimes are decided according to the damage done in terms of social status and on such consideration whether one is free from *akim* (claims or payments) or not.

(i) If a man commits or attempts to commit rape on a woman or a girl and sufficient number of witnesses are available to confirm the act, then he must pay a sum of Rs. 60/- and an additional sum of Rs. 120/- as *dai* to the girl or to the *mahari*, as the case may be.

(ii) If a man having a wife commits rape on another women or girl, he will be required to pay a sum of Rs. 60/- as *dai* to his wife. In addition, he will pay the same amount of money to the girl or to the *mahari* she belongs to.

RAPE OF A MINOR GIRL

If a man commits rape on a minor girl, who has not attained the age of puberty, he shall have to pay a sum of Rs. 1000/- to the girl and in addition, a sum of Rs. 50/- to the *jat* (tribe).

If the girl is found to have consented to the act, she too will pay a sum of Rs. 50/- to the *jat* (tribe) and a sum of Rs. 30/-as *dai* plus Rs. 6/- to be paid as *gitok* to the wife of the man, in case he is having a wife. The man also pays to his wife the same amount of money as paid by the girl. In such cases, the concerned *chra* and *mahari* should come together in a *Melaa* and decide the case, which is binding on both the offending parties. But in all such cases, the future of the girl becomes the foremost consideration.

'TILEKRAMRAM GIPANI DAI'

If a man or a woman commits adultery with someone who has a wife or a husband, then he or she shall have to pay a sum of Rs. 30/- as *dai* to the persons offended. Over and above, the person, who had committed such an act, must pay a sum of Rs. 100/- to the *jat* (tribe) for creating a public offence (*jatko kratchaatani*).

DIVORCE

The Garo customary laws do not strictly restrict a person from divorcing a man or a woman on sufficient and proper grounds under certain unavoidable circumstances. But the Christians do not strictly follow it.

(i) If a person divorces his/her wife/husband without sufficient reasons, he or she has to pay a sum of Rs. 60/- as *dai* and a sum of Rs. 25/- each to the *jat* (tribe) and to the husband or wife divorced.

(ii) If a man having a wife and children neglects them continuously for a period of at least one year and if due to such negligence the family suffers badly, the wife can divorce her husband. The *dai* of Rs. 60/- and an additional amount of Rs. 25/-, normally earmarked for the *jat* (tribe), will have to be paid by the husband to his wife and children in the event of divorce.

(iii) If a man, after having divorced his wife, stays away from the family for sometime and then returns again to his former wife and children, then in such a case he will be required to pay a sum of Rs. 15/- as *dai* for *chu'dap waltim romtomani* (breach of trust and restoration of ties) to her. In the same manner, his wife also pays the sum of Rs. 15/- as *dai* to her husband or to his *mahari*, in case she comes back to her husband after having been divorced. This, however, needs to be approved by her *chra* in a combined meeting of both the *maharis*.

REDUCING THE IMPORTANCE OF '*NOKKROM*' (HEIRESS)

(i) If a person seduces and elopes the girl who has been selected *nokkrom* (heiress), he will have to pay the sum of Rs. 60/- as *dai* to the *mahari* of the family or as decided by her *chra* and the *mahari*.

(ii) If a girl selected as *nokkrom* becomes engaged with a boy, but later deserts him and selects another boy, then she has to pay a sum of Rs. 60/- to the boy with whos she was engaged or to his *mahari*. In the same manner, if the boy goes away with another girl after breaking the engagement, it would be his tum to pay the *dai* of Rs. 60/- to the *mahari* of the girl or decided by her *chra* and *mahari*.

'SKODO KANDIA'

A man or a woman eloping with someone's wife or husband even when remaining as husband and wife is called *skodo kandia*. The man who elopes another man's wife, but returns to his wife in course of time, will pay Rs. 30/- as *so'mal dai* and a sum of Rs. 6/- as *gitok* to his wife as well as to the husband of the woman he has eloped. In the same way, the woman also has to pay the same amount as that of a man to her husband and her opponent. In case of refusal by the concerned husband or wife to take back their respective spouses on the ground of elopement, a sum of Rs. 60/- will have to be paid by the offender to the aggrieved party or as decided by the *chra* and *mahari*.

'AGANTOREA' OR *'KAWATE KUDIKGILA'*

(i) It means a person who boasts himself by telling the people that he has committed adultery with somebody or uses some such defamatory words against any person, which may or may not be true. Later, on enquiry, if it is found that those outspoken words are not true, he (or she) will be asked to pay a sum of Rs. 15/- as *dai* to one against whom such words were first used *(kratcha'atani)*.

(ii) If such defamatory words used against a married man or woman could be established, then the person who had uttered those words will pay a sum of Rs. 15/- as *dai* to the persons offended.

'AMITA' (ACCUSED OR SUSPECTED OF ADULTERY)'

If a man or woman brings *amita* (accusation of adultery) on his wife or her husband as the case may be, but if it is found to be untrue on proper enquiry, then the person who has accused or suspected the other of adultery has to pay a sum of Rs. 15/- as *dai* to the offended party for *kratcha'atani*. But if such words of *amita* are found true on proper enquiry, then the man or the woman involved will have to pay the *dai* according to the nature of offence committed .

In addition to the aforesaid conditions, *dai* may imposed for various other reasons. The following is a list of specific cases when *dai* could be imposed.

(a) A person accused of giving false witness against someone will be required to pay a sum of Rs. 15/- as *dai* to the person offended.

(b) Any person speaking ill (*agan mitakjojoa*) against someone, which is not true, pays a sum of Rs. 25/- as *dai*, when detected, to the person offended.

(c) If a person causes shame (*ramram kratcha'ata*) on any other person not by his or her actual deeds but by means of words, then such a person will be required to pay a sum of Rs. 15/- as *dai* to the person offended.

(d) If a woman beats her husband or tears his clothes or burns them or throws away in anger any of the materials used by him, she will have to pay a sum of Rs. 15/- as *dai* to the husband or his *mahari*.

(e) If a man in course of beating his wife with a view to exercise control over her, causes injury to her, then he will be forced to pay a sum of Rs. 25/- as *dai* to his wife or to her *mahari*. In addition, he pays a sum of Rs..15/- to the *a'song* (village).

(f) If a man or a woman, while beating a person with a view to control him or her, encroaches on the compound of another man or woman, then he or she will be required to pay a sum of Rs.15/- as *dai* to the owner of the compound plus a sum of Rs. 15/- to the *a'song* (village).

(g) A person scolding or abusing someone without any valid reason (*sairamrama*) has to pay a sum of Rs. 15/- as *dai* to the person offended.

(h) If a man or a woman is provoked to beat a person other than his or her relative causing injury to him or her, then the one who has caused injury by beating must pay a sum of Rs. 15/- as *dai* to the person offended. In addition, he or she will have to bear all the expenses for giving him or her necessary medical treatment.

(i) If a man or woman threatens to kill someone before causing serious injury to him or her (*agantorea*) and if such an action could be proved in due course with sufficient evidence and witnesses, then he or she will pay a sum of Rs. 25/- to the person threatened even though he or she may not act upon. In addition, he or she will be asked to pay a sum of Rs. 15/ - to the *a'song* (village).

(j) A person who steals in the village must return the stolen goods. Besides, he or she will have to pay a sum of Rs. 15/- to the *a'song* (village). In case the stolen goods cannot be returned but the act of stealing is proved beyond doubt, the person concerned has to pay Rs. 25/- as *dai* plus the exact value of the materials stolen to the owner.

(k) Any person causing disharmony and disturbances to the village (*songko golmal k. gipa*) will have to pay a sum of Rs.15/- to the *a'song*.

(l) Any person who disregards the judgment given following customary laws and traditions will be required to pay a sum of Rs. 50/- as *dai* to the *jat* (tribe) for contempt of customary laws.

(m) If a man or a woman, after accepting the judgment passed according to the customary law, appeals to other courts without the leave of the first court where he or she may have to return later, will be required to pay a sum of Rs.50/- to the *jat* (tribe) even before his or her case is taken up.

Over and above, there are some other social offences to which the fines or *dais* are fixed according to the nature and seriousness of the act committed. The following are few examples of how *dai* could be fixed in this way.

(i) The person who has committed the offence of *noksam mala do ja ga'a or chambua* (entering the house stealthily with the intention of committing adultery) has to pay a sum of Rs. 25/ - as *dai* to the person offended.

(ii) The person who has committed the offence of *sok se. eta ganna kika* or *kilte aka na. ring moa* (violating the dignity of a woman by tormenting her) has to pay a sum of Rs. 30/ - as *dai* to the woman or to her *mahari*.

(iii) The person committing the offence of *kritomo sika jakgitoko rim.a* (attempted rape) will have to pay a sum of Rs.15/- as *dai* to the woman.

(iv) The person committing the offence of *miknia mikjapa* (teasing) has to pay a sum of Rs. 15/- to the woman/girl or to her *mahari*.

(v) The person committing the offence of *muc.chi monga. Jakchi jakjipa* (seduction) must a pay a sum of Rs. 15/- as *dai* to the woman/girl.

(vi) The person committing the offence of *tilek nagendea ja. o rongkantea* (a girl becoming pregnant as a result of adultery) will have to pay a sum of Rs. 60/- as *dai* to the girl or *mahari* plus an additional amount of Rs. 15/- for *kratcha'atani* to the girl or as demanded by her *chra* and *mahari.*

Generally speaking, all social, criminal and religious offences are judged in consonance with the nature of offence and the *dai* is fixed accordingly by the *chra* and the *mahari* in the *Melaa.* But it is to be noted that although the same principles of customary laws, usages and practices are followed everywhere, we find a list of difference in the amount of *dai* imposed on every offender from one place to another or even from one locality to the other. Even then, it may be pointed out that the Garo customary laws and their usages and practices are the most elaborate one. They function in a way which is suggestive of both rigidity and flexibility as demanded by the situation.

For example, the marital customs of the Garos are regulated mainly by the principle of exogamy and *a'kim*, which are being strictly adhered to. The breach of these rules is a matter of serious concern and the penalty imposed on the offences are heavy which are decided by their respective *chra*, parents and the *mahari* in the *Melaa.* The Garo society, being a matrilineal one, gives the rights of inheritance to the property of the parents to the woman and never to a man. Boys remain empty-handed when they go out of their parent's house after marriage. But even then there is scope for the son to get a share of the property after marriage. The property given to the son and the time of marriage by his parents may be decided after due consultation with the *chra* and *mahari.* The husband can utilise this property during his lifetime. After his death, all immovable property given to be him will return to the motherhood. Again, there is some protection for the Garo woman married to a non-Garo provided by the society. For the legal protection of Garo woman married to man outside the periphery of the community, and with a view to proper legitimization of children born out of non-Garo man, such children should be named after the names and surnames of the family *ma'chong* (motherhood) or *chatchi* (clan) of the mother, but never of the father.

Every Garo attaches great value to the honour, prestige of their community and to their ancestor and tries to avoid doing anything which may cause harm to them. The general feeling is that the Garo ancestors are the lucky ones who had lived and died before the large-scale contamination of the present generation and they deserve to be honoured. Today, almost all criminal cases are taken to law courts and tried accordingly. Most of the cases are no longer tried and settled within the villages according to the existing customary laws. "How could we be wiser when our minds are lost? How could we be better placed when we have hardly any fear to break the laws our forefathers held most dear?" – wondered a knowledgeable Garo. There is, however, a feeling that the disposal of the cases according to customary laws, their usages and practices should be continued in right spirit and practised with a view to preserving and revitalizing the ancient heritage of the Garo.

REFERENCES

A. PRIMARY SOURCES

1. Roston R. *Marak and Anjang A. Marak, Village: Mariampur, Goalpara District,* Assam : 3.2.1979
2. Rohondi Marak, *Village: Mallang, West Khasi Hills District, Meghalaya,* 12.1.1980.
3. Dewaning S. Rongmuthu, *Village: Wa, gesik (Baghmara) West Garo Hills District, Meghalaya,* 1.10.1980.
4. Roghunath Areng, *Village Court Member, Village : A. gropatal, East Garo Hills District, Meghalaya,* 21.5.1979.
5. Kaising G. Momin, *Village: Wakgok Daring, East Garo Hills District, Meghalaya,* 15.4.1979.
6. Justine R. Marak, *Secretary Village Court, Village : Kujikura, West Garo Hills District, Meghalaya* 13.8.1980.
7. Sotneng Sangma, Nokma and Debin Marak, Nokma, *Village : Sasatgre, West Garo Hills District, Meghalaya.* 27.11.1980.

B. JOURNALS AND MAGAZINES

1. Rongmuthu, Dewansing 1978, *Marriage & Customs of the Garos,* North-Eastern Spectrum & Book Supplement, Vol. 1 No. 9.11. Gauhati, Assam.
2. *Matrilineal System in Meghalaya* (An Appreciation), North-Eastern Spectrum & Book Supplement, Vol. 1 No.5. Gauhati, Assam.

C. SECONDARY SOURCES

1. G.N.C. Goalpara District, 1965, *The Garo Customary Law of Inheritance and Punishment and the Village Court Act* – Nisangram Village.
2. Fr. Cpstp Giulio, 1975, *The Garo Code of Law. Anthropos,* II. 1041-1066.
3. Bose, J. K. 1941, *The Garo Law of Inheritance, An thropological Papers,* Calcutta University, New series, VI, 81-150.
4. Sangma, Jangsan (Advocate), 1973, *Principles of Garo Laws*, Gauhati, Assam.

17

The Purum: Cultural Drift and the Problem of Identity

MANIS KUMAR RAHA

India as a vast country has accommodated as may as 4693 communities including 461 scheduled tribes. Of these scheduled tribes, some are numerically very large, while there are some others who have only a marginal representation. Again, some are very little known as hardly any literature or research paper is available on them. But some others have thoroughly been studied by a number of scholars and academicians. The Purum of Manipur are one such group, who have been extensively studied and who have occupied a permanent place in the discourses of Social Anthropology. For a long time after the publication of articles (1955, 1939, 1941) and the book entitled The Purum : An Old Kuki Tribe of Manipur (Assam) (1945) by Prof. T. C. Das, there was for sometime no ripple in the academic circle over the very special and complicated marriage and kindship systems of this tribe. Needham was possibly the first person to realise the importance of the systems and he initiated an academic exercise of great importance through structural analysis of this society in 1958 and then critically analysing the Purum rinship and marriage systems in his book, *Structure and Sentiments : A Test Case in Social Anthropology in 1962*. Thereafter, a good number of scholars and academicians like Ackerman (1964), Cowgirl (1964), Geoghegan & Kay (1964), Wilder (1964), Muller (1964) and also Needham (1964) were involved in the debate on these unique features of this tribe.

Apart from the above scholars, White (1963) also tried to analyse the Purum marriage system mathematically using the graph theory. In 1965, Schneider made an attempt to analyse the Purum data. Livingstone in 1969 'applied matrix analysis on Purum data and classified the relationship between sibs that are predominantly either wife-giving or wife-taking' (Gupta, 1985:34).

All the above scholars and academicians have analysed mainly the data on the systems of marriage and kinship as presented by Das in his book and have engaged themselves in the ensuing debate centering around the marriage and kinship systems of the Purum and their implications on social structure. In 1975, the Anthropological Survey of India sent a team of anthropologists to study the Purum society in the context of 1971 Census figures where the Purum population was shown as 'nil'. In 1982-85 the Survey organised a symposium on the Purum (Chote). Discussion in this symposium, though devoted mainly to issues like marriage system, also brought into focus the identity problem of the Purums and the Purum-Chote-Kuki-Naga controversy. Admittedly, both the issues are equally important. In this paper I have made an attempt to highlight the culture of the Purums as depicted by T.C. Das and reassessment of the same as done by Das Gupta and others after a span of forty years and, of course, the Purum-Chote-Kuki-Naga controversy, which for sometime has engaged the attention of social scientists more than the structural features of the earlier Purum society.

At present, the Purum represent a scheduled tribe of Manipur with supposed Chote link. In fact, the Chote stand for another scheduled tribe of the same State. According to MaCulloch (1959), the Purum belong to the Kuki group of tribes. Hodson (1911), Das (1945) and Grierson (Das, 1935) have considered them as the Old Kuki. But to Shakespeare (1912), they belong to a clan of the Old Kuki. Brown, on the other hand, has expressed a different view. He has accepted them as a branch of the Kom tribe. Whatever may be their identity and affiliation with other tribes, it must be because of some of their unique features that the Purum have been able to draw the attention of so many leading anthropologists and other social scientists. No doubt, they are one of the most discussed tribes. Very few tribes from any other part of the world could evoke so much of interest in the academic circle as the Purum did. So it is imperative to know first of all what is unique about the Purum social formation.

The Purums were found to occupy homogeneous villages, meaning thereby that their villages were inhabited only by the members of this tribe. The families of other communities were not allowed to stay there. The name of each Purum village was prefixed with the name of the tribe. Consequently, the four villages studied by Das were named as Purum Khullen, Purum Tampak, Purum Changninglong and Purum Chumbang. In 1936 when Das studied these villages, the village Khullen had forty houses, Tampak had twenty nine, Chumbang had 'twelve or thirteen' and Changninglong consisted of 'eight or nine' houses. Each of these houses represented a family 'whether biological or joint' (1945 : 40).

The village Khullen was situated on the top of a ridge at a height of about 4000 ft above mean sea level. The village Tampak was situated on the southern slope of a low hillock. Changninglong lied on the top of a fairly high hillock and the village Chumbang was spread over on the `eastern side of the ridge on which Khullen' lied.

The Purums were mainly agriculturists. Both dry and wet types of cultivation were practised by them. Paddy was the main crop grown by them as their staple food was rice. Besides, they also cultivated a few vegetables like maize, onion, sesame, mustand, etc. The JHUM plots were in most cases situated near the village and are never far away from the village 'as cultivation of such land is carried out from village' (Das, 1945 : 53). Any villager had the right to select a particular plot within the villages as JHUM land provided the same plot was not occupied by others. Members of both sexes used to take equal part in all the operations of the JHUM field. A Purum householder could not harvest the yield before his *pipa* or head of the sub-sib had offered the first yield to the deity, *Senamahi*. Besides agriculture, the Purums practised fishing, hunting and animal husbandry as other sources to suppement their income.

Shakespeare (1912) considered the Purums as a 'clan' of the Lushei Kuki group. He also mentioned that the Old Kuki clans like the Aimol, Anal, Chawte, Kolhen, Kom, Lamgang, Purum, Tikhup and the Vaiphei did not intermarry and also lived in separate villages (1912 : 149). But Das considered the Purum as a tribe and stressed that it did not possess any characteristic feature of the clan. Rather, according to him, the Purum represented an endogamous group, a tribe divided into a number of exogamous clans (1945 : 106—107). These exogamous clans or sibs were Marrim, Makan, Kheyang, Thao and Parpa. All of these clans except Parpa were again sub-divided into sub-clans. Marrim had four sub-sibs, namely Rimphung—Chong, Rimkhung, Rim-ke-leek and Pilling, Maken had Kankung and Makan-te, Kheyang had Jullung, Aibung, Impi and Ingte and Thao had Thao-Kung, Thao-rum, Teyu and Rangshai as sub-sibs. But earlier Das spoke of another clan, Julhung in addition to these five clans or sibs (1935:3).

The sibs among the Purum were patrilineal in nature. The children belonged to their father's sib. Even the daughters did not give it up even after their marriage but continued to retain it till death. Another important feature of the sibs was in connection with inheritance.

> 'When a man dies without anybody in the male line of the family to inherit him, the members of the sib inhabiting the same village step in and divide the property among themselves. Daughters have no right to any kind of property of their father' (Das, 1945:139).

The main function of these clans or sibs was to regulate marriage. As Das (1945 : 122) states, "The Purum sib is primarily responsible for regulation of marriage though now-a-days some of its functions have been taken over by the sub-sib". While the Purum sibs regulated the marriage, these also debarred the Purum boys and girls from their free choice of marrying in any clan or sib except their own. Therefore, the Purum boys and girls could marry only in one or more prescribed sibs. Such unions between the different sibs were fixed by the traditional customs (Das, 1945 : 123). Again, the boys and girls had to find out spouses from two different sibs. The brother and sister could, therefore, marry not in the same sib but in different sibs. For example, Marrim family could give their daughters to Kheyang, Makan and Parpa, but could take girl only from Thao. Similarly, Makan could take girl from Marrim, Kheyang and Parpa but could give girl only to Thao. Kheyang could take girl from Marrim Thao and Parpa but could give girl only to Makan, Thao, on the other hand, could give girl to Marrim and Kheyang but could take girl from Makan and Parpa and finally, Parpa could give girl to Thao, Kheyang and Makan but could take girl only from Marrim. On the other hand, the Marrim boys could marry only Thao girls, but the Marrim girls could go for Makan, Parpa or Kheyang boys. The Makan boys had the option to marry Marrim, Kheyang or Parpa girls, whereas Makan girls had no option but to marry only Thao boys. The Kheyang boys could select girls from either Marrim or Thao or Parpa, but the Kheyang girls had no choice but to go for Makan boys. Similarly, the Thao boys could select either Makan or Parpa girls and Thao girls could only marry Marrim or Kheyang boys. And lastly, the Parpa boys had no option but to marry Marrim girls, but this was not so for the Parpa girls. They could marry Makan, Kheyang or Thao boys.

It is thus seen that among the Purum for each man 'the sibs are divided into 3 groups, namely, (1) his own, rather his father's sib, (2) his mother's group of sibs, or rather the group of sibs from which his wife is recruited and (3) his sister's husband's sibs *i.e.*, the group of sibs in which his sisters are married (sometimes his mother's mother's or mother's mother's mother's sib') (1945 : 25). Similarly, for a woman there are three sets of sibs :

(1) her own sib, or rather her father's sib,

(2) her mother's group of sibs, and

(3) her husband's group of sibs (sometimes her mother's mother's or mother's mother's mother's sib).

Needham after analysing the data found that 'the total society is divided by the Purums themselves into : (1) lineally related descent groups, (2) wife-giving groups, (3) wife-taking groups : and the fundamental cycle of alliance is exhibited by the specific statement that a wife-taking group may be identical with a wife-giving group of one's own wife-givers'(1960 : 78).

The family, being the smallest social unit of the Purum society, consisted of 'a man his wife and unmarried children born of their union (1945 : 111). The joint family on the other hand, consisted of the parents and one or more married sons with their wives and children. The family among the Purums was patrilocal in residence. One of the characteristics of the Purum family was that its composition was influenced by the laws of inheritance and also by marriage customers (*ibid*).

Normally, after completion of *yaun-gimba* period (service for marriage) a young man was to bring his wife to the house of his father where he used to stay till the marriage of his next younger brother or till his father died. The usual practice for him was to construct a separate house for his family and cultivate land given to him (both forest land for shifting cultivation and also plains land). After marriage, all the brothers, except the youngest one, used to leave the parental house to set up their own establishment. Only the youngest brother normally lived with his parents. The elder brothers did not like to remain dependent on their parents. On their separation from the parental house, they used to construct their new houses with the help of the villagers. As per rule of the society, they used to select a piece of forest land and begin cultivation on their own. So as the parents grew old, they had no option but to keep their youngest son to remain with them after marriage so that they could receive assistance from the youngest son in the field of cultivation. Thus, the youngest son was not allowed to live separately from his father like his other elder brothers. The youngest son was also required to look after his parents at their old age, and so take the responsibility of the parental or core household. "This perhaps, explains the custom of inheritance by the youngest son among this .prople ...."(Das 1945 : 112).

The family among the Purum was patrilineal. "The children of a man live among his agnatic relations and look up to them for help in times of difficulty. The father's brother is shown respect as accorded to the father" (*ibid* : 113). Similarly, they used to think that the sons of the father's brothers were nearer and closer to them than the sons of the mother's brothers.

Another speciality of the Purum family was that it was not homogeneous in the true sense of the term. In a Purum family due to patrilocal residence the daughters were to leave after marriage and sons, at least the youngest son, used to bring wife to his parental house from the prescribed families and sibs. Over and above, because of the prevalence of marriage by service, youngmen from other prescribed families and sibs used to stay in the families of the bride, at least temporarily.

In the Purum society the youngest son used to inherit the entire property of his father, who during his life time was the owner of all the family property. The youngest son, in addition to all his father's property, also got his father's domestic animals, grains, looms, house, land, etc. Das (1945 : 167) explains, "The economic basis of Purum society and the type of social organization are mainly responsible for this kind of inheritance". The youngest son used to remain with his parents when they were old as the other brothers had to establish separate establishment after their marriage. "Moral, social and economic factors combined to set up this system of inheritance among the Puruin" (ibid). But now some Purums think that other sons should also get a share of the property, even though less than that received by the youngest son. The daughters, on the other hand, were not entitled to get any property—movable or immovable, from their father.

Every Purum village had a village council which consisted of eight village officials. They were *Khullakpa, Luplakpa, Khunjahanba, Pakhanlakpa, Zupanba (Yalpalpa), Kairungba, Selungba and Changlai.* These officials were meant for looking after the temporal affairs of the village as they formed the judicial council of the village. The *Khullakpa* was the village headman who used to preside over this council. Normally, the sittings of the village council took place at *ruishang, i.e.*, the village council chamber or court house. This chamber was also used for discussion on social, political and religious affairs by the villagers whenever such problems arose. The posts of the village officials were not hereditary.

When a village officer dies or resigns from his post he is succeeded by the next lower officer who is, in turn, again is succeeded by the next lower officer. Thus each of the officers lower in rank to the man who died or resigned, is automatically promoted to the next higher post. Thus, on the death or resignation of the *Khullakpa*, his post goes to Luplakpa, and the *Khunjahanba* becomes the *Luplakpa*, and so on, till *Changlai* is raised to the rank of *Selungba* (Das, 1945 : 173).

The recruitment to the lowest post *i.e., Changlai*, when fell vacant, was made from the villagers. Normally, if the *Khullakpa* had a son, he was given the post: in his absence, any male member of the *Khullakpa's* sib was selected as the next incumbent.

The religious beliefs and practices of the Purum were based on their faith on the supernatural beings, different natural phenomena, soul, and the other world, etc. They have a number of deities and spirits. These deities and spirits were of three years : firstly, those which were recently introduced and were not fully assimilated with their culture ; the second set of deities and spirits was comparatively older, which the Purums had adopted fully ; the third set of deities and spirits was purely Purum in origin. But with the passage of time many non-Purum elements got infiltrated into their religion. Their contact with the neighbouring Meiteis, who had a Hindu identity, compelled them to adopt many traits from the former. "The religious beliefs and practices of the Purums show undesirable traces of loans from their Hindu neighbours' (Das, 1945 : 188). Among them, there were thus three sets of deities. The gods and goddesses whom they have recently borrowed from the Hindus are *Krishoa (Krishna), Mahadeo, Aram (Rama), Durga, Kali, Yama* and others. But the deities like *Senamahi*, the clan-god and an important deity among them, was adopted 'at a much earlier date either from the

Meiteis or from some other people from whom the Meiteis also borrowed this deity' (*ibid*). The deity like *Nungchungba* was a pure Purum deity and was considered as the most important one. The Purums also had a number of evil spirits and godlings supposed to be responsible for specific diseases. These evil spirits were responsible for harming the human beings and domestic animals and birds through disease, death and other ways. They could also damage the crops of the field if they were enraged. They were appeased through propitiation, offerings and sacrifices. The Purums also had spirits of the forest (*Haihru*) and water (*Irai-ningthan*). The ancestral worship was an important aspect of the Purum religion. These ancestral spirits (*Kasha-lai*) were worshipped annually, through they were not given much attention (Das, 1945 : 210). The Purums had a number of festivals. Through these festivals they used to worship various deities and spirits to protect them and their animals and birds from disease, death and physical harm and also from the destruction of the crops.

The above description of the culture of the Purums has been given by Prof. T. C. Das in his book, 'The Purums : An Old Kuki Tribe of Manipur'. The data for this book were collected between 1931 and 1936, and the manuscript was ready in 1941. In 1945 the book was published by the University of Calcutta. In 1975, thirty years after the publication of the book by Das, the Anthropological Survey of India sent a team of anthropologists to restudy this group of people. This team of anthropologists could locate and contact all the Purum villages studied by Das. During their fieldwork they found altogether nine villages of which seven were close to the valley. These are Tampak, Lairingkhul, Purumkhullen, Chandropotr, Chumbang, Wangparal and Punthapopki (Das Gupta, 1985 : 54).

Like every human society, the Purum society has also undergone changes. Every aspect of this society is changing in different degrees. The structured features and cultural attriocities of the Purum when Das studied them they were definitely different from what they are now. Different internal and/or external factors are definitely responsible for these changes. These changes at least point to one particular development *i.e.*, a newfound openness which has now pervaded their society. the Purums now hardly function as a closed system as they used to do in the past. There have been changes in the cultural values, which have been reflected in their social behaviors and practices followed at the community and inter-community levels.

During 1936 and after when Das undertook field work among the Purum the presence of the Christian missions were not perceptible and Christianity did not have any effect on the life on the Purum. But it started changing after the World War–II. In 1975. 'all the villagers except those of Lamlonghupi were converted to Christianity (Das Gupta, 1985:55). The entry of the Chiristian Missions in the Purum/Chote land has tremendous impact on these people.

The missions belong either to the American Baptist of Roman Catholic. But whatever Church they might have belonged to, there is no doubt about the fact that Christianity has brought significant changes in their life.

Hiyang and others have also admitted that "all the Chote villages are now changed into Christian villages in which they gave up all the rituals which they had been following since a distant past". They have further noted that 'the worship of their traditional gods, Pu-Soraren, Pu-Pakhangba and their customary festivals had been changed and their places have been taken over by the Christian festivals in the Christian villages of Chote' (*ibid* 29).

During Das's time there were two schools of lower primary standard, but in 1975 every village has two or more number of schools of primary, middle or junior high' (Das Gupta. 1995 : 56). That means the Purum/ Chote have started receiving better opportunities for modern education. These schools were opened either by the Church or by the state administration and the church-run schools are quite popular.

In 1975, the research team of the Authropological Survey of India visited all the nine Purum villages, of which seven were in the neighbourhood of the valley. These villages were Tampak, Lairingkhul, Purumkhullen, Chandropoto, Chumbang, Wangparal,. Punthapopki, Khongkhang and Lamlanghupi. At that time Punthapopki had the lowest population (60 only), whereas Chumbang had 251 inhabitants (Basu, 1895 : 38). But recently Arun Kumar could trace 12 Purum villages (1998 : 71).

The Purum now practise settled cultivation. Due to denudation of forests they have gradually given up slash and burn method and adopted wet rice cultivation, So agriculture has been the mainstay of these people. Though rice is the main product of cultivation, those who do not have land for wet cultivation produce cash crops which they sell to the vendors or agents. As a result, they are now getting quite a good amount of much needed cash in their hand. Prompted by the rise of ceash and market economy. Das Gupta (1985) noted the formation of two classes among them—*achongpa* (rich) and *saranpa* (poor). The class system of this type was unheard of in the Purum sociey when Das worked among them. In addition to agriculture, the Purum/Chote also collect edible roots, tubers, wild vegetables and other forest products and also hunt minor animals. Some of them have taken to service, blacksmithy, baskerty and weaving as subsidiary occupations. Another interesting development is the formation of some rich households (*achongpa*) in every village because of the change from shifting to settled cultivation. Hiyang and his co-workers have also admitted that though traditionally the Chotes were shifting cultivators, now most of them have shifted to wet rice cultivation (1985 a:16).

Hiyang and his co-authors have mentioned about seven village officials who run the village administration. These officials are *hulakpa* (Chief), *luplakpa* (Asstt. Chief). *juhpaipa, keirungpa, hachari*, keirungnaha and *macharinaha*. But Das Gupta has used some what different terms for the composition the village council (*Hupal*). They are *hulak, luklak, hunchal, yupal, heirung selrung* and *changrui*. Of these seven officials, all males, as mentioned by Das Gupta, *hulak* is the head who is elected by the village elders for five years, The *luklak* is next to *hulak*, who assists the latter. The duty of *yupal* is to prepare and serve wine. At present, instead of wine tea is served. The *keirung* is to take care of the *granaries*. The *selrung* acts as the treasurer and the changrui is in charge of community forest.

The *Hupal* or the village council has two wings—*hlouka* for the elderly persons and *loumi* formed by the youngsters. The members of the Hupal, form huklak to *changrui*, are all members of *hlouka*. But *loumi* has a separate set of officials. It has the following officials; one *hancha* (Chief) one *hitchang* (Asstt Chief), one *hunchal* (Asstt. Chief), one *yupal* (serving wine or tea), one *ashu arang* (announcer), four *thongchoieopong* (who serves leaf cups) and five *rui* (aides). The last named officials *i.e.*, *rui* are, in fact, guards and carry out the instructions of higher officials (Das Gupta, 1985 : 68). The Purum customary laws do not allow any two of the seven members of *hloukal* to come from the same clan. All of them should come from different clans.

Apart from the above village council, the Purums have another set up, that is the 'Chote General Union', which binds all the Purum villages (*ibid* : 71). It was formed in 1946 and its objective is to bring unity among all the Purum (Chote) people. Arun Kumar has also mentioned about 'Chothe General Union, Manipur' (CGUM) (1998 : 73). In 1987 this union was bifurcated and a new set up 'Chothe Naga Union, Manipur' was formed.

Though originally the Purum (Chote) had five sibs and five subsibs, in all 10, at present they have as many as 27 sibs and subsibs. It is also becoming difficult to follow a rigid system of classification of unilineal groups. No clan other than Marrim Rimkung and Makam Kankung, has a ubiquitous distribution (Das Gupta, 1985 : 74). It is also important to note that no village has all the clans and sub-clans/sub-sibs. The direct exchange is found only at the sub-sib level and not at the sib-level. During his field work Das Gupta found 21 cases of direct exchange and of these 21 cases, in 17 cases one way flow of bride was allowed as per norms and in 4 cases flow of bride in either way, though disallowed by the societal norm, took place. In 8 cases there was direct exchange of bride within the sib. In another 30 cases flow of bride took place deviating from the customary law (1985: 74–75).

No doubt, the Purum/Chote society has undergone marked change. Unlike in the past, they are now practising wet cultivation and are also involved in other types of occupation. Most of them have now accepted Christaianity giving up their traditional religious beliefs and practices. Their population has been increasing, so also is the number of their villages. The number of sibs and sub-sibs has also multiplied in number. In case of marriage, they sometimes do not follow the social norms or customary laws. So the present day Purum/Chote have developed a culture which is not quite in time with their past tradition. The point of consideration is, the Purm/Chote of today show a marked departure from the Purum as reported by T.C.Das some sixty years back, which had earned them so much of importance in the academic circle.

The controversy relating to Purum/Chote identity which had created a stir in the academic field with obvious political implications gives a new twist to the Purum existence. The Census figures also lend substance to the controversy.

The Census figures of different decades clearly indicate that from 1931 to 1961 the Purum population had steadily decreased in number and ultimately, in 1971 Census there was no trace of any Purum. They reappeared again in 1981 Census with 447 individuals, but in 1991 they were again reduced to 388.

On the other hand, the population of the Chote/Chothe, who were only 250 individuals in 1931, steadily increased in number reaching 2571 individuals in 1991. In 1995 – 96 Arun Kumar undertook field work in 14 Purum-Chote villages and could count 2464 individuals (Purum / Chote) in these villages (1998 : 71). In 1936 when Das visited the Purum villages, he could court the Purum population up to 303. But he never mentioned any Purum shifting his allegiance to the Chote. He oniy mentioned about 'a community called Chote' who had lived in Lamlanghupi village near Bisenpur.

TABLE 17.1. The Population of the Purum and Chote in Different Census Periods.

Year	*Purum*	*Chote*
1931	305	250
1951	43	695
1961	82	1035
1971	Nil	1905
1981	447	1687
1991	388	2571

Now with the gradual decrease of the Purum population and consequent increase of the Chote population and with the total disappearance of the Purum as indicated in 1971 Census, several questions have been raised. The question that automatically comes to the mind is whether all the Purums got finally transformed into Chote and were therefore non-existent ? Or was it that the Purum as a separate tribe never actually existed? They were rather misrepresented. In this connection Das Gupta writes:

> . . .all the Purum villages have the prefix Purum because Purum is the type of land in which they inhabit (Purum-hilly and forest land). Thus the Purum villages of Tampak, Lairingkhul, Chandropoto are better known as Purum Tampak, Purum Laiingkhul, Purum Chandropoto and so on, though villagers call themselves as Chote. To the Meitei or to any valley group, Chote or Purum Tampak may be known as only Purum, and this might have resulted to the confusion for others (1985 : 53).

Hiyang (Khiyang) and others belonging to the 'Original Customs and Cultural Research Committee' of Lamlanghupi village, Manipur South district, have clearly stated that the Chote or Chothe is the original name of the tribe which is now oscillating between two words 'Chothe' and 'Purum' (1985b : 25). They further state,

> "The Chote people have been known by that name since the days they came into being on the earth. The confusion on the issue of the name of the tribes prevailed only after the Chote people settled in some places called Purum which are the geographical surname of the places" (*ibid*: 25 – 26)

They have further pointed out that the confusion between the Purum and the Chote is due to the fact that Das mentioned this tribe in his book as the Purum. The Chote people since the very beginning of their existence never used their tribe name as Purum. Chothe was the original name of the tribe and the name Chote is still in use to refer to them. Purum is the name of certain places known to the Chote people. It was nothing but misinterpretation of fact that the tribe was named as Purum. So, according to Hiyang (Khiyang) and the other members of the above Committee, there was no tribe called Purum and still there is no tribe bearing such a name, though constitutionally the Purum have been recognized as a Scheduled Tribe of Manipur.

It is thus seen that there was a controversy regarding the identity of these people as to whether they considered them to be Purum or Chote (Chothe). Now, the question that automatically comes up is how could an eminent anthropologist like T.C. Das fail to find out the real identity of the people. According to Hiyang (Khiyang), it could be due lack of 'well-educated persons among the Chote to interpret the real name of the tribe' (*ibid* : 27) at that time. But Das at one place has mentioned that 'the Purums are very nearly related to the Chauthes near Bishenpore on the western bank of the Loglak Lake' (1935 : 2– 3). So it cannot be said that the Chote (Das's Chauthe) question had totally escaped his attention. Arun Kumar, who undertook research work among the Purum-Chote of Manipur during 1995-1996, sounds more positive on this issue. He has the following explanation to offer :

> At the time of the preparation of the list of Scheduled Tribes in 1950s', The Purum also reconsidered their identity and they took themselves as Chothe and another tribe was listed. According to them, the Purum is geographically localized

Chothe and the name of the tribe as such is Chothe (Chote as spelled by their own leaders). All the Purums are identifying themselves as Chothe; they accept the Chothe identity without any hesitation. To them, Chothe and Purum are one and the same ....' (1998 : 69 – 70).

Even then, the confusion has not cleared and a number of questions have remained unanswered. One very pertinent and relevant point is, when the Purum and the Chote have been enlisted as two distincet and separate tribes, then how could they be considered as one and the same tribe by the researchers? Another relevant question is, how the Purums whose number had steadily declined since 1931 before finally disappearing in 1971, again reappeared in 1981 or 1991? If the Purum and the Chote/Chothe are related or are one and the same, why have they been separately enumerated? Is it that the census enumerators did the same 'mistake' in identifying a tribe? Or did they find the Purum and the Chothe as two different tribes? Or did they keep both the names of the same tribe misidentifying them as two different tribes and therefore enumerated the two populations separately? Or did they fail to identify them as 'one and the same tribe' as recognised by Arun Kumar? Or were there other reasons too? Of course, the matter did not depend on the understanding (or misunderstanding) of the census enumerators, who could not be expected to have a sound knowledge of the problem. But even the members of the team of anthropologists, who visited the so-called Purum areas, failed to recognise the identity of the tribe clearly. Basu, after mentioning this group as the Purum (Chote), defines the Purum as 'a small tribe of virtually isolated population of 1464 individuals, who inhabit nine villages in the southern part of Manipur Valley' (1985 : 36). At one place he has mentioned this group of people as the Purum (Chote), and at another he has recognised them as simply Purum. Das Gupta, on the other hand, has mentioned that Purum is the type of land on which the villages are situated. He observes, 'people are often called by the village they inhabit' (1985 : 53). So the members of the team sent by Anthropological Survey of India 'deliberately decided to refer the group as Purum (Chote) because the people refer themselves to Chote, while others call themselves as Purum, (*ibid*). That means the 'Purum' (Chote) may not be the correct identity of these people.

There is another controversy with regard to the identification of the Purum with the Kuki group, Shakespeare (1912), Hodson (1911) and Das (1945) have identified the Purum / Chote as the Old Kuki tribe whereas Mc Culloch (1859) considered Purum as the Kuki tribe. Hiyang and others think that the Purum/Chote are identified as the Old Kuki because firstly, the Purum/Chote are found in the southern district of Manipur which is dominated by Kuki (1985 b : 28). The culture of the Purum/Chote has much been influenced by the Kuki because of contact of these two groups for a long time.

> "The Chote are called Old Kuki because they are the oldest tribe found in the southern Manipur. When the British and Indian scholars appeared on the spot they found the Chote people in close contact with the Kuki" '(Hiyang et al 1985 b : 29).

That is the reason why the Purum/Chote were wrongly identified as the Old Kuki.

> '. . . the Chote by no reason have any resemblance with the so called Kuki in their tribe. The Chote have a great difference with the Kuki in their traditional culture, religion and social life' (ibid).

In a similar way, Hiyang and others dismiss the idea that the Purum/Chote belong to the Naga group.

> 'There are wide ranges of differences between the cultural tradition of the Chote and the Nagas, and in respect to their origin, custom, manners, dress, laws and traditional organizations, there were little similarities in certain aspects' (*ibid*) :

But at the same time Hiyang and others acknowledge the fact that for several decades the Chotes are in favour of the Naga. According to them, there were 'political reasons' for this.

Arun Kumar, on the other hand, could find the process of 'Nagaization of Purum/Chothe identity'. He has also observed that the Purum/Chothe (Chote) 'villages are polarized to the acceptance of Naga ethnicity' (1998 : 71).

He observes, "Unlike other Old Kuki tribes [among the Purum/Chothe] there is no unanimous decision, at tribe level, in accepting Naga identity. Again unlike some other smaller tribes such as Tarao, Kharam, Kom, there is no collective decision of the Chothe to maintain neutrality. Therefore, the social tensions and conflicts even among the Chothe are manifested now and then, over its relation to the Naga movement" (Arun Kumar, 1998 : 72 – 73).

That the Purum could not evoke the same type of interest as they could do earlier may not be so much because of the changes that have swept their land and society, but because of the change in emphasis involving their identity. But this process in itself is an exciting preposition, the proper understanding of which would be able to add a new dimension to group dynamics in the context of North-East India.

REFERENCES

Ackarman, C., *1964: Structure and Statistics : The Purum case. American Anthropologist* Vol - 66, No. 1

Arun Kumar, M.C., *1998: Debate among the Purums, Man and Life* Vol-24, No. 1 & 2.

Basu, A., 1985: *Contemporary Demographic Pattern of the Purum (Chote) with Special Reference to Fertility and Mortality. In Purum (Chote)* Revisited (Ed.) Biman K. Das Gupta and others, Calcutta, Anthropological Survey of India.

Brown, R., 1873: *Statistical Account of the Native State of Manipur,* London.

Cowgill, G.L., 1964: *Statistics and Sense: More on Purum Case, American Anthropologist,* Vol. 66, No. 6.

Das, T. C., 1935: *Kinship and Social Organization of the Purum Kukis of Manipur. Journal of the Department of Letters,* Univ. of Calcutta.

Das, T. C., 1939: *Clan monopoly of personal names among the Purum.* Kuki, *Man.* Vol. 39. No. 2.

Das, T. C., 1941· *Possible Relic of Matrilocal Residence Among the Old Kuki Tribes* of Manipur (Assam). *Anthropological Papers,* Univ. of Calcutta.

Das, T. C., 1945: *The Purums : An Old Kuki Tribe of Manipur.*Calcutta, Univ. of Calcutta.

Das Gupta, B.K., 1985: *Present day Purum (Chote) Society with special Reference to Marriage alliance.* In *Purum (Chote) Revisited.* (eds.) Biman K. Das Gupta and others. Calcutta, Anthropological Survey of India.

Geoghegan, W.H. & P. Kay, 1964: *More Structure and Statistics: A Critique of C. Ackerman's analysis of Purum. American Anthropologist* Vol. 66. No. 6.

Gupta, P., 1985: *Analysis of Critiques of Chothe (Chote) tribe.* In *Purum (Chote) Revisted* (eds.) Biman K. Das Gupta and others, Calcutta. Anthropological Survey of India.

Hiyang (Khiyang) T. and others. 1985a: *The Original Custom and Culture of the Chote Tribe.* In *Purum (Chote) Revisited* (eds) Biman K. Das Gupta and others, Calcutta. Anthropological Survey of India.

Survey of India, 1985b: *The Original History of the Chothe (Chote) Tribe.* In *Purum (Chote) Revisited* (eds.) Biman K. Das Gupta and others. Calcutta, Anthropological Survey of India.

Hodson T.C., 1911: *The Naga Tribes of Manipur,* London.

Livingstone, 1969: *The Applicability of structural model in marriage system.* In *Anthropxology in Some Theory in Behavioral Section* (eds). I Buchler and H. Nitini. Pitsburgh, Pittsburgh Univ. Press.

McCulloch, W., 1859: *Account of the Valley of Manipur.* London.

M. Mullar, E.W. , 1964: *Structure and Statistics: Some remarks on the Puram Case. American Anthropologist.* Vol. 66 No. 6

Needham, R., *1958: A structural analysis of Purum Society. Americal Anthropologist,* Vol. 60(1).

Needham, R., 1962: *Structure and Sentiment: A Test case in Social Anthropology,* Chicago, Chicago Univ. Press.

Needham, R., 1964: *Explanatory Notes on Prescriptive Alliance and the Purum. American Anthropologist,* Vol. 66 No. 6.

Schneider, D., 1965: *Some muddles in the model or how the system really works.* In *The Relevances of Models in Social Anthropology* (Ed.) V. R. Banton, ASA Monograph series No. 1, London.

Shakespeare, 1912: *The Lushai-Kuki Clans.* London.

Wilder, W., *1964 Confusion versus classification in the study of Purum society. American Anthropologist,* Vol. 66 No.6

White, H.C., 1963: *An Anatomy of Kinship: Mathematical structure of accumulated rules.* N. J.: Prentice-Hall.

18

A Note on the Cultural Background of Kamtapur Movement in North Bengal

RAJATSUBHRA MUKHOPADHYAY

Over the past few decades, there has been an upsurge of regional movements launched by different communities in different parts of India. The particular community or ethnic group involved in these movements is found quite assertive to lay their demand for autonomy, sovereignty, and at times for secession. This has become a major concern in social science discourse in recent times.

The present note examines the ongoing Kamtapur movement in North Bengal from cultural perspective. It probes into the prevailing cultural differentiation and rift between the indigenous Rajbansis and so-called alien (mainly immigrant Bengalis locally called *Bhatias*) people, and the consolidation of linguo-cultural identity of the former community in the wake of this movement.

Despite the controversy over their story of origin, numerically, Rajbansis form the largest Scheduled Caste Community of West Bengal. As per 1991 Census, out of a total of 2852951 Rajbansis in the state, about 78 per cent are found to live in the northern territory, known as North Bengal in common parlance. It is believed Rajbansis are the early settlers of this clime. History reveals, as an off-shoot of great Bodo family they entered India in the 10th century B.C. from the east and settled on the bank of Brahmaputra river, and gradually spread over Assam and the whole of North and East Bengal (Sanyal, 1965 : 10). Amongst the six North Bengal districts, the Rajbansis have greater concentration in the Cooch Behar and Jalpaiguri districts. These two districts together account for 69 of the total Rajbansis of North Bengal. The proportion of the Rajbansis to total population of North Bengal is about 19 per cent. But they account for the highest percentage (60%) of Scheduled Caste population in this region. The Rajbansis (Koch-Rajbansis) are also in occupation of vast areas of the districts of Goalpara, Kamrup and Nowgaon in Assam, and West Garo Hills district of Meghalaya.

The major sentiment articulated in favour of Kamtapur movement is – apart from other existing socio-economic disparities and deprivation, the Rajbansis, being an indigenous community, are at present facing a lot of hardships and are fast loosing their ethnic identity, culture, language and civilizational attributes under pressure of alien Bengalis (*Bhatias*), who mostly came from downstream region of southern East Bengal (now Bangladesh) to this territory. This fresh surge of consciousness has provoked them to demand a separate statehood and 'self-rule' over an area that covers all North Bengal districts—Malda, North Dinajpur, South Dinajpur, Jalpaiguri, Cooch Behar and parts of Darjeeling. In defence of such a claim, the protagonists of this movement project their vulnerability in the socio-cultural enclave to the dominant Bengalis, who, as they perceive, are threatening to overwhelm them. They consider that Rajbansis have nothing in common with the alien Bengalis either in terms of physical appearance, language or culture, and they do not belong to the Bengali community. The Bengalis are further accused of their super-coordinating posture and ethnocentric attitude displayed towards the Rajbansis.

Like many other ethnic movements, Kamtapur movement also sees cultural self-determination as a prerequisite to the attainment of the desired political freedom and distributive justice. The form of language called Kamtapuri constitutes an essential part of the politics of Kamtapur. The fancy which has been floated is, North Bengal belongs to the Kamtapuri speaking people and it is their homeland. So there is a need to form a separate Kamtapur state. In addition, the constitutional recognition of this particular language, its mandatory inclusion in educational curricula, and the introduction of Kamtapuri programmers in AIR and TV have been demanded by the leaders of this movement.

The constitutional recognition of their language under the 8th schedule is the immediate goal of the Kamtapuri activists, while their political opponents hold that their agitation will serve as a convenient 'route' to a 'dangerous' destination. The issue of ethnicity and language of the Kamtapuris have often been debated by the State government, which maintains that Kamtapuri is a dialect and a derivative of Bangla. But the Kamtapuris do not subscribe to this view. The language issue has, in fact, been the single biggest factor behind the Kamtapur movement (Dey, 1999 : 1, Chaudhuri, 2000 : 35-36).

As a part of ascriptive mobilization, the leaders of Kamtapur Peoples' Party (KPP) have adopted a strategy of cultural revivalism. Several outfits like *All Kamtapur Students Union* (AKSU), *Kamtapur Vasha Sahitya Parisad* (KVSP) are now quite active to revitalize the past history, language, culture and traditional customs of thee Rajbansis. The AKSU asserts that constitutionally the Rajbansis have every right to protect and promote their glorious history, language, culture and traditional custom in a dignified way. Otherwise, the rich cultural heritage of the Rajbansis will ultimately face extinction because of the onslaught by the alien Bengali culture. The AKSU demands caught the fancy of the Kamtapuris. Among its 13 demands, AKSU further added inclusion of Kamtapuri in the University syllabus, and the setting up of a central University in Cooch Behar in the name of Roy Saheb Thakur Panchanan Barma (a charismatic leader of the Rajbansi community).

It is often claimed that the KPP represents the aspiration of not only the Rajbansi community but also of those who speak Kamtapuri language such as Khens, Suris, Muslims and some of those having titles of Das, Nath, Gope etc. who occupy a peripheral position within a Bengali community. These communities may not necessarily share a uniform culture and identity, but they have a language in common. This could hold them together developing a sense of mutual interest and prompting them to go for agreements of one type or another. They also demanded the inclusion of Kamtapuri as their mother tongue during the Census operation of 2001. The claim of Kamtapuri as a distinct language could find immediate support from three political parties, namely CPI-ML (Santosh Rana faction), UKD (*Uttar-Khand Dal*), and UBJSS (*Uttarbanga Jharkhand Sangram Samity*).

Under the direct patronage of *Kamtapur Vasa Sahity Parisad*, recently the *Bhagavatt Gita* has been translated in Kamtapuri language under the title *ayee gita*. A Kamtapuri grammar book has already been published and there is also one almanac (*Kamta Panji*) in Kamtapuri. The preparations of a Kamtapuri dictionary, and a translation of the 16th century Hindu classic in verse, *Chandi*, are in progress. The language issue has gathered fresh momentum with these publications.

Kamtapur Vasa Sahitya Parisad is actively involved in publishing periodicals, bulletins, booklets, novels, poems and audiocassettes in Kamtapuri language. It also organized seminars and meetings at various places of North Bengal in demand of their cultural and economic rights. In a convention organized by the *Kamtapur Sahitya Sabha* in early '99 at Shibmandir, near North Bengal University, the nerve-centre of the movement, fifteen thousand people belonging to the Rajbansi community assembled to chalk out a future course of action to reanimate their lost cultural heritage. In this convention, along with the display of songs, dances and dramas, traditional to the Rajbansis, the prospect of the Kamtapuri language had also been discussed by a section of intelligentsia of the community. Some learned participants further observed with anxiety that Rajbansis being the earliest settlers of North Bengal have lost their language, culture, land and pride. Bengali has swamped the Rajbansi dialect, which is now facing the threat of extinction. Very few Rajbansis of the present generation are well versed about their traditions and culture, and they have hardly any knowledge of their language and history. They are fast loosing their linguistic—cultural identity. Recently KPP has organized cultural programmes across Malda and South Dinajpur districts to gain popular support and revive its party activities.

The Kamtapur movement tends to consolidate linguo-cultural identity of the Rajbansis with an aim to attain a separate homeland for Rajbansis, the indigenous settlers of the area. Yet, it is true that this particular regional movement should not be seen solely in cultural terms. Interestingly, there is a resemblance between the ongoing Kamtapur movement and earlier Assam movement. In the latter case, the Assamese speaking people, like that of the Rajbansis of North Bengal, felt threatened first by the Bengali domination and then by the increasing number of Bangladeshi refugees (Gupta, 1995 : 59). So processually there emerged *Kamtapur Gana Parisad* (KGP) in North Bengal on the lines of *Ahom Gana Parisad* (AGP) of that of Assam.

The premise from which the leaders want to mobilize their community members in favour of Kamtapur movement is that of 'cultural rights' *i.e.*, the rights of the indigenous Rajbansis to preserve their culture and language. So they demanded appropriate constitutional and administrative recognition of their language called Kamtapuri. The KPP leaders, thus potently make use of the linguistic affinity and sentiments to cultivate 'we' feeling among the Rajbansis across North Bengal. And the appealing slogan "Kamtapuri is a language of the heart, a medium of self-expression" has been used as booster to hasten the mood of protest and keep their community members somewhat emotionally charged. On language issue, the very term 'Kamtapuri' has thus ultimately turned into a marker of their identity for both staying in and outside the community.

The Kamtapuri asked for an official recognition of their cultural autonomy in the regional-linguistic context of North Bengal. Such a claim tends to instigate some kind of animosity or rather ill feeling towards outsiders (mainly alien Bengalis) and other linguistic groups long settled in this region. That may turn the Kamtapur movement to an 'isolationist' one. In fact, the protagonists of this movement have expressed resentments against their vulnerability in the face of dominant Bengali cultures which threaten (as they apprehend) to overwhelm them.

The Kamtapur case again justifies the necessity to study the symbolic and cultural aspects of ethnic movements in India. It is a case in point to show why and how this particular movement identifies cultural self-determination as a pre-requisite to the attainment of the real (?) political freedom and distributive justice. This apart, some of the controversial issues pertaining to the cultural rights of diverse ethnic groups in a multicultural society like India *vis-à-vis* the role of the state in fostering political and cultural homogeneity cannot be totally ignored at the present juncture.

The Kamtapur movement has cherished some kind of 'cultural nationalism'. It attempts to articulate popular aspirations of the Rajbansis to nurture and preserve their 'natural bonds' rooted in ethnic affinity, religion, culture, language and territoriality. Specific cultural attributes like history of ancestry, distinctive beliefs, institutions, customs, social and religious practices are often brought forward to display their ethnic distinction. On the basis of that they want to function as a solidarity interest group and put forward the claim that the Rajbansis are quite different from the Bengalis, and culturally they have nothing in common. That has added a new dimension to the already vexed problems of the overall economic backwardness of the region, unhealthy scramble for limited goods and services, incursion and unabated influx of refugees, land alienation, and a feeling of relative deprivation and discrimination (genuine or otherwise) among a section of Rajbansis. It is true that ethnocentrism or revivalism itself may not lead to ethnic conflict if the groups are not involved in competition for a larger share to economic resources and products, and for a greater part of a decision making process. But in North Bengal the situation is somewhat opposite. Under such a state, the Kamtapur movement calls for a separate statehood in keeping with the modern discourse of nationalism and emancipation.

Cultural revivalism, and particularly revitalization of certain selected aspects of tradition of a community in a region is often perceived as assertion of 'melting pot' approach for cultural homogenization. Bandyopadhyay emphatically states, "In certain concrete terms it raises its ugly face in demanding separation of a particular region from what it considers the clutches of a dominant nationality" (1998 : 156-57). On the other hand, D'Souza argues that whereas territorial segregation of cultural groups leads to nativist and secessionist demands, territorial intermingling of cultural groups in a social climate of structuralism gives rise to the hegemonic claim on the part of the majority group, justifying it on the principle of majority rule in a democracy. The hegemonic rule of a cultural group is totally undemocratic. The regional autonomy based on cultural nationalism reduces the chance of domination of one group over the others (1995 : 165). Thus the debate goes on among the pundits in the perspectives of ethnic movements in India.

The Kamtapur case clearly reveals that the linguo-cultural aspects of any regional movement are important in themselves as they often reflect the sentiments of original settlers of a territory who otherwise feel threatened by the overwhelming majority and cultural supremacy of the alien population. At this juncture, the question of 'cultural rights' appears to them as an issue of political mobilization. During this movement for cultural revivalism, they obviously come in conflict with the alien 'majority' group. Their particular attitude of mind and struggle for cultural rights are somehow abrogated, ignored or repressed by the dominant power. Therefore, there is a need to critically look into the challenge, if any, posed by the indigenous communities to the hegemony of the state, especially the attempts to stabilise their distinct linguo-cultural identity with reference to the dominant mainstream culture.

Admittedly, North Bengal has very typical ethnic problems and tensions rooted in cultural subordination and super-ordination. The vanity, immodesty and pride of the so-called culturally advanced communities accompanied by a sense of economic insecurity by the Rajbansis have contributed substantially to the emergence of Kamtapur movement in

North Bengal (Nandy : 1999; Das : 1999). Though it is too early to predict about the fate of this particular movement, there is no denying the fact that it has succeeded in making considerable dent among the Rajbansis of North Bengal invigorating them to pursue their cultural and political goals.

REFERENCES

Bandyopadhyay, Bholanath, 1998. *The Politics of Regionalism in India*, in Sobhanlal Datta Gupta (ed.), *India:Politics and Society Today and Tomorrow*. Calcutta : K.P. Bagchi, pp.155-177.

Chaudhury, Kalyan, 2000. *The demand for Kamtapuri : North Bengal faces a secessionist movement, Frontline*, May 26, pp. 35-36.

Das, Dhirendra Nath, 1999, *Ethno-Political Aspects of Regional Movements. A study in the Context of Some Regional Movements in the Plains of North Bengal.* Unpublished Ph.D Thesis, North Bengal University.

Dey, Pabitra, 1999. *The Politics of Language. The Statesman* (NB plus), Feb.12,p.I.

D'Souza, Victor S. 1995. *Towards a Cultural Policy in India : A Socio-Cultural Perspective. Sociological Bulletin*, 44 (2), pp.159-167.

Gupta, Dipankar, 1995. *Political Sociology in India : Contemporary Trends.* Bombay : Orient Long man.

Nandy, Vaskar, 1999. *Uttarbange Bengali, Kamtapuri ebong Adibasi-Jharkhandi Parichiti* (in Bengali), *Bitarkika*(3), PP.147-168.

Sanyal, Charu Chandra, 1965. *The Rajbansi of North Bengal A Study of a Hindu Social Group*, Calcutta : The Asiatic Society.

19

Prospects and Problems of Tribal Development: A Case Study from Arunachal Pradesh

GEETANJALI BARUAH

Namsai is a small town situated in the sub-montane area of the Lohit district of Arunachal Pradesh bordering Assam at an altitude of 143 metres on the right bank of Noa-Dihing river, one of the major rivers of Arunachal Pradesh. An attempt has been made here to bring into focus the potentialities along with various problems faced by the people of this area, which hamper the overall development of the region in terms of improving the well-being of the residents and raising their socio-economic conditions of life.

Arunachal Pradesh is in the north-eastern extremity of the Indian sub-continent having an area of 83,743 sq.km. It is a thinly populated hilly tract with a long international border with Bhutan to the west, China to the north and north-east, Myanmar to the east. It is the twenty fourth state of the Indian Union which has attained statehood on the 20th February, 1987. At present the state is having thirteen districts, of which Lohit is the largest one. The Lohit district is situated on the north-eastern extremity of Arunachal Pradesh. It is bounded on the north by China (Tibet), on the east by Myanmar, on the west by the Dibang Valley district of Arunachal Pradesh and Tinsukia district of Assam and on the south by the Tirap district of Arunachal Pradesh. It occupies an area of 24,427 sq. km. and its total population is 109,632, of whom 61,022 are men and 48,610 are women (Census of India : 1991). The district is divided into five sub-divisions-Namsai, Tezu, Hayuliang, Anini and Roing. These are further sub-divided into fifteen circles. The Namsai sub-division stretches along the southern part of the district comprising three circles, viz. Namsai, Wakro and Chowkham. An extra-assistant commissioner functions as the head of the sub-division, who discharges his duties from the sub-divisional head quarters at Namsai. The entire area of Arunachal Pradesh was treated as rural in 1961 Census. In 1971 Census only four districts and sub-divisional head quarters (Bomdi-La, Along, Tezu and Pasighat) were recognised as towns. In 1981 Census two more centres, namely, Itanagar (New Itanagarh) and Naharlagun (Old Itanagarh) were added to the earlier four towns, as a result of which the number of urban centres rose to six. In 1991, the number of urban centres increased further with the inclusion of Namsai, Zero and Khonsa.

It has been mentioned in the Lohit District Gazetteer (1978) that though Khamtis and Singphos are the two major dominating populations of the district, there was a probability that originally Namsai was an Ahom settlement. According to the Gazetteer, "Nam" is a Shan word for river or water. In Assam as well as in Arunachal Pradesh, there are many places having the name originating with the word "Nam". However, Namsai in Khamti means "sandy water" (*Nam*-water : *sai*-sand).

Before discussing about the potentialities and various other problems of the Namsai town, it will be pertinent to deal with the major problem, faced by the town, which is the annual flood. In the Lohit district there are innumerable rivers and rivulets of which Lohit is the main one. The name of the district is also derived from it. Apart from Lohit, another important river is the Noa-Dihing. It flows southward towards the plains region of the district, i.e., the Namsai area. The main tributaries of the Noa-Dihing in the Lohit district are Dirak and Tengapani. The Namsai town suffers every year because of the vagaries of the Noa-Dihing. During monsoon, the river overflows it's banks, causing serious erosions and considerable damages to the roads and bridges almost every year. As a result, surface communication in the district is frequently disrupted during monsoon. Another problem associated with flood is waterlogging of Namsai area. The floodwater of the Noa-Dihing river overflows the swamps and low-lying areas causing water—logging in a vast area of about 14 km. from the village Ningrau to Namsai township. Considerable damage to the cultivating fields is caused by it.

It has already been mentioned that Namsai area is mostly inhabited by Khamtis and Singphos. They fall in the category of advanced cultivators. In the whole district they are the only communities, beside Mishing and Chakma, who practise wet rice cultivation. Irrigation is done by means of canals dug from the nearby streams. These two communities not only make a good harvest every year but also produce surplus. The production of good quality rice, popularly known as Khamti rice, is well known in the region and is in great demand. High yielding varieties of rice like 'taichung' and IR-8 are also cultivated in this area. However, such possibilities have a limited application and could not be extended to most of the areas, which are hilly and not favourable for wet rice cultivation.

Forest plays a very important role in the economy of the district as a whole, Lohit is the second highest forest revenue-earning district in the state. There are four forest-based industries including a major plywood industry in the district. Namsai itself is having a reserve forest with an area of 2,375,58 hectares, firewood, timber and other materials made out of timber (posts, poles, etc.) from the major forest products. The minor forest products include cane, bamboo, thatch, *dhuna* (incense powder), etc. The famous medicinal herb *Coptis teeta* , widely known as *Mishmi teeta*, is available only in the Lohit District and it earns a substantial revenue every year.

Even a few decades back, the whole of Lohit district was economically isolated from the rest of the country. The difficult and inaccessible terrain and uncompromising ecological conditions are the main constrains in the development of trade and commerce not only is Namsai but in the district as a whole. Naturally, no large scale industry exists in the area. The industrial activities are centered around small scale cottage industries only, such as, weaving, cane and bamboo works, smithery. However, a wood-based industrial enterprise, the Assam Saw Mills and Timber Company which has a plywood factory and produces veneers and tea chests, is functioning at Namsai. This is the only medium scale industry in the whole district producing almost 3, 50,000 tea chests annually. The factory was originally established at Murkong-Selek in the Pasighat sub-division in the year 1918 under the managing agency of the British Company Private Ltd. The earthquake of 1950 damaged it and the subsequent flood of 1951 swept away a part of the Company's establishments. As a result, the factory was shifted to Namsai in the year 1952. In 1959, it became a Company under Messrs, Jalan Industries Private Limited. Beside tea chests, plywood panels and sawn timber, the Company also manufactures commercial and decorative ply-board, black boards, railway sleepers, etc. One of the important factors of development of the wood-based industry in the district is the role played by the elephants in providing easy transportation. Elephants are still found in considerable number in the foothill areas (including Namsai), some of which are tamed and are found to be quite useful for pulling together logs and heavy timber and loading the same in trollies and trucks. A saw mill, a few ricemills, rice hullars and one brick clin are also situated at Namsai. Those stand out as examples of machine-run industries.

Forest is undoubtedly the main source of economy. Forest-based industries hold prospect. But before that forest has to be nurtured, protected and replenished. The Arunachal Government has taken some measures to develop the forests, such as, rising of plantation and forestation, construction and improvement of forest roads. Still, further attention is needed in a way which could sustain the growth of forest. Needless to say, development of the area industrially as well as improvement of the general economic condition of the people depends to a great extent on the forest wealth. But side by side it needs to be remembered that uncontrolled utilisation of forest wealth has disastrous human and ecological consequences too.

Weaving is another important enterprise of the people of this region, which, however, needs proper support and patronage. Women of this region are expert weavers, they weave almost all their required garments in their looms. Girls are trained right from their teens in weaving. This traditional form of art is thus allowed to survive from one generation to another. Weaving has now been introduced in the government centres as one of the courses for training and for its increased production in pursuance of the government policy to preserve and popularise this beautiful form of art before it disappears from their society altogether. Because of high cost of the yarn, majority of the women are now finding it difficult to continue with weaving at the household level. As a result, it tends to be limited to a few well-to-do families only. The State Government may take initiative to supply yarn at a subsidised rate to the needy families so that this beautiful traditional form of art continues to flourish. However, it will also be very helpful to the women of the area if weaving is commercialised and the number of weaving centres is increased. Initiative may be taken to revive the non-fictional weaving centres which could come to the benefit of the Arunachal women in general and the women of Namsai area in particular, providing them

Life of the people in Namsai area in one of continuous struggle. People are trying hard to come to terms with the vagaries of nature. However, if the natural resources like river water can be utilised in a constructive way it will be of benefit to the people. One Micro-hydel project for electricity generation has been installed in the district with the capacity of 400 K.W. Namsai has been electrified in the year 1976. The total generating capacity of the unit is 930.10 K.W., which is hardly sufficient. More such Micro-hydel projects need to be installed. Admittedly, the water power potential in this area is immense because countless number of rivers and rivulets are flowing through Namsai and Lohit district as a whole. It only demands proper utilisation and harnessing to meet the growing needs of the industrial units and urban centres. The rural electrification programme may also be expeditiously implemented. These are the measures necessary to boost up development potentialities of the area by way of creating resources for technological advancement.

Regarding the economy of the region, it may be mentioned here that the people now find it very hard to depend solely on agriculture for subsistence. Even some time back it was their mainstay of life. Their old method of agricultural production with antiquated tools is holding the economy backward. This is one of the main reasons behind lack of progress and falling standard of living with the result that a substantial number of persons have come under the poverty level. The block development office at Namsai was established in the year 1953. It covers three circles including Namsai. The total number of villages under the block is 109, of which Namsai circle alone covers 50 villages. Out of a total number of 5057 households at Namsai, 4332 families live below poverty line. Circlewise break-up reveals that Namsai circle itself has 1801 families living below poverty line. The present situation may directly be linked with the state of economy, which among other factors, is singularly the most important one. No doubt, their economy has to be improved. *Jhum* cultivation by which almost the entire population subsisted can no longer meet the growing needs of the people. So a change for a better and more effective productive system is very much essential. Though Khamtis, Singphos, Mishings and Chakmas of Namsai area have started practising wet rice cultivation, others still cling to the age-old *jhum* cultivation as is prevalent in the hilly areas of Lohit district, Of late, the state government has taken up a few programmes for the improvement of agriculture, which are listed below :

(1) Development of land under permanent cultivation;

(2) Distribution of improved agricultural implements and machines amongst progressive farmers;

(3) Irrigation by canals and construction of minor irrigation projects;

(4) Implementation of rural water supply schemes;

(5) Supply of fertilizers and improved seeds.

Without questioning their long-term effects, it may be possible to get immediate results, if these programmes are implemented properly and in right earnest. But, first of all, the problem of recurring flood has to be controlled on a priority basis because it is the source of various other problems.

Last but not the least, one of the major problems facing Namsai town is communication. It is true that construction of roads and bridges in Lohit district as a whole poses a great challenge to the engineering skill and resources. Turbulent rivers which often change courses are great obstacles to developing easy communication in the area. During monsoon, these rivers and streams invariably cause floods and landslides which are very frequent in the region. Submerging of roads and washing away of bridges are a regular feature. As a result, it becomes very difficult to maintain roads and bridges causing serious disruption to communication not only to Namsai town but to the whole of the Lohit district. It is worth mentioning here that in a way Namsai town could be regarded as one of the gateways to the district via Assam. This makes it all the more important from the locational point of view.

Though road communication has developed considerably from the state of porter tracks and mule paths of pre-independence days and of early fifties, still in almost every summer the whole district remains virtually cut off from the rest of the country.

An uninterrupted supply line capable of carrying goods and services to distant and less accessible areas is essential for development programmes to bear fruit. How far the development process would affect the cohesive structure of the community is another question. After all, a growing town as a centre of economic activities seems to nurture the sphere of community of strangers competing among themselves instead of creating a new sense of community living out of the old one. From North-East Indian perspective, this type of development is considered to be the source of many complexities creating unforeseen human problems.

REFERENCES

Dalton, E.J. 1972. *Descriptive Ethnology of Bengal (Reprint).* In: *Indian Studies : Past and Present*, Calcutta 1973.

Dutta Choudhury, S. 1978. *Lohit District Gazeteer*, Govt. of Arunachal Pradesh, Shillong.

Sarkar, S.R. 1991. *Census of India : Arunachal Pradesh*.. Series 3, paper 1. Provisional Population Totals. Director of Census Operations, Arunachal Pradesh.

Index

C

U